# BLACK MAN'S DILEMMA

## REVISED EDITION

## UPDATE OF EVENTS, 1976-2002

### BY

Chief Areoye Oyebola

*Black Man's Dilemma*

# BLACK MAN'S DILEMMA

## REVISED EDITION

## UPDATE OF EVENTS, 1976-2002

*Black Man's Dilemma*

# BLACK MAN'S DILEMMA

## REVISED EDITION

## UPDATE OF EVENTS, 1976-2002

By

**Chief Areoye Oyebola**

B.Sc. Econ. (Lond.); Dip.Ed. (Ib).); Dip. Journ. (Plymouth) F.R. Econ. S.; LL.D, Newport University; WATSON Scholar, Haggai Institute, Singapore, Editor, Daily Times, 1972-1975, Managing Editor, Daily Times, 1975; Commissioner for Home Affairs and Information, Western State of Nigeria, November 1975 - February 1976; Commisioner for Local Government and Information, Oyo State of Nigeria, March 1, 1976 - November 30, 1977; now a full time Author and Publisher.

BLACK MAN'S DILEMMA
COPYRIGHT BY AREOYE OYEBOLA.
ALL RIGHTS RESERVED.

FIRST PUBLISHED IN 1976
2024 EDITION PUBLISHED BY
BTB PRESS
WESTCHESTER NEW YORK
ISBN: 978-1-63652-387-3

# ACKNOWLEDGEMENT

## REVISED EDITION

## UPDATE OF EVENTS, 1976-2002

Glory, honour and praise to my dear heavenly Father, who through the Holy Spirit, gave me the inspiration to write Black Man's Dilemma. He provided the content, an appropriate title and the success in the publication of the 1976 and 2002 editions.

Thanks to the two great black leaders, Ahmed Sekou Toure, late President of Guinea, and Nwalimu Julius Nyerere, Late President of Tanzania, for the encouraging letters they wrote to me after they had read copies of the 1976 edition which I sent to them.

Deep gratitude to one of the most thoughtful, disciplined and far-sighted black leaders who ever lived, the late Chief Obafemi Awolowo, one of the three pillars of Nigerian nationalism, for his great love for me. For two hours at his residence, Park Lane Apapa, Lagos, that great leader discussed the content of the first edition of Black Man's Dilemma with me shortly before it was sent to the press. His profound thought was that education has made all the major difference between the black race and other races. He shared my concern for the underdog position of the blacks in the world.

My appreciation goes to my friend, President Olusegun Obasanjo, for the keen interest he showed in the 1976 edition of Black Man's Dillemma. For despite his very tight schedule as the then Military Head of State of Nigeria, he willingly, in late 1975, accepted my request that he should read the manuscript. He painstakingly read the manuscript and returned it with a seven-page hand-written suggestions and criticisms, some of which I accepted. Generally, he believed that I was too harsh on the black race and that there were far too many more things to civilisation than technology.

To my political science teacher at the University of Ibadan, Professor Essien Udom and his black American wife, I say "thank you". I was relaxing at a restaurant in Calabar in Cross River State of Nigeria, shortly on my return from the Obudu Cattle Ranch holiday resort, where I had written the first four chapters of the 1976 edition of Black Man's Dilemma, when I had a chance meeting with the couple.

Professor Udom and his wife confirmed to me that the issues I raised in the book had agitated their minds for many years before our meeting. Their thoughtful contributions strengthened my belief that the book was worth all the efforts.

Also, I have been greatly encouraged to work harder on the revised 2002 edition of **BLACK MAN'S DELIMMA** by the writing of a deep and highly reflective Nigerian journalist and columnist, **KAYODE AWE**. In his column, **KAWE**, of May 30, 1983 published in the **EVENING SKETCH**, he wrote as follows about me and Black Man's Dilemma: "if you ask who is my man of the century in Nigeria, I will tip Chief Areoye Oyebola, journalist, educationist, author and lover of objective appraisal of issues. I pick him because of his downright objectivity and frankness in his book - **BLACK MAN'S DILEMMA**. Chief Oyebola is the only one having the courage to express the truth about black man's backwardness". Thank you for your kind appraisal.

Similar encouragement was received by me in December 1996, when I turned 60. Nigerian's authoritative and highly respected newspaper - The **GUARDIAN,** gave, among other things the following assessment of my contributions to journalism in my country: "The strength of a nation lies in its idea and there are not many people who can claim to have done better at enriching Nigeria with sound ideas, than Chief Areoye Oyebola, who celebrated his 60th birthday recently. In journalism where he rose to the very pinnacle of the profession, as the managing editor of Daily Times and as one-time president of the Nigerian Guild of Editors, Oyebola gave new meaning to the power of ideas. His perception of a greater tomorrow was infinite."


CHIEF AREOYE OYEBOLA
DECEMBER, 2002.

*Black Man's Dilemma*

## PREFACE TO THE 1976 EDITION

This book is about the problems of the black race. I have tried to find reasons why black man's membership of the human family has never been on the basis of genuine equality and the reasons why the black race is backward.

I have examined the black man's past, his stupidities and unexplored challenges. I have raised many hard questions, questions which challenge the very nature of the black society, its long-standing values, beliefs and institutions.

My observations and conclusions have relevance to all black peoples who lived in Africa in the period before the slave trade and colonialism, the black peoples of the new nations of Africa and those who are still under foreign domination as well as the blacks in the United States, South America, the Caribbean and Europe. In short, this book is about black peoples throughout the world.

The concept of black personality is becoming increasingly popular. Culturally, the concept is believed to be the deep-seated desire of the black race to reach out for its past and the peculiar contributions which our race had made and may make to world culture and civilisation. Politically, the concept of black personality connotes the assertion of equality of black peoples with other races. And the political aspect of black concept has become increasingly important with the attainment of independence by many African countries.

But I believe that concepts like black personality or Negritude will remain empty slogans unless it helps black peoples to embark on a candid self-examination of their past, their present and their future. It is the belief that black peoples are today leaving the substance for the shadow that prompted me to write this book.

And in this study, I have come up with the sad discovery that the much-vaunted black man's contributions to civilisation are comparatively negligible. Africa, in particular and the black world, in general, have contributed very little to modern world and the enrichment to civilisation. For if the truth be known, we are just backward.

This view is based on the assumption that the different races of the world came into existence at the same time. Of great significance is the possibility that our contributions to civilisation may continue to be insignificant hundreds of years from now unless we critically and honestly find out the reason why in all the crises of man's story, our race has always been the underdog.

We must admit the fact of our backwardness. We must ignore the liberal white scholars who exaggerate our past contributions to civilisation. After all, if our black ancestors were as civilised as some liberal scholars would want us to believe, we must be able to find unmistakable evidence of their concrete achievements in Africa. For instance, the English, the Chinese, the Egyptians or the Japanese can point to their ancestors' great achievements in terms of buildings, works of art and inventions.

Some writers have attributed our relative backwardness to black man's mental inferiority in comparison with Caucasian and other races. These are, to my mind, extreme views. These are theories which regard the black man as sub-human and genetically inferior to other races. But after an elaborate examination of the intelligence test studies, I have come to the conclusion that there is no genetical intellectual superiority of the white man over the black man as such. The range of mental groups is the same among all races and throughout the world. There is abundant evidence of black men who have clearly excelled white men in various aspects of human endeavours. Even then, I have come to the inescapable conclusion that factors like the black man's colonial past, the crippling effect of the slave trade on him, nature's kindness to him, his isolation, climatic conditions and neo-colonialism in the new black states of Africa, the Caribbean and South America have, to varying degrees, conditioned our intellect, our life outlook and our indentity. These factors have adversely affected our creativity and originality.

For instance, the social effects of colonialism have degraded and dehumanised the black peoples. The great historical wrong done to blacks through the slave trade and colonialism constitutes an important explanation for our backwardness.

But the strange thing about our race is that other races have, in the past, been similarly enslaved and colonised. But these other races broke the shackles of slavery and domination, reached great heights and in many cases excelled their oppressors in contributions to civilisation.

But the black man has, for too long, looked for scapegoats for his many problems. He has, therefore, become his own worst enemy. It means our salvation as a race depends on our ability to honestly and candidly examine our limitations and weaknesses. We must find out why we have, for centuries, remained poor imitators of the Caucasian race. The present great pride in our cultural heritage is significant only if it helps us to reshape towards new goals and purposes.

Pride in our past is meaningful only if it becomes a source of strength for great achievements in science and technology by some of the free black nations of the world. Pride in our past is meaningful if it enables, at least, a black nation to make an original breakthrough to modernity. Nkrumah's Ghana, Guinea, Tanzania, Guyana and Nigeria since the July, 1975 coup, had sought or have been seeking original solutions to their problems of development. They have thinking and progressive leaders, but these are so few in relation to many black states that are helpless and have no sense of direction.

Civilisation is a heritage of mankind. It is not a native of any region. It is not an exclusive contribution of any race. Many races have contributed to civilisation through contacts. But unless the black race makes its own significant contributions to civilisation, our race will continue to be pitied or at best merely tolerated like all beggars. We will continue to be the world's underdog. To make it, the black man needs a hurricane of change known as revolution. He needs a complete mental revolution. But it appears to me that a great majority of the black middle class are not ready for this. Here lies the black man's dilemma.

# UPDATE OF EVENTS 1976 TO 2002

## PREFACE TO THE REVISED EDITION

Since 1976, when this book was published, my thought has been stimulated further on the problems of the black race. Thousands of readers of Black Man's Dilemma reacted to its content through personal letters they wrote to me, newspaper reviews, letters to editors and quotations of its extracts in other books. These people can never fully understand how deeply encouraged I have been by their interest in the book.

Some even wrote letters of appreciation under trying circumstances. One such letter came from one of the most outstanding Nigerians, Dr. Tai Solarin, now late, a renowned educationist and founder of the famous Mayflower Secondary School, Ikenne, Ogun State of Nigeria. Dr. Solarin was a close senior friend of mine, whose biography – *TO MOTHER WITH LOVE* – my company published. In his life time, he was the most outstanding Nigerian campaigner for democracy, justice and fairplay. A courageous social critic, he confronted the military authorities who, for many years usurped and gravely abused political power and human rights in Nigeria. He led street demonstrations and rallies against military governments. He was imprisoned many times by Nigerian soldiers.

While Dr. Tai Solarin was, as usual, detained without trial in Jos prison, he sent a hand-written letter, dated June 28, 1985, to me in which he wrote.

> "I have just gone through Black Man's Dilemma. I have been using the book side by side with a publication written half a century ago by Zik (that is the popular abbreviation of the name of Dr. Nnamdi Azikiwe-first President of Nigeria) Renascent Africa, written in 1937."
>
> It makes one weep for Nigeria for it so clearly shows that Nigeria has not moved a foot in half a century,"

Concluding his letter, Dr. Solarin promised:

> "When one day I walk into freedom again, I am going to go round Nigeria and get all our University undergraduates to make the reading of your Black Man's Dilemma a must before they emerge into the national struggle."

And he fulfilled his promise because in every one of the several lectures he delivered at tertiary institutions all over the country, he always introduced Black Man's Dilemma to his audience.

On his release from prison after a lot of public outcry against his unjustified detention, Dr. Solarin wrote, in the Nigerian Tribune newspaper, an elaborate two-part review of Black Man's Dilemma in which he emphasised that the black race occupy a world's climatic zone that is so debilitating, thereby causing our race's persistent backwardness. His review of Black Man's Dilemma, more than five years after publication, is in appendix 1.

There are other encouraging writings on this controversial book.

In his 314 page book, AFRICAN AMBIT, published by Pentland Press in the United Kingdom, in 1995, Reginald Dickenson the Author who, for many years, served as an administrator and engineer in colonial Africa and different parts of the world said:

> *"Chief Areoye Oyebola has written the most objective book I have read about the problems of Africa as seen from the African viewpoint". His full comments can be found in Appendix II.*

Also, Professor J.I. Okogun of the University of Ibadan, a very brilliant scholar, who obtained a first class degree in Chemistry, my very good friend, concluded his newspaper write-up on Black Man's Dilemma with the following recommendation:

> *"Let Areoye Oyebola's Black Man's Dilemma be made a prescribed reading for every Nigerian Secondary School Child. The main suggestions in the book should aid the rapid achievement of those attitudes recently recommended to Nigerians by the Head of State (who, in 1977, was General Olusegun Obasanjo) at Jaji and on several other previous occasions".*

The full text of Professor Okogun's comment is published in Appendix III.

A very famous British journalist and for many years Editor of the London based West Africa Magazine, David Williams, wrote, among other views, as follows on Black Man's Dilemma:

> *"Many of Mr. Areoye Oyebola's judgments can be disputed, but he brings to the support of his thesis a mass of detailed information. And nobody could fail to be stimulated by so earnest and uncompromising a writer....*
>
> *"Some might find this a curious book to publish on the eve of FESTAC (Festival of African Arts and Civilisation). Yet in a way, General Olusegun Obasanjo, in his speech opening the festival made one of the points which Mr. Oyebola seeks to get across. For a*

*long time the place of Africans in the world was "mapped, analysed, and interpreted by others", the Head of State said. "To succeed Africans must "restore the link between culture, creativity and the mastery of modern technology and industrialism." Some of the letters, comments, appreciation and criticisms are in Appendix IV.*

I was thrilled to receive from a highly educated Ghanaian lady, who was trained in Germany and had travelled extensively to other nations of the world. She is also a very successful manufacturer based in Tema, Ghana, Mrs. Osafo-Addo who explained that she had for a long time "been thinking of writing a book on the Black-race, with special emphasis on Africans". Having "read Black Man's Dilemma several times", she wrote to thank me on my "wonderful work". Her letter and my reply are found in Appendix V.

Regrettably, an ostensibly eminent black African, at present the world's most important international administrator, has proved to be a disappointment as far as an objective and candid appreciation of black race's position in the world is concerned. He is the present United Nations Organisation's Secretary General, Kofi Annan, a Ghanaian, who seems unwilling to admit that his race has any problem. I sent to Annan, by registered express airmail postage, copies of Black Man's Dilemma with a two page letter dated January 20, 1998 and some relevant documents. One of my requests was that Kofi Annan should encourage the Paris based United Nations Educational, Scientific and Cultural Organisation (UNESCO), which has always canvassed the view that all races of the world are equal, to give me a chance to put my contentions on the black race across to UNESCO researchers, experts and scientists.

The second request is that Annan should give me the benefit of sharing his thought on what he regards as a way out of black race's dilemma. Annan ignored both my first letter and the second reminder dated July 1, 1998 sent to him through the UNO office in Nigeria when he visited our country in 1998. The two letters to Kofi Annan are published as Appendix VI.

However, unlike Kofi Annan's unfortunate silence and indifference, a white man, The Director-General of UNESCO, sent a prompt reply to my letter of October 25, 1997, on Black Man's Dilemma.

The white Director-General of UNESCO did not accept my suggested dialogue or seminar with its scientists on the black race. He did not also invite me to the 2001 UN conference against racism held in Durban, South Africa.

His silence is understandable because many white men do not want the black man to embark on any critical examination of his past, present and future so that he can, for all time, be kept in economic, social and mental bondage and backwardness. But how do you explain the silence and indifference of Kofi Annan, a so called eminent black man?

As expected, other readers were very critical of the views expressed in Black Man's Dilemma.

There was the very critical view of Mr. Adebayo Bello , which was published in all the leading newspapers in Nigeria. He regarded the views I expressed in Black Man's Dilemma as *"a tenuous web of half-truths with utterly demoralising conclusions. Going through the book page by page, I cannot pinpoint what philosophy Mr. Oyebola is trying to postulate"*.

And a reviewer in the Nigerian Daily Times wrote: "If there was ever any hypercritical and searing criticism of the lot of black man the world over in recent years, that book is the one written by Areoye Oyebola titled, "Black Man's Dilemma.... The book is worth reading for the violent views and its politically provocative tirade against the black man".

*A reader of the Ibadan based Daily Sketch newspaper also wrote: The reader of this book, no matter how liberal minded, will receive occasional shocks from the electricity of the 127 page book, whose words are life wires, unprotected in many parts".* These and other views are in Appendix IV

However, over the years, as events further unfolded in Africa in particular and the black world in general, I have become fully convinced that I have no apologies whatsoever to offer any member of our race for any of my words or views my critics have regarded as harsh in the first edition of Black Man's Dilemma.

In fact, since 1976, as I observed the activities of all sorts of excessively greedy, dishonest, wicked, unintelligent, mentally sick men, mainly soldiers, who took over leadership positions as presidents, heads of state and ministers in independent African countries, I have become convinced that I did not fully appreciate how acute the dilemma of the black man was when I first wrote about him in 1976. I am convinced that these extremely bad leaders whose names and misdeeds I have mentioned in the present review of some chapters of this book and are worse than common criminals, could never have been tolerated even for a day among the other races of the world.

And even then, as our sense of crisis daily accumulates in the black countries of Africa, as the masses, especially the youth, sink deeper into agonising penury, misery and helplessness, as our countries fall into harsher neo-colonial entrapment through globalisation, economic slavery-promoting IMF loans and the hasty and dubious privatisation of the commanding heights of the national economies, which belong to the citizens, I still retain my optimism that the black race will eventually make it.

I believe that all is not lost. Afterall, there are great men among the black peoples of the world. Like the great men of the United States—the black Afro-American citizens, who, in co-operation with their bold Nigerian friends, put up an intelligent, desperate and courageous fight against the terrible tyrant, sadist and mentally ill-equipped dictator, General Sani Abacha of Nigeria, who committed many heinous crimes against Nigerians until he met his disgraceful death while in a state of stupor in 1998.

Yes, there are great men within the black race. We have our great and adorable Nelson Mandela of South Africa, a world statesman, a man of great heart and foresight, a leader of leaders. We remember the black hero, Kwame Nkrumah, a pioneer African revolutionary, a man of positive action and uncompromising integrity.

So was Nkrumah's close friend and confidant, the late Ahmed Sekou Toure of Guinea, the fierce fighter against colonialism and neo-colonialism, a great friend of the Guinean masses. We also have the other giants of African history, late Nwalimu Dr. Julius Nyerere of Tanzania, General Murtala Muhammed of Nigeria and Forbes Burnham of Guyana, South America.

And, I stand by my conclusion in the first edition of Black Man's Dilemma. That is, in order to make it among all the races of the world, black peoples everywhere need a mental revolution. Encouraged by the few deep, thoughtful and courageous elders, the black youths of the world must spearhead this revolution. Our youths must turn every idea and belief now cherished by our race completely upside down, for serious re-examination. But in this all important task, time is running out for the intensely patriotic black elders and youths.

*Black Man's Dilemma*

# REVISED EDITION

## UPDATE OF EVENTS, 1976-2002

## INTRODUCTION TO HARD COVER EDITION PUBLISHED IN NEW YORK BY VANTAGE PRESS, INC.

An African black man investigates the status of black people throughout the world in a comprehensive study that gets to the roots of his people's dilemma.

The premise of the book is one concerned with what the black man, regardless of his independence, has inherited: backwardness not progress. Progress is still exclusively white. Subjugated, exploited, and dehumanised, the black man, no matter where, still struggles to gain even a political foothold in the sheer cliff of world reality. Freedoms have been gained yes, but they are freedoms without self-reliance. Attempts at self-reliance have been stifled by white supremacy, even in such seriously determined states like Ghana, Guinea, Guyana, Tanzania and Nigeria. Whether through conspiracy or outright aggression, the world's black population continues to find itself under the heel of the imperialistic calumny of oppressive white regimes. There is also unrest and turmoil within the black leadership itself. Added together it all spells out dilemma with a capital D.

Two paths lie ahead for black people. One, they can follow the worn-out path of Western trial and error and remain neocolonial, or they can attempt original solutions to their complex problems, refusing to become white imitators. This, of course, is the most difficult path, but in the long run it will lead to solutions and not further entrapment.

This is a book of promise for the black people. It is, therefore, a primer of black hope, one that cannot be overlooked if the real problems within the black dilemma are ever to be recognised and thereby solved.

*REVISED EDITION*

*UPDATE OF EVENTS, 1976-2002*

# DEDICATION

Dedicated to all who are willing to honestly discuss the problems of the Black Race and to those at whose feet the challenge of tomorrow for our race will be laid.

*Black Man's Dilemma*

# REVISED EDITION

# UPDATE OF EVENTS 1976-2002

## CONTENTS

Chapter
1. Who is the Black Man? 1976 Edition ............................ 1
1. Who is the Black Man? An Update ............................. 7
2. Africa, the Birthplace of Man, 1976 Edition ................ 9
2. Africa the Birthplace of Man, An Update .................... 17
3. Black Man's Backwardness, 1976 Edition ..................... 19
3. Black Man's Backwardness, An Update......................... 33
4. Black Man's Negligible Contribution to Human Civilisation, 1976 Edition ............................................. 37
4. Black Man's Negligible Contribution to Human Civilisation, an Update ................................................. 57
5. Black Man's Culture And Civilisation: Myth and Reality, 1976 Edition. ..................................................... 59
5. Black Man's Culture and Civilisation: Myth and Reality, an Update. ........................................................ 77
6. The World's Underdog. 1976 Edition ............................ 79
6. The World's Underdog, An Update ............................. 93
7. The Myth of white Superiority, 1976 Edition ............... 97
7. The Myth of White Superiority. An Update ................. 113
8. The Black Americans. 1976 Edition ............................ 115
8. The Black Americans. An Update ............................... 135
9. Post-Independence Helplessness and New Hopes. 1976 Edition ........................................................ 141
9. Post-Independence Helplessness and New Hopes.

xxix

    An Update .................................................................. 167
    *William R. Tolbert Jnr and Sergeant Samuel K. .......... 169
    Doe of LIBERIA
    *Field Marshall Idi Amin of UGANDA ....................... 170
    *Mobutu Sese Seko of Democratic Republic of
    CONGO (FORMERLY ZAIRE) ................................. 172
    *Jean Bedel Bokassa of CENTRAL AFRICAN
    REPUBLIC .................................................................. 174
    *Hastings Kamuzu Banda of MALAWI ...................... 176
    *Robert Mugabe of ZIMBABWE ............................... 178
    *Arap Moi of KENYA ................................................ 180
    *Gnassingbe Eyadema of TOGO ................................ 182
9.  Post-Independence Helplessness and New
    Hopes and Nigeria's
    Betrayal of Black Hope, An Update ........................... 183
    *Nigeria 1960-79 ........................................................ 186
    *Alhaji Shehu Shagari 1979-1983 ............................... 187
    *General Muhammed Buhari 1983-1985 .................... 188
    *General Ibrahim Badamosi Babangida:1985-1993 ..... 190
    *Chief Ernest Shonekan 1993 ..................................... 195
    *General Sani Abacha ;1993-1998 .............................. 196
    *General Abdulsami Abubakar, 1998-1999 ................ 204
    *Nigeria is still in danger ........................................... 207
10. The Black Man can make it. 1976 Edition ................. 213
10. The Black Man can make it. An Update ................... 233
    APPENDIX I .............................................................. 241
    APPENDIX II ............................................................. 255
    APPENDIX III ............................................................ 261
    APPENDIX IV ........................................................... 265
    APPENDIX V ............................................................. 275
    APPENDIX VI ........................................................... 279
    BIBLIOGRAPHY ....................................................... 285

*CHAPTER ONE*

## 1976 EDITION

## WHO IS THE BLACK MAN?

EXPERTS have never been unanimous about the classification of racial types. But in race classification emphasis is usually placed on variations in the external physical characteristics.

Hence, any definition of race, no matter how loose, implies the existence of groups which have certain physical similarities which are perpetuated according to the laws of biological inheritance. However, an allowance is usually made for a margin of individual variations.

A national community cannot be a race while a race cannot be defined in terms of common culture, religion or language. And although language may be helpful in race classification, it is not entirely a safe guide to race.

Further, the slave trade and emigration by various races have made it impossible to classify major racial groups on clear lines of geographical demarcation.

For several years, men have given different racial classifications. As far back as 1738, the Swedish naturalist, Carolus Linnaeus who assigned all men to the species, HOMO SAPIENS, (HOMO for man, SAPIENS for wise) also divided human beings into the following four categories:

AMERICANUS  –  (American India) –Tenacious, contented, free, ruled by custom.
EUROPAEUS  –  Light, lively, inventive, ruled by rites.
ASIATICUS  –  Stern, haughty, stingy, ruled by opinion.
AFTER (African)  –  Cunning, slow, negligent; ruled by caprice.

Linnaeus classification has an obvious fault. It is based on characters of the mind. And contrary to his belief, negligent, lively and contented individuals can be found everywhere in the world and not among any particular race.

Also in 1775, a German scholar, Otto Blumenbach, divided men into five racial groups according to colour of their skin.

Blumenbach's five racial groups are:
CAUCASIAN or White
MONGOLIAN or Yellow
ETHIOPIAN or Black
AMERICAN or Red
MALAYAN or Brown

Other anthropologists later measured parts and proportions of the body, particularly of the head and gave a great multiplication of races.

For instance, in 1889, J. Deniker, classified human beings into 29 races who were distinguished by forms of hair, colours of skin and shape of nose.

In 1933, Eickstedt classified human beings into three basic races Europid, Negroid and Mongolid and with what he described as 18 "sub-races", three "collateral races", 11 "collateral sub-races" and three "intermediate forms".

In 1950, three American anthropologists, Coon, Garn and Birdsell classified human groups into six "putative stocks" – Mongoloid, Negroid, White, Australoid, American India, Polynesia-and 30 different races. Some of the 30 races like American coloured, South African coloured and Neo-Hawaiian are interesting as examples of races in the making.

Also, in 1950, Boyd, classified mankind on the basis of frequency of the gene and recognized five major races. The groups, which are as follows, represent those that are found in different geographical areas.

EUROPEAN or Caucasoid
AFRICAN or Negroid
ASIATIC or Mongoloid
AMERICAN INDIAN
AUSTRALOID.

At present, it is difficult to say that one racial classification is more correct than the other. But either the five categories listed above which Boyd recognised or the following three major racial groups are generally recognised by anthropologists and scientists because they are clearly based on geographical isolation. The three major groups are:

CAUCASIANS (or Whites). They derive from Europe and are typified by our present day European.
MONGOLS. They derive from Asia and the Chinese and Indians are two of their great sub-divisions.

NEGROES. They derive from Africa and are typified by West Africans.

In this book, I will use the words Negro race, Negroes, Black race and black men interchangeably. The main physical characteristics of the Negroes are their dark or dark-brown skin, short frizzy or spiralled hair, a flat broad nose, a measure of projecting jaws and thick lips that are often everted.

The home of the Negro race is the African continent. Sub-groups of the race have been given linguistic classification by anthropologists, notably Professor C.G. Seligman in RACES OF AFRICA. These are the Sudanic speaking blacks of West Africa, the Bantu speaking blacks of the Southern, Eastern and Central Africa, and two other smaller groups-the Bushman, Hottentot, and Negrillos of Southern Africa. They are all remarkably uniform in appearance.

The Hamites (Berbers) and Semites who are found mainly in Northern Africa do not belong to the Negro or black race. They are light-skinned. These, as well as the Moors or Arabs found in the North African countries, are entirely different from the black race.

Apart from the difference in skin colour between the inhabitants of North African countries and the black race, the white North Africans, sometimes described as dark-skinned Caucasians, are also separated from the Negroes of black Africa by their difference in culture and history. White Africa is also Mediterranean and it is a continuation of Europe.

However, through the ages, the Hamites and later Semites have, in different degrees, intermingled with the black race. So, among the Negroes in Africa are millions who have been hamiticised to a varying degree. In this book, I regard the hamiticised Negroes as part of the black race because they have the general physical characteristics and culture of the Negroes.

Intermingling of races, which has been going on during the whole of recorded history, has also affected negroes who inhabit large areas of the earth surface. Those who are affected include the "mullatto" or "coloured" in South America, the Caribbean, United States, South Africa and Europe. They have one white and one black parent. Many of the 80 million Negroes in the Western World fall into this category.

In this book, they are treated as part of the black race. Although this is an arbitrary classification, most White people include "coloured men" among the black and a great majority of the "coloured" peoples have identified themselves with the blacks, especially in the United States, the Caribbean and South America.

*Black Man's Dilemma*

# CHAPTER ONE

## *REVISED EDITION*

# *Who Is The Black Man?*

## *AN UPDATE*

There are no new findings which contradict the facts and conclusions in this chapter.

*Black Man's Dilemma*

## CHAPTER TWO

## 1976 EDITION

## AFRICA: THE BIRTH-PLACE OF MAN

IN the 18th century, fossils were accepted as the petrified remains of former living organisms. This led to two kinds of con troversy. There were those who believed in the 'catastrophic theory' which says that different fossils found in different geological strata in different periods of time came into being as a result of series of destructions and creations. And that the creation of man came last. The second view about fossils is that of the `Diluvialists` who argued that fossils represented creatures destroyed during Noah`s flood.

With the increasing discovery of human bones, remains of extinct animals and artifacts in Europe during the first half of the 19th century, more geological evidence became available about the evolution of animals and man. These findings destroyed the validity of the Diluvial theory which believed in a single universal deluge throughout the earth and the catastrophic theory.

But in 1859, when Charles Darwin published his great work, *Origin of Species,* a strong support was given to a belief in organic evolution. Darwin established that one living form could arise out of another ancestral form, instead of being a separate creation. He showed that the varieties of living organisms had reached their present condition by a process of descent with modification, guided by the principle of natural selection. Darwin propounded the theory that hereditary variations, of unknown origins, provided the raw materials from which the environment selected the fittest or adapted characters and combinations for survival.

Later, in 1871, Charles Darwin published another great work, *The Descent of Man*, in which his theory of evolution was applied to the origin of man. The work refuted the idea that human beings were specially created by God and endowed from the very beginning with all mental and physical qualities for their existence. This means that man had evolved over a period of hundreds of thousands of years from the lowly animal form.

Darwin then observed that human beings "had risen to the summit of the organic scale, and had developed a god-like intellect, he still bears in his bodily frame the indelible stamp of his lowly origin"

Darwin further submitted that human beings descended from the same stock as the old World Monkeys, which like human beings, have 32 set of teeth. He argued that all living mammals in any specific area were usually closely related to the fossilized remains of extinct species discovered in the specific area. Darwin, therefore, concluded that because the gorilla and the chimpanzee which are the two living primates that most closely resemble human beings are both found in Africa, man's birthplace would, in all probability, be discovered on the continent of Africa.

Inspired by Darwin's writings, scientists looked forward to the discovery of an intermediate form between human beings and the apes. This hypothetical "missing link" is known as the " Ape

## Africa: The Birth-Place of Man

Man" He is described as pithecanthropus in 1866 by Ernst Heackel, a German evolutionist. With time, experts discovered there are many of such "missing links" between the ape and man. And to a world waiting for a clue to the "missing link" the discovery by a young Dutch army doctor, Eugene Dubois, in 1891, aroused great interest. Dubois found at Trinil in Java a low-vaulted skull with prominent brow-ridges, a femur and a premolar tooth which were believed to belong to the same individual. The femur showed that the individual was an upright walking one. But the size of the brain case was estimated to be half-way between that of a gorilla and man. Dubois named the java man he founded " pithecanthropus erectus" because it was "an erect missing link" The java find was more ape-like than any known man but more human than any known ape.

This find became important in the study of human evolution. It was believed that man emerged as a recognisable human creature a few hundred thousand years ago in Asia in the form of upright walking man-like animal known as HOMO ERECTUS. After several years this 'man' acquired increasing sophistication in his use of tools. His brain size roughly doubled and the shape of his skull changed from that of the ape to the one similar to that of man, HOMO SAPIENS.

Also in the 1920s, remains of primitive four-foot tall ape-men were discovered in South Africa. But the most profound archeological discoveries so far about the origin of man were that of the late Dr Louis Seymour Bazett Leakey (1903-1972) and his family. The findings of Dr. L. S. B Leakey and his colleagues proved that it was on the African continent that man's ancestor was lifted from the animal level to the status of man.

In July 1959, Louis and Mary Leakey unearthed primitive stone tools and an almost complete skull in Olduvia gorge in Tanzania.

*Black Man's Dilemma*

Late in 1961, the Leakeys found a skull that looked far more similar to that of modern man. Its teeth were the size of human teeth. Its brain case was much bigger than that of the 1959 find and lacked the gorilla-like crest at the top of the head. This was named HOMO HABILIS. He was believed to be the true ancestor of man. Louis Leakey's son Richard, later made significant finds at a 1,000 square mile tract of land on the eastern shore of lake Rudolf in Kenya. And just 100miles from lake Rudolf, in the Omo Valley of Ethiopia, there are excavations on a 200 square-mile area. All these archeological discoveries lead to one major conclusion: that the origins of man have now been pushed back more than 2 million years. Also, that man left in his process of evolution at least two, and perhaps three species of man-like creatures-all long extinct.

But the finds in Africa could not mean that man evolved there alone even though the recent finds confirm that Africa has remarkable claim to being the cradle of mankind. Africa gave the world the human race. Hence, human history began in Africa and spread round the earth. The conclusion has also been drawn from discoveries in Africa that the Old Stone Age Africa (Paleolithic Africa) led the rest of the world in man's early development. Africa thus became the birth-place of man because it was there that our near man ancestor emerged into human status about two and half million years ago. And for several centuries after the emergence Africa was believed to be in the forefront of all world progress.

But if man originated from Africa, it is strange indeed that the black man has remained far behind the other races of the world in his ability to conquer nature or improve his environment. In terms of inventions, discovery of better means of production and the conquest of harsh climatic and physical conditions (like the cold climate spurring the white races to invent heaters and mine coal), the black man has made no remarkable progress. It has

## Africa: The Birth-Place of Man

been particularly noticeable that since the Industrial Revolution, Europe and America have remained the world's centers of progress. The Chinese had for centuries made their own significant contributions to civilisation. And in terms of effective and rapid adaptation of modern science and technology to production techniques, the Chinese and Japanese have made and are still making important contributions to modern civilisation and progress.

The relative backwardness of the black man also leads to another intriguing question. If all men living are descended from common ancestors, whose birthplace has been established to be mainly, if not entirely in Africa, how has mankind become divided into the Caucasian, Mongolian and black races? History alone cannot answer this question. For the major groups of human beings had already become different before written history began. The differences arose through heredity when the genes sometimes changed by a process called mutation which gives rise to a great variety of genes. But this alone cannot explain differences in races for the gene proportions may remain relatively the same in different populations.

A significant point is that the different populations in different parts of the world seem to be fitted for or adapted to the conditions under which they live. Certain hereditary characters such as white skins seem to have been more successful in Europe and the Mediterranean while dark skins seem more successful in Africa South of the Sahara. Various studies have shown that the proportion of animal or plant population which have those combinations of characters that are advantageous in certain places, for example in a desert or riverine area, tend to increase in the place from one generation to another until they form the bulk of the population. They gradually supplant other combinations.

Darwin explained that the necessary changes occur through differential reproduction by which certain genotypes leave more offspring than others. He described this process as that of natural selection. It tends to produce local races and eventually species which are adapted to or fitted for life in the particular area. It means that not all genotypes have equal chances of leaving offspring in all environments. This view supports the conclusions of several experts, especially Professor Claude Levi-Strauss, who says that "natural selection, favouring some genes in certain places and others in other environments has probably been the most potent factor in causing change in gene frequency and thus in producing racial differences."

In the light of the foregoing facts, I have always wondered why the black man has done relatively little in changing his environment and making it a better place to live in. And why he has failed to provide significant comforts for himself without foreign assistance or influence. He has not been able, at least solely on his own, to modernise his methods of providing basic needs like food, shelter and water. He has also not been able to make his own system of farming, weaving, house construction and cooking less tedious and laborious as other races have done through a thoughtful application of scientific principle and technology to human endeavours. And science and technology have become an inheritance of mankind.

Besides, if all races, including the black race, have behind them a past of approximately equal length, why must our own race remain behind in material progress? Why must black societies remain comfortable with the sad fact that we are just reaching the stages in development which the Caucasian and Mongolian races had reached centuries back? It means we must admit the distressing but incontrovertible fact that while progress was being made among other races, no progress or very little progress was being made among the black peoples. And Africa is believed to be the birthplace of man. It also means we have wasted our time while others were battling day and night to conquer nature and make their environments better than they found them. While others were running fast in the race for progress, it appears we were loitering along the road. It is sad. But it is the unfortunate situation.

*Black Man's Dilemma*

## CHAPTER TWO

## *REVISED EDITION*

## *AFRICA: THE BIRTHPLACE OF MAN*

### *AN UPDATE*

I have been very unhappy because since I published Black Man's Dilemma in 1976, black countries have not made even rudimentary efforts to adapt modern science and technology to suit their peculiar underdeveloped needs.

With the developed world embarking on increasingly advanced technological innovation in printing, computer, information equipments, engineering and industrial machines, I had hoped that, like Japan did, black countries would begin some meaningful adaptation of modern technology to their needs even if it is in their crudest form. By doing this we could be described as the poor imitators of the other races. This should not bother our race. Afterall, science and technology are an inheritance of mankind. All that should be important to us is that we have successfully adapted science and technology to change our environment and improve our methods of providing basic needs.

But with the world striving to occupy the moon and arrange regular shuttle between it and the earth, why must the black race have    difficulties in crossing the fence? This calls for a deeper reflection and positive actions by thoughtful members of our race.

*Black Man's Dilemma*

## CHAPTER THREE

## 1976 EDITION

## BLACK MAN'S BACKWARDNESS

THERE are three intriguing facts about the black race. They are facts which most black and "coloured" peoples and some liberal whites would prefer not to face honestly and squarely.

One such fact is that no black country has ever made a breakthrough to modernity. As black peoples, we have no country to be proud of in terms of its great inventions and discoveries, its technical equipment and political power. No black country has successfully developed or adapted the technology of industrial civilisation to assure its citizens of a high standard of living. I don't know of any black country which has made any meaningful beginning in the development of at least, parts of modern technology and science. No black country has solved the problem of poverty among a great majority of its citizens. None has found any concrete solution to the problem of poor nutrition, endemic diseases, inadequate basic education and infrastructural facilities. Countries like Guinea, Tanzania, Guyana and Nigeria since July, 1975, are trying to be original but they face great odds and they are few.

But both the Caucasians (the whites) and the Mongolians (the

Asians) have built modern nations. Of recent, China and Japan have taken over modern technology. They have adopted their own tools and systems of organisation which allow skill to develop. They have recorded great achievements, attained high productivity and assured their citizens of basic essentials of life and even a modicum of comfort.

And the whites have a lot to be proud of. Great Britain was a pioneer in industrialisation. She developed a technology, initiated an agricultural revolution and exploration and built a modern nation. Other whites like the French and Germans built modern nations. Countries like Denmark, Norway and Sweden which have no history of colonial exploitation also had a breakthrough to modernity and their peoples attained some of the highest standards of living in the world.

And the white peoples of the Union of the Soviet Socialist Republics (USSR) have built a modern nation in two generations by making peoples with a nomadic and pastoral way of life to operate an industrial economy based on machines.

Above all, the whites have penetrated into the remotest parts of the world and their technology and social organisation have lasted for at least four centuries. In the United States, the same Caucasians (the whites) have created a civilisation based on the most up-to-date innovations in science and technology and unparalleled development of infrastructure. They have built a modern nation with the highest standards of living in the world.

## Black Slavery

The second intriguing fact about the black race is that it was the only race in history which has between 14.6 million and 20 million of its members physically transported as slaves from Africa to a completely new area (the Americas) and with the period of transportation lasting about 300 years.

Dr. W.E.B. Du Bois, the famous Afro-American historian, calculated that from about 1510 when the first slaves were transported to the New World till the 19$^{th}$ Century, a total of 14,650,000 blacks were taken to America from Africa as slaves. Later estimates put the number of black slaves removed from Africa from the sixteenth century onward at 20 million.

Dr. Du Bois also said Africa lost 100,000,000 people as a result of the slave trade. This might appear an exaggeration if account is not taken of millions who died before embarking on or during the passage to America and the fact that slaves had been shipped out of Africa even before America was discovered.

Equally strange was the active support which the African chiefs and middle class gave to the capturing and transportation of their fellow blacks to America. All along the East and West African coasts trading stations sprang up. These were manned by African chiefs and entrepreneurs who sold black slaves to the whites on trade by barter basis.

The Africans offered for sale were ostensibly supposed to be condemned criminals, people who had voluntarily sold themselves into slavery or war captives. This explanation was false although to African slave dealers, it was a convenient rationalisation. However, with this explanation, the Europeans were relieved of moral responsibility for their heinous crime. And African slave dealers even claimed credit for saving their victims from death.

The motivation of the chiefs and entrepreneurs who sold fellow Africans into slavery was ridiculous. African rulers found European wines, Venetian glass beads, French brandy, cast-off uniforms, outdated firearms, scarlet handkerchiefs and other goods sufficiently desirable to hand over captives which they had taken in tribal warfare. Wars were fought between various tribes with the sole aim of getting fellow blacks for sale to Europeans. Many chiefs also sold their own subjects when the offer of shoddy consumer goods from Europe became quite attractive. Some scholars argue that the blacks who sold their subjects didn't know the extent of hazards to which the subjects would be exposed. But even then, they were motivated by selfish considerations.

The black people of Africa could not muster enough courage to counter the decisive advantage which the Europeans initially had in their possession of crude cannons, firearms and boats. So the slave trade lasted about 300 years. The helplessness of black Africans about stopping the slave trade and their active interest in its continuation has no precedence in history.

Admittedly, Agaja Trudo, the great King of Dahomey, believed that slave trade was inimical to the best interest of his territory. And in the 1720s, King Trudo opposed the White slave traders. But his was a solo effort. He struggled. For between 1724 and 1726, Trudo looted and burnt European slave camps and forts. Efforts of white slave traders to crush the kingdom of Dahomey by instigating fellow Africans to raid it also failed. They could not unseat Agaja Trudo. But with time, the urge to acquire cowries and firearms and the desire to safeguard his throne became too strong for Trudo. He agreed to the resumption of slave of trade in 1730.

### The Black Man is Always Behind other Races

The third perplexing fact will undoubtedly arouse the resentment of my black and 'coloured' brothers and sisters.

*Black Man's Backwardness*

Relying on the fact that the different races of the world came into existence at the same time, I have come to the sad, but valid conclusion that the black man has made little or no contribution to world civilisation. And civilisation is a heritage of mankind. It is not a native of any region. It is not an exclusive contribution of any race. It entails achievements in government, law, religion, art, science and social philosophy and the means and circumstance that render these achievements possible. When civilisation is viewed as the wonderful variety of the achievements of man, the black man must admit the fact of his negligible contribution. To appreciate the fact that the Caucasian and Mongolian races have always moved far ahead of the black race, the black peoples of the world require a revolution. It is a revolution of the mind. It is the conquest of the right to think and admit that in all the crisis of man's history, our race has always been the underdog. Ours is the only race that has never made it anywhere in the world. We have for too long remained poor immitators of the other races.

Throughout history, the black man has shown an appalling loss and lack of integrity in position and intellect and the thinking world cannot fail to be struck by the negativity, opportunism and parochialism of black people's activities. This is no racism. I am black. I am not even "coloured". But this is the truth. Its also an admission of the fact that a few blacks and black nations which are doing well have a great task ahead.

From a cooler and quite rational viewpoint of self interest, liberal white scholars in the economically advanced countries of Europe and America, have for so long hesitated to tell the black man clearly that he is backward. For Centuries the whites have ruthlessly exploited the black man. They want to continue to oppress and exploit him. And to put a complete end to this subjugation, oppression, and exploitation the black man needs a determined and unusual effort. Which means that he must be realistic and truthful about his past and present situation. And this the whites don't want him to do.

Rather than urge black peoples to accept the fact of their centuries of backwardness vis-à-vis, the other races of the world, take more positive steps to right the great historical wrongs done to them and put their membership of human family on the basis of genuine equality, Western scholars tell us we have nothing to be ashamed of, that the black man can change his underdog position in the world without a radical change in his attitude. For instance, Michel Leris of the Centre National de la Recherche Scientifique and Musee de l'Homme in Paris puts forth this view clearly in **RACE AND CULTURE:**

> *From the History of Europe as well, we can learn how much the customs of peoples can change without major alteration of their racial composition, and how fluid is 'national character'. Who would suspect that the peaceable farmers of modern Scandinavia were the descendants of the dreaded Vikings, whose long ships raided so much of Europe in the nineth century? Or would a Frenchman of 1950 recognise as his fellow countrymen the contemporaries of Charles Martel, who conquered the Arabs at Poitiers if he had not learned it in the schools? It is also worth remembering that when Julius Ceasar first landed in Great Britain in 52 B.C. the Britons struck the invaders as so barbarious that Cicero, writing to his friend Atticus, advised him against buying any of them as slaves because 'they are so stupid and incapable of learning'. Nor should we forget that, after the fall of the Roman Empire, the inhabitants of Europe took many centuries to establish solidly organised and militarily formidable states....*

## Black Man's Backwardness

This kind of thinking is, strangely enough, actively encouraged by a world organisation – UNESCO – and the thought is prevalent among Western liberal scholars. It is not a helpful idea to we the black people in the serious dilemma we face. For instance, if as Michel Leris puts it, Britons were so "utterly stupid and incapable of learning" when Caesar first landed in their country over 2,000 years ago, the black peoples were probably then thousands of years from their own evolution from the animal kingdom of apes into HOMO SAPIENS. We were possibly not as developed as the Stone Age cave dwellers 2,000 years ago. Besides, black peoples cannot wait for 2,000 years to catch up with the rest of the world.

A world that is right there on the moon when we have not crossed the fence. It means we must achieve what took other races centuries to achieve, in two or three decades. This will entail a critical self examination. It will require a mental revolution.

The Caucasian race in Russia did not, after the 1917 revolution, decide to wait for centuries before they could catch up with the civilised world. They had their breakthrough to modernity in two decades. And the Mongolian race in the Communist Republic of China also joined the rest of civilised humanity in less than two decades after the 1949 Communist victory.

Equally obvious is the deceit in the statement credited to Lord Olivier in 1905 that "The Negro is progressing and that disposes of all the arguments in the world that he is incapable of progress". I admit that we are making some progress. But whatever progress we are making is little and very slow.

As peoples who are just emerging from centuries of backwardness, foreign domination and dehumanisation, the concept of African personality is a constructive force for the blacks. It helps us to re-create the past, build up some myths that can be of relevance to our future aspirations. But the idea that black man's past, his religious and spiritual life, his respect for elders and communal spirit are more important than his technology is inimical to our progress. If the black race is going to understand how the Caucasian and Mongolian races created their various achievements, how their beautiful cities came to be built, and writing came to be invented, how they adapted science and technology to all areas of production, our race must examine how these other races created their great past and civilisation to strengthen their own present and future. I agree with the view that industrialisation and technology may not necessarily bring happiness or social peace but they bring higher standard of living.

Technological and social advancement, especially the former, which stems from scientific discoveries and progress, have always received great emphasis as clear marks of civilisation. There was a period when man's grandeur, his religious and spiritual life were regarded as being far more important than his technology. But while arts and religion are important in the assessment of civilisation, there is a great danger in just looking at them in isolation. Various cultures and races have contributed to civilisation through mutual contact and influences.

The earliest civilisations were based on agriculture. These grew in areas made fertile by the following rivers – the Nile, the Euphrates, the Tigris, the Blue and Yellow Rivers, the Ganges and the Indus. Trading civilisations which centred around inland seas or seas with land masses followed.

Those involved in these early commerce were the Greeks and Phoenicians in the Mediterranean and the Malays in the China seas. The early commercial civilisations were later displaced by those based on large-scale industrial enterprises centred around the coal deposits of Europe, North America and Asia.

Contacts between various races both within and outside nations have resulted in the enrichment of various civilizations and the growth of world civilization. Various nations have borrowed from different cultures while cooperation and intermingling between people have resulted in new cultures. In his work, RACE AND CULTURE, Michel Leris gives the following vivid explanation on how the present Western civilisation has borrowed a great deal from other civilisations:

*"The civilisation of which the Western world is so proud has been built of a myriad contributions, of which many are non-European in origin. The alphabet first reached the Phoenicians from the Semitic communities bordering the Sinai Peninsula, travelled from them to the Greeks and Romans and then spread through the Westernmost parts of Europe. Our numerals and algebra came to us from the Arabs whose philosophers and scientists incidentally played an important part in the various renaissances of mediaeval Europe. The earliest astronomers were Chaldeans; steel was invented in India or Turkistan; coffee comes from Ethiopia; tea, porcelain, gunpowder, silk, and the compass were given us by the Chinese who also were acquainted with printing centuries before Gutenberg, and early discovered how to make paper. Maize, tobacco, the potato, quinine, vanilla and cacao we owe to the American Indians. The explanation, of the 'miracle of Greece' is really that Greece was a crossroad, where vast numbers of different peoples and culture met. Lastly, we should recollect that the wall paintings and engravings of the Aurignacian and Magdalenia ages (the most ancient works of art known in Europe, of which it may be said with truth that their beauty has*

*never been exceeded) were the works of men of the Grimaldi type, probably not unlike the Negro races of today; that in another aesthetic sphere, the jazz which plays so important a part in our leisure, was evolved by the descendants of Negroes taken to the United States as slaves, to whom that country also owes the oral literature on which the famous Uncle Remus stories are based".*

Undoubtedly, human civilisation, not just Western civilisation, owes a great debt to many countries which were first with the discoveries of many crucial products and processes and those who were initiators of great arts, music and religions. For instance, India was the first with the use of the so called Arabic numbers and with glass and steel. China was first for the manufacture of silk and the discovery of paper. The world also owes a debt to China for the magnetic compass and gunpowder which had been in use in that country in the twelfth century.

The Phoenicians were the first with the use of alphabet, and the ancient Mexicans were perfectly familiar with the wheel in the manufacture of toy animals on wheels for children to play with. Greece, Rome, Carthage, Egypt, Palestine, Assyria and Persia also made significant contributions to civilisation.

Civilisation has its universality and the world has been made richer by the variety of contributions to civilisation by different peoples at different periods. What is good, true and valuable in human civilisation has never been a monopoly of any country or culture. In this respect, the error of the Chinese Emperor who sent the following written message to the King of England is quite obvious! "We possess all things. I set no value on objects strange or ingenious."

Many scholars have put great emphasis on the universality of Culture. They argue that culture is flexible and provisional. It is constantly transformed. It also accumulates new elements while all innovations in culture are never entirely original. Claude Levi-Strauss says: "Civilisation implies and indeed consists in the coexistence of culture exhibiting the maximum possible diversities." And Michel Leris elaborates as follows on this point in RACE AND CULTURE.

*"Innovations in culture never 'start from scratch'. For instance, the invention of the loom not merely implied prior knowledge of certain laws and of other simpler mechanisms, but also the response to a need arising at a particular moment in the evolution of modern industry. Similarly, the discovery of America would have been impossible without the compass, while Christopher Columbus would never even have thought of sailing westwards if the march of events had not made a maritime trade route to the Indies a felt need.*

*In the aesthetic sphere, the work of Phidias could never have come about without Polycletes, nor Andalusian folk music of today have developed without Arab music; and as a last example, in the sphere of government, it was on Athenian life and aspirations already existing that Solon drew to endow his fellow citizens with a new constitution, which in fact was no more than a codification of the social complex.*

*Thus, no invention, discovery or innovation can be ascribed exclusively to one individual. Inventors, or pioneers on other lines, are, found in all civilisations. However, an invention is not the result of a single flash of genius, but the last stage in a gradual advance, as the following sequence exemplifies: in 1663, the Marquess of Worcester devised a 'steam fountain' on his estate near London, based on principles suggested about 50 years earlier by a Frenchman, Salomon de Caus. Later came the invention of the pressure boiler by another Frenchman, Denis Pain, leading in turn to that of the reciprocating engine by James Watt and the final step was by George Stephenson's construction of the 'Rocket locomotive in 1814.*

*Neither inventions nor discoveries are ever more than modifications, variable in their degree and their repercussions, which are the latest of a long series of earlier inventions and discoveries in a culture which is itself the work of a community and the product of indigenous innovations or borrowings from abroad by earlier generations."*

It is true that civilization is mankind's inheritance and inventions often occur in stages in response to felt needs. However, the idea that human civilisation entails carrying forward and change has received other interpretations. An example is the diffusionist idea which sometimes became extravagant. Like Lord Raglan's school which states that all civilisation started in Mesopotamia. Or the Elliot Smith school which says that everything about civilisation started in Egypt. So were a group of German archaeologists who believe that everything started in Germany.

Also, the idea of the origin and spread of human civilisation has been given some deep racial overtones. Take the racist Gobineau who regarded the mixing of cultures as a disaster for mankind. Gobineau made the claim that out of the 10 most brilliant civilisations known to mankind, six belong to the 'Aryans' who are regarded by him as the 'higher' brand of the Caucasian (white)race. These are Greek, Roman, Hindu, Egyptian, German and Assyrian. The other four major civilisations, according to Gobineau, are Mexican, Chinese, Maya and Peruvian.

*Black Man's Dilemma*

## CHAPTER THREE

# REVISED EDITION

# BLACK MAN'S BACKWARDNESS

### AN UPDATE

In the first edition of Black Man's Dilemma, I mentioned three facts about the black race that I have always found most intriguing. The first is that no black country has, in terms of scientific and technological development, provision of high standard of living for its citizens and an enduring political structure and power, made a breakthrough to modernity.

The second fact was our ancestors' helplessness in the face of years of black slavery until a motley of contradictions among the European slave dealers and the elite forced them to have a rethink on their heinous crime.

The third fact is the relative backwardness of the black race vis-à-vis the other races of the world.

Of the three points mentioned above, the point that has always kept me sad is that after so many years of political independence, there is still very slim possibility of a black country making a breakthrough to mordernity. The high hope I nursed in 1976 that black African countries like Nigeria, Guinea, Ghana and Tanzania would take giant steps towards technological, economic and socio-political development, has turned out to be a misplaced hope.

While South Korea, China, Japan, Brazil, Germany, the United States and other far-sighted countries are massively investing their human and material resources in the application of scientific, engineering and technological research, thereby transforming their production, industrial and social welfare systems, Nigeria and other black countries pay minimal attention to research. They also attach little importance to the application of research findings to their countries' needs.

While countries in Europe, America and Asia have yearly used scientific, engineering and technological research and application to astronomically raise their gross domestic product and achieve economic transformation, Nigeria and other black African countries prod on with their stunted growth in science, engineering and technology.

And achieving any meaningful application of the research findings in Nigeria's 60 research and development centres, institutes and the more than 30 Federal Universities, is a big problem for the country. Policy makers do not see the direct connection between massive research findings and application on one hand and a country's spectacular breakthrough to modernity on the other hand. It is very sad.

But far more painful is the failure of black countries to insist that the multinational companies, which have their headquarters in the highly developed economies of Europe and America, must devote a goo percentage of their earnings to scientific, engineering and technological research. Strangely though, these foreign-owned multinationals invest heavily in research and the application of research findings in their home countries. This explains the yearly technological advancement their countries record in manufacturing and engineering.

*Black Man's Dilemma*

CHAPTER FOUR

# 1976 EDITION

# BLACK MAN'S NEGLIGIBLE CONTRIBUTION TO HUMAN CIVILISATION

FROM the research I did for this book and concrete evidence of the great civilisations of the Caucasian and Mongolian races which I saw during my journeys to different parts of the world, I have become fully convinced that the much vaunted black civilisations of ancient Ghana, Shonghai, Mali, Zimbabwe, Hausa/Fulani, Yoruba, Benin and other areas were quite inferior to the civilisations of the other races. The black race did not make any significant contribution to human civilisation which is a common inheritance of mankind. Even if one agrees with Claude Levi-Strauss that "world civilisation represents no more than a worldwide coalition of cultures, each of which would preserve its own originality", yet, our contribution has been comparatively negligible.

I regard the writings of Western liberal scholars and black historians on the greatness, glory and achievements of ancient African kingdoms, empires and emirates as a deliberate morale booster for the dehumanised black race. Ours is a race that has always been the underdog and is now just trying to reach out for its past. Some have argued that Western morale booster is better than morale killer. However, I believe that our morale will be meaningfully boosted if we admit that our achievements were modest in the past but strive hard for great achievements now and in future. Black intelligentsia merely want to go beyond the black man's misery of today to discover a past of glory, grandeur and beauty. But let us make no mistake about it, there was not much to be proud of in our past. We are exaggerating our past achievements while the overwhelming majority of blacks all over the world, heirs to the Zimbabwe, Mali, Borno, Shonghai, Fulani, Yoruba and Benin civilisations have no access to basic essentials of modern living. They are today underfed and illiterate. They are in poor health. And our present backwardness reflects yesterday's backwardness.

All talks about our past greatness are myths. They are empty dreams. And it is a vain hope to think that myths are a substitute for the great strength which the black race must today call forth for its rapid breakthrough to modernity, our lack of a worthwhile past notwithstanding. Some say colonialism has distorted our great past. But if ours was a solid past like that of the other races it would have been indestructable.

Claude Levi-Strauss in his work, *RACE AND HISTORY*, stresses that there is no culture without its own basic values and that it is wrong to put too much emphasis on "mere external features" or concentrate too much attention on isolated contributions of different cultures to civilisation. He said:

> *The originality of each culture consists rather in its individual way of solving problems, and in the perspective in which it views the general values which must be approximately the same for all mankind,*

*since all men, without exception, possess a language, technique, a form of art, some sort of scientific knowledge, religious beliefs, and some form of social, economic and political organisation. The relations are never quite the same. However, in every culture, and modern ethnology is concentrating increasingly on discovering the underlying reasons for the choices made, rather than on listing mere external features.*

Levi-Strauss is right that all men possess a language, techniques and some sorts of art, religion and knowledge of science. But on the basis of his own argument, while it is admitted that in the past, the black peoples of Africa possessed these general values, they possessed them in a most rudimentary form. The black peoples of Africa had oral and not written language. Their techniques of production were far cruder than those prevalent among the Caucasian and Mongolian races at the same periods of history and they possessed no knowledge of technology comparable to that found among the other races.

My aim is not to base the assessment of black culture and civilisation on the impressive technological progress of the West in the last six centuries. But even then, the black man's contribution to world civilisation is virtually non-existent in relation to the noteworthy architectural, technological, scientific, political and aesthetic contributions and remains of the classical world (Greece and Rome), Eastern Europe, Western Asia and the Eastern civilisations of India, Ancient China, classical Japan and their neighbours.

I agree with Professor Juan Comas' observation in his work, *RACIAL MYTHS*, that the insignificant contribution of the Negroes as a race is not due to "the supposed racial inferiority of the coloured peoples" (this point is discussed fully in chapter 7 which is on race theories). I also agree with his view that "it is unfavourable environmental, political and socio-economic factors which alone keep these groups at their present level." But the incontrovertible fact is that the other races have conquered adverse physical environments. They have triumphed over the most unfavourable political and socio-economic situation. I can share the following optimism of Professor Comas that the black race could easily conquer the adverse environmental factors which have made his history a non-event only on condition that the black elite will accept the pressing need for mental revolution and originality:

> *The contributions of Negroes as a race or as individuals to world civilisation are not an adequate basis for prognostication of what the race may be able to achieve in the future in terms of its own aptitudes and under more satisfactory environmental, social and economic conditions.*

The more I travel to various cities in Asia and Europe and see the great landmarks of mankind's contributions to world civilisation, the more convinced I became that the black man's claim to any significant contributions to civilisation is hollow and false.

At best, black peoples have remained the poor immitators of the other races since their isolation from the world was broken some five centuries ago. Before then, we had shown no evidence of any originality that wasn't foreign inspired or influenced. The really creative individual was never an organic and dynamic part of the ancient African societies.

In several relics, museums and monuments in Asia, Europe and North Africa, I saw concrete proofs of the existence of the rich Western, Eastern and Middle Eastern civilisations. These are uncontested and incontestable proofs of the unique contributions which the Greeks, Romans, Chinese, Indians, Japanese, Egyptians, Mesopotamians, English and Germans made to world civilisation through contacts and the mobility and mixture of highly developed culture which these contacts brought.

Nowhere in Africa can one find the type of heritage I have seen in Europe and Asia. Intriguing questions that have persistently crossed my mind are: What efforts were my black ancestors making when such great architectural, aesthetic, technological and scientific achievements were taking place in Europe and Asia? Did my black ancestors achieve any original and durable form of political and social organisation comparable to those whose written records I have seen in Europe, Asia and North Africa?

From one city to another in China, I saw numerous records and concrete evidence of the wonderful achievement of the Mongolian race. Some of those achievements date back to over 2,000 years ago. There is the great wall built with solid stones and concrete over rugged mountains and valleys and stretching for thousands of miles. It is one of the wonders of the world.

I saw the intricate architecture of the huge underground palaces which the Chinese built over a thousand years ago. Luxuries like chinawares, gold and silver works, sophisticated household utensils, paintings and sculptures created by the Chinese in and around these palaces are just bewildering. I saw abundant evidence of the Chinese invention of gunpowder and compass at a time when Europe could rightly be described as a dark continent. The Chinese perfected their own system of writing and printing.

While in Europe, I had a feeling that the ancient city of Anthens - the great city of Plato and Pericles- is no more. Yet, the inherent value of the intellectual, social and artistic achievements of the

Greek city-states vividly struck me. I had a feeling of the continued existence of the Greek achievements that is independent of time and use.

Everywhere in Europe and white Northern Africa I saw monuments and relics which showed the achievements of the Caucasian race in architecture, inventions and their sustained efforts to accumulate capital equipment and improve on methods of production of both the capital and consumer goods. There was nothing comparable to these unique developments in black Africa at the same periods of history.

In Exeter, England, I saw the solid walls which Caesar built when he landed in Britain about two thousand years ago. Also in Britain, which was a pioneer in industrialisation, I saw concrete evidence of effort of Britons to harness energy from the wind, water and later coal in order to meet their felt need for industrialisation. I saw the huge castles of the manorial lords and other public buildings which in their architectural grandeur and in the sophistication of the furniture in them today constitute a clear forward march in man's quest for civilisation.

Other contributions of which abundant evidence exists were in the areas of exploration, production of arms and ammunition, construction of macadamised roads and improved housing units.

But in all the centers of the so-called black Africa civilisations I had visited - Oyo, Benin, Sokoto, Maiduguri, Ile-Ife, the acient cities of modern Ghana, e.t.c., I found mud walls and dilapidated buildings not in any way comparable to the solid stones and concrete buildings - the great monuments I found in Europe, Asia and the Middle East. I have found no evidence of profound inventions and skilled human activities in black Africa. Bare-footed, scantily dressed descendants of the ancient African Kings and

Emirs squat round the old palaces still cherishing out-moded institutions and values.

Having visited some of these black African centres of development, I have come to the conclusion that the Dutch who visited Benin City in Nigeria in the 15th Century and described it as follows were more interested in trade success and diplomatic deceit than in the reality of Africa. The Dutch visitors wrote:

> *"the town (Benin) seems to be very great. When you enter into it, you go into a great broad street, not paved, which seems to be seven or eight times broader than the Warmoes Street in Amsterdam....*
>
> *The King's palace is a collection of buildings which occupy as much space as the town of Harlem, and which is enclosed with walls. There are numerous apartments for the prince's ministers and fine gallaries, most of which are as big as those on the Exchange at Amsterdam. They are supported by wooden pillars encased with copper, where their victories are depicted, and which are carefully kept clean.*
>
> *The town is composed of thirty main streets, very straight and 120 feet wide, apart from an infinity of small intersecting streets. The houses are close to one another, arranged in good order. These people are in no way inferior to the Dutch as regards cleanliness; they wash and scrub their houses so well that they are polished and shining like a looking-glass.*

The clownish Dutch adventurers who saw "houses that were so well polished and shining in Benin" in the 15th century and who saw that things were exactly equal in Benin and Holland must be fraudulent people who wanted to cash on the ignorance of the people of Holland. The Benin of today should, at least, in some ways, reflect the Benin of yesterday. But there is no evidence of the beautifully planned city which these Dutch adventurers described so vividly. Even if great destruction had occurred, the ruin should at least reflect the remarkable achievements in the architecture and town planning portrayed by the Dutch.

Today, in the old African centres of civilisation, there are carvings and terracotta. There is also a direct evidence of the ancient African methods of working bronze and ivory. But these were in no way superior to the great artistic works which other races had created for centuries. In Zimbabwe and old Timbuktu where some monuments and written records of enduring value exist, there are grave doubts whether they were original creations of black Africans or were Arab inspired.

Many Western liberal scholars are aware of the fact that the white countries have a lot to lose if the black man faces the reality of his situation and if he accepts the fact that he hasn't a past that he can be too proud of. The whites have a lot to lose if the blacks henceforth work hard to place their membership of human family on the basis of genuine equality. White experts publish books about our past glory, grandeur and achievements. They've got willing disciples among black intelligentsia who have lost the candour of any critical self- searching.

They create myths about the great past of black Africa. Listen to a leading black African leader and poet, Leopold Sedar Senghor, creating a myth in 1972, on Ile- Ife, the spiritual center for the Yorubas in Nigeria. Leopold Senghor says:

Ife is essentially the crossroads where, in olden times, flourished the Negro soul and imagination, creating myths, composing prayers, developing art.

In other words, I entirely agree with Professor Idowu when he says that religion is the foundation of Yoruba culture. Yes, religion expressed in terms of mythical image and symbols which, when given clearer meaning with the help of rhymes, became real works of art. In those days, the visible world was a sheet of water. It was then that Olodumare (God) decided to send Oduduwa (father of the Yorubas) as an emissary there. Carrying a bag of sand and holding in his hand two birds, symbols of peace and fruitfulness, Oduduwa had been instructed to spread his charge upon the surface of the water. From that gesture sprang Ile-Ife where, for the first time, man appeared as Oyo had fashioned him, in the shape of a creator of life and beauty. This particular man used the most authentic form of writing. He had no need to make books or building museums. His function was to express life through prayer and art, by symbolism. Thus he helped other men, all men to lead a better life. The man of Ile-Ife who was greeted by the West through the voice of Leo Frobenius, the German, was endowed with poetic powers. His mission was to help to shape the world for, as it has long been known in Africa, the world and, indeed, the universe, have to be fashioned constantly by man. It was that man who appeared at Ile-Ife who made it possible for the Blacks of America deported from mother Africa, to stand upright, rejecting the offer of humiliation and a slow lingering death. Moulded, as they were, in the clay of Ile-Ife, their refusal triumphed over all *weapons which decimated other races or worse still, condemned them to a dull, toneless, languishing existence, this is the virtue that lies behind the passion of Black men, and I use the world in all its varied meanings.*

President Leopold Sedar Senghor of Senegal had the best in French education and mode of life. He was assimilated into French culture. He probably refused to be dehumanised the way the French wanted him to be.

I agree with poet Senghor that it is sometimes good to have a myth, a black myth in particular. China has. Japan has. But Senghor's Ife myth and others are futile and irrelevant unless they become a source of strength.

As black peoples we need realistic myths. We need myths that can assure the blacks of a decent place among all races. We need myths that will be translated into concrete achievements in science, technology, industrialisation and military power. These are myths that can enable black peoples to raise their heads erect in Zimbabwe, South Africa, Namibia, USA, Nigeria and Senegal.

These must be myths that can make whatever we lack in a rich cultural heritage irrelevant. Our myths would become sources of strength once we could transform our present misery into achievements in a spectacular way.

Otherwise, Senghor's praise for "the vision of the man at Ile-Ife" may be dismissed as an over-simplification of a serious matter and an empty rhetoric.

The absurd view has also been expressed that colonialism and slavery led to the 'death' of black Africa's cultural heritage. A culture can only die if a whole people can be exterminated as the Romans did in the annihilation of Carthage. And even if, like Athens, black Africa's great monuments were destroyed and our languages were changed, we would still have the ruins of the monuments to show and our genius and forms of thought would still live on. For instance, in the book, *CULTURE PATTERNS AND TECHNICAL CHANGE*, a group of UNESCO experts made an interesting study of the uniqueness of the culture of the Greeks. They say:

> *The Greeks have the most ancient civilisation of the European continent, yet their technical development at present is one of the lowest. The history of their industries and factories goes back more than 2,500 years, yet they now resist industrialisation.*

But even then, there is today incontrovertible evidence of the great achievements of the Greek city-States. Besides, the absorption of the rich cultures of the Greeks into first, Romans, then medieval and now modern civilisation, has left the genius of the ancient Greece as mankind's heritage. No one can sincerely say this of any of the black kingdoms, empires and emirates of the African continent.

### False Claims on Black Man's Contribution to Civilisation

I appreciate the fact that our 25 million black and 'coloured' brothers and sisters in the United States need a morale booster. They need to be told that their black ancestors had a past that was as great and eventful as that of the Caucasian (white) race. For far more than in any other place, the back man has, for about 300 years, been mercilessly exploited and dehumanised in the United States.

He has been called all sorts of names by the whites. They've told him, his ancestors' continent was a vast haunt of savages, a continent of cannibals who live on trees. That the Negro is a link between the monkey and man - meaning, of course, the Caucasian (white) man. He has no historical past he can be proud of. The black man in America was also forced to lose his language, his dress and soul. He was made to substitute the white man's culture for these. And it will be shown later in this book that the black Americans have done far more than any other group of blacks anywhere in the world in their ability to show great resilience, courage and ingenuity in the face of some of the worst exploitation and persecution in history. It is therefore understandable why the late black American militant, Malcolm X, displayed such a frenzied outburst of emotion in the speech he made in New York on Afro-American History shortly before his assassination. Malcolm X gives the following version of black civilisation:

> On the African continent there was always a higher level of history, rather a higher level of culture and civilisation, than that which existed in Europe at the same time. At least 5,000 years ago, they had a black civilisation in the Middle East called the Sumerians. Now when they show you pictures of the Sumerians they try and make you think that they were white people. But if you go and read some of the ancient manuscripts or even read between the lines of some of the current writers, you'll find that the Sumerian civilisation was a very dark-skinned civilisation, and it existed prior even to the existence of Babylonian empire, right in the same area where you find Iraq and the Tigris-Euphrates Rivers there. It was a black-skinned people who lived there, who had a high state of culture way back then.
>
> And at a time even beyond this, there was a black-skinned people in India, who were black, just as black as you and I, called Dravidians. They inhabited the

## Black Man's Negligible Contribution to Human Civilisation

subcontinent of Indian even before the present people that you see living there today and they had a high state of culture. The present people of India even looked upon them as gods; most of their statutes, if you'll notice, have pronounced African features. You go right to India today – in their religion, which is called Buddhism, they give all their Buddhas the image of a black man, with his lips and his nose, and even show his hair curled up on his head; they didn't curl it up, he was born that way. And these people lived in that area before the present people of India lived there.

The black man lived in the Middle East before the present people who are now living there. And he had a high culture and civilisation, to say nothing about the oldest civilisation of all that he had in Egypt along the banks of the Nile. And in Carthage in Northwest Africa, another part of the continent, and at a later date in Mali, Ghana and Shonghai and Moorish civilisation - all of these civilisations existed on the African continent before America was discovered.

Now the black civilisation that shook the white man up the most was the Egyptian civilisation, and it was a black civilisation. It was along the banks of the Nile which runs through the heart of Africa. But again this tricky white man, and he is tricky- and mind you again, when I say this, it's not a racist statement. Some of them might not be tricky. And his civilisation shows his trickiness. This tricky white man was able to take the Egytian civilisation, write books about 't, put pictures in those books, make movies for television and the theatre - so skillfully that he has even convinced other white people that the ancient Egyptians were white people themselves. They were African, they were as much African as you and I. And he even gave the clue away when he made his movie, "King Solomon's Mines", and he showed the Watusis, you know, with their black selves, and he outrightly admitted in there that they looked like the ancient Pharaohs of ancient Egypt. Which means that the white man himself, he knows that the black man had his high civilisation in Egypt, whose remains today show the black man in that area had mastered architecture, the science of building things, had even mastered astronomy.

Malcolm X also talked about the civilisation of the Moors. He said: "the Moors were also dark-skinned people of the African continent". They were such great warriors that they crossed the straits of Gibraltar in the 8th Century, conquered Portugal, Spain and Southern France. In the same speech, Malcolm X claimed that Hannibal was a black man and implied that Carthage was a black civilisation. He summed up his claims on Carthage as follows:

Also as I said earlier, at that same time there was another African civilisation called Carthage. One of the most famous persons in Carthage was a man named Hannibal. You and I have been taught that he was a white man. This is how they steal your history, they steal your culture, they steal your civilisation - just by Hollywood producing a movie showing a black man as a white man. I remember one day I told some one that Hannibal was black - some Negro, he was in college, you understand - I told him Hannibal was a black man, and he had a fit. Really, he did, he wanted to fight me on that. "I know better than that".

*"How do you know"? He said, "I saw him" "Where'd you see him"? He said, "In the movies". And he was in college, really, he was a highly educated "Negro" - and some of you all right now are having a fit because you didn't know it either. Hannibal was famous for crossing the Alps on foot by themselves - no, they couldn't. Hannibal found a way to cross the Alps with elephants. You know what an elephant is - a great big old animal, it's hard to move him down the road. They moved him across the mountains. And he had with him 90,000 African troops, defeated Rome and occupied Italy for between 15 and 20 years. This is why you find many Italians dark-some of that Hannibal blood.*

Malcolm X said many things that are not true. But as a militant leader of an oppressed and dehumanised black Americans, his exaggeration and bitterness should be understandable. As I will show in the next chapter, he was right in his observation that there was some authentic black African civilisation in the old Ghana, Mali and Shonghai empires.

That the Dravidians of India are dark-skinned is correct. But it is not true that the Dravidians were black Africans. For at no time did black Africans migrate to India. Besides, that the Dravidians were dark-skinned is not strange because differences in colour of the skin exist among members of all races. For instance, among the darkest peoples of Nigeria, one finds light-skinned people without any kind of Hamitic or White intermingling. Among some sections of the Indian population and in the Southern part of India are dark peoples with strikingly Negro features. But it is not known when and how they got there.

Malcolm X is right to say that the Egyptian civilisation was African.

But the ancient Egyptians were "white" and not "black" Africans. Some black writers also make the mistake that because the river Nile which meant everything to the ancient Egyptian civilisation rises from the Negro region of Central Africa and brings aluvium from parts of Ethiopia (ancient KUSH), that all the great civilisations along the River Nile were black. Besides, the existence of some black population in North African countries for centuries did not make the major civilisation in that region black.

The civilisations found in Egypt between the Neo-lithic age and the Third Century, when Christianity spread over the country, was mainly Hamitic. Excavation of tombs has shown that from the polished stone Age onwards, the Hamites constituted the bulk of the population. But from the beginning of the dynastic epoch, the country was invaded at different periods by nomads from Asia known as Hyksos, the Libyans, the Achaeans, the Persians and Assyrians. When Egypt was annexed by Alexander in 332 B. C, it entered into the Greek orbit and this ended the sway of the Persians and Assyrians. Egypt had a period of relative isolation as from 31 B.C. during which she had contacts with the Near East.

From the 7th Century onwards, Egypt was under Arab and Turkish rule. Arabs and Turks became the ruling class and formed military oligarchy. Under the Fahmid dynasty (969 A.D. to 1170 A.D.) industry and science developed a great deal in Egypt. In the 10th Century, water wheels and windmills were introduced from Persia. Old industries of leather, metal and textiles were improved while sugar refinery, gasoline distillation, paper making and porcelain were introduced. The Mamluks held power from the 13th Century onwards. Under their dynasty and that of Ayyubids, trade contacts with Europe increased while many bridges, aqueducts, dams and canals were built.

Egyptologists and historians say that between 5869 to 3500 B.C., during the reign of Dynastic Egyptians, some of the ruling class had Negroid features. They were believed to have invaded Egypt from the direction of Ethiopia. The invaders appear to be some what mixed. It has also been stated that during the thirteenth Dynasty a full-blooded Negro known as Neshsira, forced his way on to the throne of Egypt. Although regarded as a usurper by some historians, it is believed that he ruled for some period.

It is not correct that the Moors were "dark-skinned people" as Malcom X claimed. It is however true that the Moors were great warriors and they had a highly developed civilisation. The Moors were the Maghreb Moslems and they were white. The Maghreb are the lands at the Western extremity of the Islamic empires which stretched across Europe, Asia and Africa within the years of Prophet Mohammed's death in the 7th Century. When the Moors were ejected from Spain in the 1230's they continued to maintain vigorous nations in North Africa.

The civilisation of Carthage was also not a black one. Although it was African. Carthage was the seat of a great civilisation which flourished between 1200 B.C and 200 B.C. The Phoenicians, who were Semitic people and the most daring sailors of the ancient times, built the city of Carthage. In about 822 B.C. some Phoenicians from the city of Tyre, under the leadership of a princess known as Elissar, sailed to Africa and founded Carthage. Some records show that the civilisation that eventually flourished in Carthage was a blend of influences from the Berber peoples of the Maghreb and other peoples from Eastern Mediterranean. With the Maghreb playing a dominant role in the building of Carthage, it will be understandable why there would be some black African population in Carthage. The Maghreb people were known to have used slaves, called HARRATINE, who were mainly black Africans from the South of the Sahara.

There is considerable confusion on the origin of General Hannibal. Some historians believe that he came from Ethiopia. Even then, it is not clear whether he was white or black because Ethiopians were and still are mainly Hamites (white), mixed with Semites and Negroes.

The old Ethiopian civilisation is generally assumed to be black. The original population which founded the kingdom of Axum in the first century A.D. is believed to be Negro. The consolidation of the inland Ethiopia was done in the 12th century by the Zagwe, a dynasty which invaded the area. The Zagwe rulers built several churches cut out of solid rock. The Ethiopians had great architectural achievements. The original population of Ethiopia was Negro. And today's Wattas and Manjos in Ethiopia are descendants of the original black population. The Hamites however entered the country over a long period and the population of Ethiopia eventually became a mixture of Hamites, Negroes and Semites.

Nubia or Kush was another remarkable African civilisation with a hybrid population. The people of Nubia were Negroes, Bejas and Egyptians. This composition can be ascertained from the graves of the Twelfth to the Seventeenth Dynasties. About 3,000 years B.C., Nubia had a civilisation similar to that of pre-dynastic Egypt. Nubia traded continually with Egypt and there were intermittent wars between her and Egypt. She gained prominence once more in the Twelfth Dynasty. Nubia declined in the 4th century A.D. Three smaller states arose after her decline. The three Nubian States were consolidated to two by the 8th Century. These states achieved a lot in brick-making, architecture, pottery and painting from the 9th to the 11th Centuries. They successfully withstood great pressures from the Arabs. Nubia was eventually dominated by the Muslims by the 15th Century. Kush was one of the earliest and most vigorous centres of iron mining and smelting in Africa. The famous Middle Nile State of Kush or Meroe had its beautiful brass-work reproduced later in West Africa. The special casting of West Africa brass, believed to have originated from Egypt, passed to that region via Kush. The point that should be emphasised here is that Ethiopian and Nubian civilisations were products of a hybrid population. They were not black civilisations.

*Black Man's Dilemma*

*CHAPTER FOUR*
*REVISED EDITION*

*BLACK MAN'S NEGLIGIBLE CONTRIBUTION TO HUMAN CIVILISATION.*

*AN UPDATE*

The renowned poet and compassionate apostle of Negritude, Leopold Sedar Senghor of Senegal, whose 1972 speech about the origin and excellence of the Yoruba race, quoted in the 1976 edition, (see page 45) died in December, 2001. He died at the age 95. Senghor was a great black leader who shunned the temptation to make himself a life President.

He was President of Senegal for twenty years. Poet Senghor rejected the theory and practice of cultural assimilation of black Africans which was a cardinal point in the French colonial policy.

He persistently advocated that African personality is distinct. It symbolises the deepest cultural values, dignity and resilience. His sustained plea for black man's mental and psychological liberation and the creation of myths on African civilisation and culture constituted an awakening among black Africans. His views, quoted in chapter four of the 1976 edition of this book, was that

Ile-Ife in Nigeria, the spiritual home of the Yorubas, was the center through which God created the world, using Oduduwa, the great ancestor of the Yorubas. These are historical and cultural myths which could become a source of strength and pride to the black race.

But black pride is not enough. Pride in our past must be a source of strength in what must be the black man's resolute endeavour to henceforth contribute more aggressively to modern civilisation, which is a heritage of mankind.

CHAPTER FIVE

## 1976 EDITION

## BLACK MAN'S CULTURE AND CIVILISATION: MYTH AND REALITY

BLACK peoples should stop claiming credit for the highly developed culture and civilisation of the Phoenicians, who were Semitic, or the civilisation of the pure Hamites or that of the Berbers of the Maghreb, the Moors and other white peoples of Northern Africa. For the blacks to hold to the idea that the Egyptian, Carthaginian, Ethiopian and the Maghreb civilisations were products of black man's ingenuity is to live in a world of illusion. And this won't help the black race.

In the old Ghana, Mali, Shonghai, Kanem-Bornu, Benin Yoruba, Bunyoro-Kitara, Zimbabwe and other empires and kingdoms, the black race can boast of some achievements in arts, religion, political organisations and production techniques. These, no doubt, were modest achievements compared with the consstributions of other races in North Africa, Middle East, Europe and Asia. The originality of some of our contributions is in serious doubt. Besides, the limited cultural progress we've made was far more recent compared with developments among other peoples who had for centuries enriched human civilisation through inventions, technological innovations and advanced social and political organisations. It will be more profitable if we accept the reality of our situation and find out why we were and are still so much behind the rest of the world, especially in contributions to science and technology.

The Arabs described the whole of Africa South of the Sahara as 'BILAD AS SUDAN' – the land of the Blacks. In early times, Western Sudan covered the areas now occupied by Upper Volta, Niger, Senegal, Mali and parts of Guinea, Nigeria and Mauritania. Among the old empires of Western Sudan, Ghana, Mali and Songhai provided evidence of black Africans' contributions to political, military and administrative organisations before the advent of the white man. The zone where the states of Ghana, Mali and Songhai were located, was a trading as well as an agricultural one. In the zone, iron was believed to have been introduced in the millennium before the birth of Christ and iron tools were known to have brought considerable benefits to farming in the area. It was an area in which several types of millet were domesticated with one type of cotton, rice and many other food crops introduced. The region also had livestock. In his observation about Western Sudan, Leo Africanus said the Negroes in that area excelled the others in civility, industry and wit. And E.W. Bovill, in his book, *CARAVANS OF THE OLD SAHARA*, observes:

*The virile peoples of the Western Sudan have always been distinguished for commercial enterprise, martial ardour, and aptitude for the art of government. From the happy combination of these qualities there sprang a number of political states to which the grandiose style of empire is often loosely assigned. None, however, can challenge the fairness of its application to the great Mandingo kingdom which is known as the empire of Mali or Mande, and is sometimes called the Mellestine.*

## GHANA

The Ghana kingdom which later expanded to become an empire was founded about A.D. 300. It extended northwards to the Sahara, Westward to the Niger and the Atlantic seaboard. The empire's principal export was gold dust which was obtained by Ghana from the Wangaras found in the region of the Senegal River. The exact area where the Wangaras then lived is unknown today but they were outside the Ghana Empire at the time of the gold trade. Ghana was well known for its famous gold nugget which was part of the empire's royal treasure. Ibn Khaldun said the nugget weighed one ton by the time it was sold to Egyptian merchants after 1076. The main imports of the empire were salt, copper, cloths and brocades and its external trade was through the caravan route that ran from Sijilmasa in the present Morocco through the important salt-mine of Taghaza in the Sahara desert. Its external trade brought prosperity and the people of Ghana were said to have worn clothes made of velvet, silk, wool and cotton while internally there was extensive trade in armour, jewels, copper, textile fabrics and dates.

The city of Ghana, from which the empire derived its name, was divided into two. There was the Moslem township with 12 mosques and several scholars, theologians, professors and priests. Arabic letters were used for official purposes throughout the empire.

The pagan township and the non-Moslem sector had sacred groves and royal burial places. Majority of state officials were moslems. Both townships were well built with some buildings made of clay and some of stone. There have been several descriptions of the pomp and pageantry which surrounded the ruling class of Ghana.

El Idris wrote about the "sculptures, paintings and glass windows which adorned the royal palace". And Al Bekri's record (1067) translated from Arabic includes the following personal account of the royal palace:

> The king of Ghana can put 200,000 warriors in the field, more than 40,000 armed with bow and arrows.
>
> ...When he gives audience to his people, to listen to their complaints and set them to rights, he sits in a pavilion around which stand 10 pages holding shields and gold-mounted swords, and on the right there are the sons of the princes of his empire, splendidly clad with gold plaited into their hair. The Governor of the city is seated on the ground: in front of the King and all round him are vizirs of an excellent breed, who never leave the king's seat; they wear collars of gold and silk, ornamented with the same metals. The beginning of the royal audience is announced by the beating of a kind of drum which they call DEBA, made of a long piece of hollowed wood. The people gather when they hear this sound....

In Tarikh-el-Fettach (Fettassi) one of the two old histories of the Sudan published in Timbuktu, the following account of the royal stables of the King of Ghana at the end of the 7th Century is also found:

> None of the one thousand horses slept except upon a carpet, nor was he tied except by a silken rope round his neck and to his foot. Each of them had a copper pot into which he urinated. No drop of urine should fall except into the receptacle, were it night or day. One would never see beneath these horses the slightest droppings. Each horse had three persons attached to his service and seated near him. One

*took charge of his food, the second of his drink, and the third took charge of urine and droppings.*

Ghana survived the first attacks by the North African forces with Arabs' assistance in 1020 and that by Almoravids in 1042. But the empire was eventually destroyed in 1076 by the forces of Almoravids under Abu Bakr. Many of the various tribes later marched southwards.

## MALI

The name Mali applies to the town which later formed the basis of the old Mali Empire. The first capital of the empire was Djeriba and this was later transferred to Niani. The capital city Niani no longer exists but a small village by the same name now occupies the former site, about 300 miles North-East of the present Sierra Leone. After the downfall of Ghana, the empire of Mali replaced it as the pre-eminent power in West Africa. After Sundiata ascended the throne of Mali in 1230, the empire expanded and he later moved the capital from Djeriba to Niani on the Upper Niger. Sundiata's general later expanded Mali Empire to the Gambia River, Northwards far into the Sahara desert, into the thick forests of the South and from Atlantic to Katsina, Zaria and Kano in modern Nigeria. At its peak, Mali stretched for 1,000 miles from north to South. Sundiata had brought a lot of improvement to Mali by the time he died in 1255, having reigned for twenty-five years. On his achievements, Professor C.P. Groves wrote in his book, *THE PLANTING OF CHRISTIANITY IN AFRICA.*

*It was Sundiata, the conqueror of Ghana, who laid the foundation of Mali's imperial greatness in the thirteenth century. He not only pursued a vigorous policy of military conquest that raised his little kingdom to a powerful state, but developed a wide administration of his territories, and is said, for example, to have encouraged agriculture, and the* more extensive cultivation of cotton.

Another remarkable ruler who ascended the throne of Mali in 1307 was Mansa Musa. By his activities Mali became well known in Europe and Asia. In 1324, seventeen years after Mansa Musa became King of Mali, he made an astounding pilgrimage to Mecca. Mansa Musa was a cónvert to Islam and decided to make a pilgrimage to the Holy Land. His caravan consisted of 60,000 men. The caravan included a retinue of 12,000 slaves all dressed in Persian silk and brocade. And each of the 500 slaves who were directly behind the horse of Mansa Musa carried a staff of gold weighing about six pounds. The caravan also included 100 camels, many horsemen and the King's wives.

His baggage-train consisted of 80 camels and each carried 300 pounds weight of gold dust. The caravan travelled from Niani on the Upper Niger to Walata, then to Tuat, and then to Cairo. Mansa Musa's wealth caused a sensation in Cairo and his gifts of gold was reported by an Egyptian official, El-Omari, to have lowered the value of gold in the Middle East for 12 years. And for years after Mansa Musa's return, ordinary people in the streets of Mecca, Baghdad and Cairo talked about the wonderful pilgrimage. While Mansa Musa was in Mecca, some of his generals captured Gao, the capital of Shonghai Empire and Timbuktu, Shonghai's second largest town. So Mali Empire expanded.

On his way back home, Mansa Musa recruited some learned men who returned to Mali with him and brought a lot of improvements to the empire. One of those recruited was a poet and architect, Es Saheli, whom he had met in Mecca. Es Saheli was from Andalusia and he brought to Mali the skill of building with burnt brick. The scholars Mansa Musa brought started colleges and libraries which came to rival those existing anywhere in the Islamic world. It was on Mansa Musa's return with these scholars that Timbuktu first acquired its great reputation as a centre of learning. Koranic theologians and Islamic law experts hereafter laid the foundations of the University of Sankore, an institution that later became an important centre of learning and culture for Africa and the Middle East. Mansa Musa also developed Timbuktu as a big commercial centre from which regular caravan journeys were made to Egypt, Ghadamer, Sus, Tuat, Sijilmasa, Fezzan, Dra'a and Fez. Mansa Musa died 1n 1332 having succeeded in transforming his empire into a centre of culture, learning and trade well known in different parts of the world.

After Musa's death, Mali empire began to crumble under the rule of his weak son, Maghan. Maghan was however succeeded as emperor by a brother of Mansa Musa. He strengthened the position of Mali and restored it to its former glory. For instance, when the famous Tunisian historian, Ibn Banttuta, visited Mali in 1352 he was highly impressed. He wrote:

> *The Negroes possess some admirable qualities. They are seldom unjust, and have a greater abhorrence of injustice than any other people. Their Sultan shows no mercy to anyone who is guilty of the least act of it. There is complete security in their country. Neither traveller nor in habitant in it has anything to fear from robbers or men of violence.*
>
> *They do not confiscate the property of any white man who dies in their country, even if it be uncounted wealth. On the contrary, they give it into the charge of some trust-worthy person among the whites, until the rightful heir takes possession of it. They are careful to observe the hours of prayer, and assiduous in attending them in congregations, and in bringing up their children to them.*

Emperor Sulayman died in 1359 and civil war broke out in Mali immediately after his death. Mari Jata who eventually won in the civil war cultivated the friendship of Egypt and the Sultan of Morocco. He was extravagant and Ibn Khaldun reported that Mari Jata II sold the huge and famous gold nugget of Ghana to Egyptian merchants. He died in 1374.

## SONGHAI

The city of Timbuktu which was the second largest city in the Songhai Empire and which Mali once conquered with Gao remained under Mali domination until 1433, when the Tuaregs who had earlier captured Timbuktu, abandoned it and returned to the Sahara desert. The capital of Songhai, the city of Gao, had earlier become once again independent of the Mali empire. In 1468, the King of Gao and Ruler of the Songhai empire, Sonni Ali, recaptured Timbuktu from Mali. The Songhai kingdom expanded under Sonni Ali and the city of Djenne was defeated. It was developed and fully fortified. It was surrounded by a network of waterways and big natural moat which gave it security against attackers but still made it easily accessible.

Sonni Ali also defeated the Mossi and expanded the empire further. He died in 1492 while crossing a river during a rasid on the Fulani and Zaghrani of Gurma. His son, Bakari Da'a succeeded him. Bakari Da'a was defeated by Mohammed Ture also known as Askia Mohammed I or Askia the GREAT, who became the new ruler of the Songhai empire. From 1498 to 1520, Askia Mohammed I, conquered territories from Mali eastward to Kano and Katsina and far into the northern desert fringes. During his 35 years rule, he conquered several new areas throughout West Africa, including the Sudan.

One remarkable point about Askia the Great was the great esteem he had for scholars. He brought back educated men of Timbuktu who had earlier fled to Walata and he turned Walata, Timbuktu, Djenne and Gao into important University towns. The University of Sankore became one of the greatest seats of learning in the world. Askia gave civil liberty to individuals and minority groups throughout the Songhai empire. He created a regular army and established regional governments in the empire. He designated officials for important public duties like forestry, fisheries and tax collection. Although a devout Moslem, he promoted religious tolerance and appreciated the good qualities in the traditional African religions. This explains his creation of the post of high priest in charge of the ancestor and spirit cult. He brought water to the desert areas of the empire by sinking wells and creating water courses. He was forced to abdicate to one of his sons, Musa in 1528.

## OTHER ANCIENT BLACK STATES IN WEST AFRICA

West Africa is notable for other highly organised nation-states, such as the Ashanti, Yoruba, Dahomey, Benin, Nupe, Bornu and Kanemi kingdoms. These states have elaborate military organisations and well developed legal systems based on local and regional councils. These councils served as both administrative and judicial bodies and they were all responsible to the king's court which was usually the apex of all organisations. These kingdoms and states had bodies of public and private law. They had elaborate systems of religious organisations and a net-work of secret cults and societies.

In Ashanti, the king was the paramount head over a confederation of provincial chiefs among a population of more than half a million. The king received levies and occasional tributes from his chiefs who in turn exercised control over the sub-chiefs and village heads of the villages in areas under their jurisdiction. The king directly administered the affairs of the capital and the surrounding villages. Provincial chiefs were semi-autonomous in the running of their capitals. The king alone could order capital punishment and he was assisted by a council composed of the queen mother and all important chiefs in taking decisions on all important matters about the state.

His was not a personal despotism but rather an aristocratic form of government. The royal stool of Ashanti-well known as the "golden stool" was introduced by Osei Tutu, the fourth king of Ashanti and founder of the empire who ruled from 1700-1730. The golden stool was the symbol of the realm.

The Yoruba kingdom extended to parts of the present-day Dahomey and the Ilorin district of the Kwara State of Nigeria, which became Islamised during this century. Modern Kwara marks the northern limits of the kingdom. The Yorubas are known to be among the most advanced peoples in West Africa. They had a single culture hero, Oduduwa, and had a marked degree of culture-uniformity, with Ile-Ife, regarded as their place of origin and religious capital. The political organisation was similar to that of the Ashantis with the Alafin of Oyo as the paramount ruler for the whole kingdom. Various obas or kings in the states of the kingdom owed allegiance to Oyo, first the seat of Oduduwa and his successors known as the Alafin. In all parts of the kingdom, the paramount chiefs, known as Obas, were aided by partly hereditary and partly appointed councils which had great authority.

In Dahomey, the king and his clan had far more autocratic powers than in Ashanti and Yoruba land. Dahomey was famous for its peculiar group of female soldiers known as the "Amazons" by white explorers but "king's wives" and "our mothers" by

Dahomeans. These female troops were sometimes more than 2,500 and about one-third were usually unarmed. Under king Gezo in 1818, the female force was re-organised and greatly enlarged. Later, king Gelele got every girl brought to him before marriage. He could enrol anyone in the army. The women soldiers were sworn to celibacy but the king had the right to take any of them to wife.

Apart from their systems of governments, these West African black states showed a considerable skill in plastic art. The art of Benin and the Yoruba areas in Nigeria are well known. These are bronzes, masks and carved ivories of Benin and Ile-Ife. When Benin City was captured in 1897, many carved elephant tusks and bronzes were found. These included the bronze head of a black woman which is now in the British museum. They showed remarkable technical skill and artistic creativity.

They were believed to have been created in the sixteenth century. It is believed that the magnificent bronze heads at Ile-Ife, the spiritual capital of the Yorubas, were indigenous although the inspiration came from North Africa from where the Yorubas were believed to have migrated to Nigeria.

## ZIMBABWE

Striking achievements were recorded by the 15th Century in the area between Rivers Limpopo and Zambezi in the territories now known as Zimbabwe (Rhodesia) and Mozambique. The empire later described as Monomotapa by European navigators existed in that area. The civilisation in the area flourished between the 11th and 14th Centuries when the most significant feature of the area, the construction of large stone palaces, flourished. The Zimbabwe culture is distinguished by the granite rocks built upon granite hills and flaked granite. The well known site of the surviving stone ruins is the Great Zimbabwe, north of the Sabi River. One of the major structures at the site is 300 feet in length, 220 feet in breadth and the wall are 30 feet in height and 20 feet in thickness. In ancient Zimbabwe, bricks were laid without lime to act as cement. One of the great buildings in brick in Zimbabwe is dated 14th Century and it is referred to as a temple because of the belief that it served religious purposes. It is believed that a lot of manual labour, skill, artistry and creativity went into the construction of the Zimbabwe walls, the doors and the inner recesses

The black peoples in Zimbabwe were also believed to have perfected the art of mining. They produced experts who had perfect knowledge of where they could find copper and gold soil. They had on a small scale mined all the copper and gold bearing strata of the area, although they had no drilling equipment. Zimbabwean craftsmen also made ornaments from the mined copper and gold. The presence of Arab traders as far as Sofala in the Mozambique channel spurred Zimbabwe to mine more gold for export in about 11th Century. It was during the period that stone building in the area started. At one time, the Khoisan type of hunters and 'Bushmen' now found in small numbers in South Africa settled in the area. From the 11th to the 14th Centuries, the Sotho-speaking peoples had migrated to Zimbabwe. Later, the Shone-speaking dynasty took control of most of the area. This was the Rozwi clan which set up the State of Mutapa between the Limpopo and the Zambezi by the time the Portuguese arrived. The ruler was Nwene Mupata and the first one ruled from about 1415 to 1450. The Rozwi dynasty which established itself about 1350. A.D. encouraged production for export and gold, copper and ivory were exported.

Zimbabwe became an important area for the Indian Ocean trade and many Arab merchants settled in the region. Trade links were fostered between Indonesia, China and India through the Indian Ocean.

## BUNYORO-KITARA

This comprised the areas now known as Ankole, Toro, Karagwe, Buganda and Bunyoro-all of which are found in modern Uganda, except Karagwe region lakes-Victoria, Edward, George and Albert. Like that of many other African peoples, the history of Bunyoro-Kitara area was passed down by oral tradition. The ruling dynasty is known as the Bachwezi whose origin is surrounded by some uncertainty although they are generally believed to be light-complexioned pastoralists who came from the north and settled in Bunyoro-Kitara region.

They became the ruling aristocracy between the 14th and 15th Centuries. The Bachwezi introduced Long-horned humped cattle and the constitution of extensive earthwork used for enclosing large herds of cattle and defence. Other major activities found in Bunyoro-Kitara were the sinking of well-shafts through rocks, the manufacture of bark-cloth and iron-working. However, before 100 A.D., i.e. before the arrival of the Bachwezi in the area, iron-using societies were known in East Africa. Near the present Tanzania/Kenya border at Engaruka, ruins of a small iron-age civilisation which flourished before 100A.D. are to be found.

## THE ZULUS

The origin of the Zulus is obscure. However, it is believed they migrated from around the Congo to Southern Africa in the 14th Century. They were among the Nguni peoples. The Zulus were among black Africans who showed tremendous capacity for organised warfare before the arrival of the Europeans. Zulus formed a warrior empire and thrived on conquests. The Ngunis had settled in Southern Africa centuries before the advent of the Europeans. After the death of their powerful leader, Chief Dingiswayo of Abatetwa in the 18th Century, a well-known Zulu,

Shaka, became the leader. Shaka was reported to have put 10,000 warriors in the field at the peak of his glory. He conquered many territories and got all the Nguni groups absorbed. He was a great disciplinarian who cruelly got many of warriors executed for flimsy reasons. Shaka was murdered by his half brothers and one of them, Dingaan became the leader of the Zulus. Under Dingaan's leadership, the Zulu army still conquered many new areas and remained unbeatable. But during the reign of Cetewayo, the Zulu army lost to the British army which had superior weapons.

## CONCLUSION

The foregoing focus on the indigenous black African culture and civilisation for which some evidence is available from about the 4th Century till the 19th Century shows that some progress was made. The progress was, however, slow and limited. Why there were no significant inventions like that of printing, compass, gunpowder, cannons and highly- developed structures like the pyramids of Egypt; the palaces and great wall of China, remains an intriguing question. Besides, there was no indigenous form of writing in Black Africa. Reliance was placed on oral tradition and the few written records that are available about black Africa's past were written mainly in Arabic.

More importantly, while other races in Asia, Europe, India and the Middle East had been authors of great inventions and builders of wonderful monuments for over four thousand years, the oldest of the even seriously arguable contributions of black Africa to civilisation were about 1,000 years old by the time the white men came to Africa. And even then, all traces of Ghana, the first indigenous empire founded in the 4th Century, had completely disappeared from Africa. Today, there is no trace of old Ghana which Sundiata was believed to have destroyed in 1240. And, if a clear evidence of the Roman and Greek civilisations, which reached their peak several centuries ago is today obtainable, it is strange indeed that the much-vaunted civilisation of the old Ghana had completely disappeared.

There were remarkable achievements in political organisation, especially in the West African region but it is unfortunate that many barbaric activities surrounded the practice of government, especially in the royal courts. Like the practice of human sacrifice and the splitting of human blood associated with either the annual harvest festivals or death of rulers, in Ashanti, Dahomey, Oyo, Benin and other areas. The death of a king was usually the signal for the women of the palace to destroy furniture and then to kill themselves with the hope of joining their husband with his belongings. A number of soldiers and eunuchs were also expected to die in some areas. This happened in some places up to the beginning of the 20th Century. In some other areas, the practice stopped at the close of the 18th Century.

The problem of foreign contributions to black Africa's significant achievements is also a major one. For while it would be right to an extent to say that Ghana, Mali and Songhai grew out of their environment and out of the efforts of their indigenous black African population, it would be a clear over-simplification of issues to ignore the impact of the trans-Saharan trade on the growth of the three empires. Besides, the literate culture and scholarship which grew around the centers of learning at Sankore University in Timbuktu, Gao and Walata were Islamic and Arabic. And a great majority of the chroniclers of the history and governmental activities in Ghana, Mali and Songhai empires were Arab scholars, Koranic theologians and other foreigners. For instance, it is a fact that Mansa Musa recruited some learned men, including the Granada architect and poet, Es Saheli from Mecca. He also brought back experts who brought new skills in construction and architecture to Mali empire. Also the so called great rulers of Songhai and

Mali had strong Arab connections at least through Islam.

Furthermore, the Ghana, Mali and Songhai empires did not provide capital for the trans-Saharan trade. The merchants of the Maghreb cities provided the capital and sent their agents to these states. It was a kind of colonial relationship and Songhai, Mali and Kanen-Borno also exported slaves to North Africa. The colonial pattern of trade and slave trade sponsored by the Arabs were inimical to the interest of the black African empires.

The significance of foreign influence on the modest civilisations we could be proud of has also been mentioned with regards to the works of art found among the Yoruba and Benin peoples of Nigeria. The carved ivories, masks, bronzes and elephant tusks found in Ile-Ife and Benin, which are of great technical skill and artistic value, echo the works of art found in the Egyptian pyramids. This would have created a serious doubt on the authenticity of these works if the influence of Egypt on Yoruba and Benin arts had not been admitted by the theory that the Yorubas migrated directly from the Nile.

Also, doubts have been expressed as to whether the 14th and 15th Centuries achievements of the Bunyoro-Kitara and Zimbabwe, especially the latter, were real products of the evolution of black societies. It has been suggested that they could be a transplant from outside. It could also be that a kind of synthesis between the indigenous and outside influences produced the skill, creativity and artistry that went into the construction of the Great Zimbabwe monuments.

Grounds exist for these doubts. From the 2nd Century, Arabs had been travelling to the East African coast. They were familiar with the natives and inter-married with them. The coast was then known to the Arabs as the Empire of Zin-a name from which Zanzibar is derived. But by the 7th Century after the death of Prophet Mohammed, large numbers of Arabs travelled to East Africa. Many of them settled on the shores of the present day Tanzania, Somalia and Kenya. They exchanged their ironware, beads and cloth for black slaves, ivory and metals.

And as far back as the 9th Century, the Chinese had visited and traded with East Africa and in that Century, a Chinese civil servant, Tuang Cheng-Shih described the East African coastline, its peoples and some ports. Excavations in Mombasa have uncovered Chinese porcelain believed to be more than 1,000 years old. A Chinese superintendent of foreign trade, Chao Ju-Kua, also mentioned 'Zangibar' in 1225 A.D. This can possibly mean the island of Zanzibar. Early in the 15th Century, a giraffe was believed to have been sent to Peking from the port of Malindi in East Africa. The strange animal received a big welcome at the Feng-tien Gate during the reign of Yung-lo emperor. Thus the Arabs and Chinese had visited East Africa before the advent of the Europeans and the contacts probably greatly influenced the achievements in the area. However, archeological evidence in black Africa is still quite tentative and fragmentary and it is believed that probably more than 80 per cent of our historical sites are yet to be investigated.

*Black Man's Dilemma*

## CHAPTER FIVE

# REVISED EDITION

# BLACK MAN'S CULTURE AND CIVILISATION: MYTH AND REALITY

## AN UPDATE

As admitted in the 1976 edition of Black Man's Dilemma, black African history reveals considerable progress in the political, economic and social organisations of the black race. In the traditional African societies, lineages, age-grades, clans, divine rulership and religious hierachies provided a cohesion in the political administration of large and small groups. There were adequate rules, regulations and sanctions which allowed the smooth running of different communities. Similarly, care of the needy, disabled and the aged within the context of extended family system, constituted the uniqueness of the political and administrative organisations. However, because emphasis was on ascribed and not achieved status, the most able and suitable persons didn't always reach the leadership positions.

However, as stressed in the first edition of this book, indigenous black African history, culture and civilisation was limited in scope and impact. For instance, there is today an absence of major hallmarks of civilisation. Black Africa lacks imperishable architectural monuments and any history of significant inventions like writing, printing, gunpowder and compass.

But the sad fact about this is that black peoples and countries have refused to be dramatically renewed inside out with wholesale embrace of modern science and technology in the past forty years or so since black countries attained political independence. If the black peoples had done this, they would have become so great and respectable among the other races. It would then have been unnecessary and irrelevant to judge us by the modesty of our past historical, scientific, and technological achievements.

The crucial point is that if black race's membership of the human family will ever be put on the basis of genuine equality, the blacks must accept a new single.minded dedication to innovations in science, engineering and technology in areas of modern communication, food and raw materials production, shelter and transportation. Above all, a black African country must explode its own atomic energy and become a world power. And to my mind, my country, Nigeria, is that country if it can muster enough courage to put an end to its perpetual wobbling. To achieve a world power status, Nigeria must, however put an end to the sad situation which allowed many criminals to rule our hapless country since independence.

CHAPTER SIX

# *1976 EDITION*

# *THE WORLD'S UNDERDOG*

WHETHER in the United States, a country where all the races of the world are represented, or in South Africa, Zimbabwe (Southern Rhodesia), Mozambique, Angola or in other independent black nations like Nigeria, Ghana, Senegal, Uganda, Lesotho, the black man has always been and is still the world's underdog. The white race has always decisively arbitrated on the pace and course of the black man's mental and material progress. The white still does so today even in a free country like Nigeria. As black peoples, we are everywhere a pawn in the power struggles of the white race.

We are even worse than that. We have always been a bone of contention among all the races of the world. We still are. It wasn't the white race alone that has always been interested in our domination and exploitation. For we noted in chapter four that from the 4th to 15th Centuries, the old empires of Ghana, Mali and Songhai sold black slaves to the White North Africa. Also, the large numbers of Arabs who travelled to East Africa after Mohammed's death in the 7th Century bought black slaves.

In the United States, more than 20 million black Americans are, to a large extent, a dehumanised people. They have always been the underdog since the beginning of that country's history. Many of them are still disenfranchised. And America is a country where all the races of the world are represented. Besides, the whites who emigrated from Europe to the New World were largely the inferior members of the Caucasian race. Millions of Europeans who emigrated to the United States from Europe between the mid-19th Century and the beginning of the 20th Century were mainly from the poorer classes. They were the poor whites who were mainly from the poorer classes. They were the poor whites who were rendered unemployed or landless by the industrial and agricultural reforms in Europe. The dynamic, ambitious and rich whites who left Western Europe for America were few relative to the poorer whites.

These inferior whites with the active support of black America's slave sellers, conquered, captured and enslaved millions of black Africans under harsh condition in which a very large proportion of black slaves died. The whites did more. For several years they have stripped the black Americans of all identity. The black culture was systematically destroyed in America. White slave owners killed children who had any knowledge of their mother tongue. The blacks were made to believe that there was no black history of any kind. Fear was instilled in the minds of the black population. Pregnant black women were made to watch their husbands tortured and put to death and they sometimes had their legs tied to trees with their stomach cut open. The aim was to dehumanize and strike fear into the black population, thereby forcing them to become docile and incompetent children of the white slave owners. There were also all forms of lynching. Some black victims had their bodies dismembered. Some were shot, hanged or burnt alive.

Slavery and the repression that went with it led to a distorted pattern of race relations in the United States, even after emancipation. White supremacy became a condition of life sanctioned by law and social custom. And even after the civil war had been fought and slaves proclaimed free, the attitude remained. White citizens refused to accept the black Americans as human beings fully endowed with human and civil rights.

It must, however, be admitted that despite their great sufferings, many black American slaves became creative. They created the Jazz music and Negro spirituals. The oppressed and persecuted black slaves found Negro spirituals an adaptive weapon in religion and evolved their own special kind of Christianity.

There was also a great deal of resistance to slavery by the Negroes in the Americas. There were rebellions too. For instance, Haiti became independent as a result of the rebellion of its slaves. In several other areas, black slaves fought to regain their status as human beings. Fugitives from slavery formed independent settlements in Guyana where they were described as "the Bush Negroes". In Jamaica, Negro insurrectionists were called "the Maroons".

Let us turn to South Africa. There also the black man is completely down. The blacks were oppressed, exploited, dispossessed of their land and treated as sub-humans by the white minority. But strangely enough, the blacks are 20 million while the whites are only 4 million. The minority whites live in great luxury based on the exploitation of black labour while the blacks live in poverty, squalor and slavery.

The South African policy of apartheid and racial discrimination is evil and abhorrent to rational and civilised peoples all over the world. Under apartheid, South African whites repress and terrorise the blacks and to an extent the Asian population. The racists have remained unyielding despite world condemnation and several

## Black Man's Dilemma

sanctions of the United Nations Organisation. Apartheid remains a serious threat to the security of the African continent and the world.

The extent of human degradation to which the black man has been subjected in South Africa has no parallel in history. Economic, social and political discriminations have been completely institutionalised in South Africa, a country which started on the process of becoming a nation about 300 years ago. Under apartheid, an African is a person who, in fact, is generally accepted as a member of any aboriginal race or tribe of Africa. And the following apartheid regulations reveal the extent of black man's degradation in South Africa:

> *No African is entitled as of right to acquire freehold title to land anywhere in South Africa; nor is it the intention of the present government ever to grant such right to the African, even in his own Bantu area.
>
> *There are no trade union rights for Africans because the term worker or employee does not apply to an African because an "employee" is any person other than an African employed by or working for an employer.
>
> *No sporting event may take place anywhere in South Africa in which white and non-white persons compete against each other whether in individual events or as teams or part of teams.
>
> * White and non-white persons may not attend the same sporting event together as spectators, unless a special permit is granted. No match in which Africans and coloured persons participate together may take place in a town anywhere in South Africa.

*No South African team composed of whites and no-whites may participate in an international tournament or competition. A permit may be granted to coloured persons to attend an international or provincial match in a town, provided separate entrances, seating and toilet facilities are available.

*An African religious leader who conducts regular classes for his congregation in which he teaches them to read the Bible is guilty of a criminal offence. Also a white man who spends a few hours each week in his own home teaching his African servant to read is guilty of a criminal offence.

* It is unlawful for a white person and a non-white person to have tea together in a café anywhere in South Africa unless they have obtained a special permit to do so.

*Unless he has obtained a special permit, an African professor delivering a lecture at a white club, which has invited him to do so, commits a criminal offence.

*A coloured person attending a public cinema in a town (even though he occupies specially separated seating), is guilty of a criminal offence, unless a special permit has been issued.

These are just a few of the repressive apartheid laws which regulate the daily lives of 20 million non-whites. They reveal the extent to which apartheid has dehumanised the blacks in particular and other non-whites in general and turned them into third rate citizens.

But it is strange indeed that for about 300 years, a minority of Europeans have ruthlessly exploited, coerced and dominated the black South African majority. It has virtually become a perpetual and total domination of the native blacks of South Africa by the minority immigrant whites. Equally strange is the fact that the efforts of the South African blacks to free themselves from bondage have been few and half-hearted. Admittedly, they are put under serious handicaps by the whites. They cannot form political, social and economic organisations.

Families and relations have been separated as a conscious policy by the apartheid regime. Several black leaders, including the late Albert Luthuli and Nelson Mandela, had been killed, suppressed, harassed and jailed. Even school children were recently killed in hundreds for protesting against the use of the racist Africana language.

Even then, one wonders why the spirit of the black man in South Africa, the divine spark in him to be free, has failed to break the shackles of his slavery and domination for so many years. For no matter how crude the weapons at their disposal, no matter their disabilities in terms of organisation and white repression, the oppressed black South Africans could become free in their God-given land if they would develop the will to be free. After a careful consideration of some facts of history, I have come to the conclusion that if, at least two million of the 20 million black South Africans are willing to pay the supreme sacrifice for their freedom, that is, if only 10 per cent of the black population are willing to die, the oppressed black population could lose their bondage completely within six months.

By spontaneous mass uprising, widespread economic sabotage and blunt refusal of black stewards, drivers, cooks, gardeners, baby sitters and others to serve their white masters, the white edifice in South-Africa could crumble within a few weeks. It is true that the frightened white settlers will use the sophisticated arms and ammunition they have acquired over the decades to wipe out many blacks if such mass uprising occurs. But South Africa's apartheid,racial discrimination and repression have, for so long, become a problem of major concern to the United Nations and the whole world that either the whole world or the Communist Countries with the support of the Third World would intervene before the white racists could kill a million blacks.

Besides, the United States, the United Kingdom ,France and other countries ,which, because of their huge investments, have for years backed the apartheid regime, would be frightened about the loss of their investment under a chaotic situation. Hence, they could, out of self-interest, force the white racists to make significant concessions to the blacks. The Soviet Union, China and other Communist countries could, should the black South Africans be courageous enough to precipitate chaos, play an active role in support of the black underdogs .And if because of ideological differences, China and USSR are not on the side of the blacks, none of the two is likely to back the racists.

This could constitute a restraining influence on the extent of ruthlessness which the apartheid regime and it's backers -the Western powers- might wish to employ.In short, South Africa would not be the same again. But the sad fact is: black South Africans are not prepared to die in thousands, if not in millions, in order to regain their freedom and put an end to the shame of being treated like animals in their God given land.

That black South Africans have a lot to gain if they put an end to their timidity and embark on widespread resistance was made clear by the profound world reactions which the Sharpeville massacre of 1960 provoked. On April 21, 1960, hundreds of unarmed blacks who demonstrated against apartheid were killed by the racist forces. It was unfortunate for the black South Africa that the Sharpeville demonstations and subsequent killings did not occur in all the major cities of South Africa. If this had happened, it would have been a decisive turning point in the history of South Africa. The white minority would not have been able to cope with the situation. At worst, they would have killed a million blacks.

For as limited in scope as the 1960 Sharpeville killings were, it marked the beginning of the whole world's deepest involvement in South African problem. For from the day of the massacre in April 1960, the Security Council has repeatedly overruled South Africa's arguments that it's apartheid policies were matters of domestic jurisdiction. The Council has since held that the racism involved in apartheid was a development which related to international peace and security.

The Council met in March and April 1960, at the request of 29 African and Asian countries concerning "the situation arising out large-scale killing of unarmed and peaceful demonstrators against racial discrimination and segregation in the Union of South Africa". The then eleven members of the Security Council eventually adopted a resolution, by nine votes in favour, none against and two abstentions (France and United Kingdom) which recognised that "the situation in the Union of South Africa is one that has led to international friction and if continued might endanger international peace and security". The Council called on South Africa "to abandon it's policies of apartheid and racial discrimination." Russia even threatened that it would possibly intervene during the Sharpeville massacre if it didn't stop.

My belief is that the black South Africans should have shown courage since 1960 and cause many more of the type of Sharpeville incident. This would have changed the pace and course of history in South Africa. But the question that is as many layered as an inion is: Is the black South African prepared to pay the supreme sacrifice so that his descendants may be free forever? The answer is unequivocal. The black man is not prepared to die despite the abundant goodwill and sympathy of the uncommitted world he had enjoyed since that memorable day- April 21, 1960,- in Sharpeville.

But even far more than it is possible in South Africa, uncompromising and widespread mass disobedience and disorder by the blacks can yield quick result in form of sudden political changes in Namibia (the former South West Africa). For that territory is a responsibility of the United Nations Organisation and if the blacks precipitate a chaotic situation, the UN would be forced to use a minimum of violence to end any repression and massacre which the white racists may unleash on the black Namibians.

Namibia was a German colony until 1919, and when the mandatory system was established after Germany's defeat, the administration of the territory was given to South Africa while the other German territories were given to Britain, France and Belgium to administer. After the Second World War, every mandated territory except South West Africa, was converted into a trusteeship territory and has subsequently gained independence. But South Africa has persistently refused to honour its international obligation of 1919 and has instead applied the inhuman apartheid policy to Namibia.

The population of Namibia has, under the apartheid system, been classified into the European or White group; the "coloureds", "basters" or people of mixed descent; and black Africans or "Natives", who are further sub-divided into different tribes. In 1966, the blacks were 485,000 while the whites were only 96,000 and the coloured and Basters were 29,000.

The travel, residence and movement of the black population are controlled by the "pass" system. Permits are issued to male natives from the northern areas to enter the police zone only when they are on labour contracts. They must carry their permits while they are within the police zone and must return to their home areas after a period of 18 months. Namibia is divided into separate "homelands" known as Bantustans by South Africa. This means that 43 per cent of Namibia's territory is set aside for Europeans who comprise only 13.97 per cent of the population.

Only 40 per cent of the land is set aside for non-whites who constitute more than 86 percent of the population. Schooling is separate for the whites, coloured people and blacks. School attendance is compulsory from the seventh to the sixteenth year for white children. For the coloured and basters' children, education there is compulsory from age 7 to 14. But there is no compulsory schooling for the blacks and only very few of them reach the lower primary school level.

Since 1946, the UNO has devoted several hours discussing Namibia. The UN General Assembly has adopted more than 80 resolutions on the territory and has devoted a special session to it. The steps taken by South Africa to incorporate Namibia have also been resisted by the UNO. On October 27, 1966, the UN General Assembly terminated the mandate under which South Africa had legal basis for its occupation and domination of Namibia. The UN thus brought the territory directly under its control.

The white racists, however, defied these moves. For in 1967, the racists brought 37 Namibians to Pretoria to try them on terrorism and subversion. Despite strong protests by the Security Council and General Assembly, heavy sentences were imposed on the Namibian political leaders and members of liberation movements. But this notwithstanding, the UN Security Council decided on March 20, 1967, that South Africa's continued presence in Namibia was illegal and contrary to the Charter of the UN and called on South Africa to withdraw its administration immediately. South Africa ignored the March resolution and on August 12, the Council called on South Africa to withdraw its administration from Namibia before October 4, 1969. This ultimatum was also ignored. All this means that the creation of a chaotic situation by the Namibians through sustained resistance and positive action would make it imperative for the UNO to intervene.

However, it must be admitted that many black Africans had shown great courage in their heroic struggles against colonial domination and racial oppression. A remarkable example was the uprising of Mau-Mau terrorists in Kenya. The Mau-Mau's sustained terrorism prompted the United Kingdom to change its idea of making that country a permanent white settlement. Kenya eventually attained independence.

Also, the stiff resistance of liberation movements to the Portuguese colonial domination in Guinea Bissau, Mozambique and Angola had led to the attainment of independence by these territories. This was, no doubt, a remarkable achievement. For since the Portuguese arrived in Mozambique in 1498, they had sought to establish themselves as a power over the various African communities which they found. They were in Africa to find new sources of wealth and control its flow to Europe. The Portuguese also dreamt of the existence of a multi-racial empire in which people of all races, cultures and religions were to live happily and harmoniously. It was an unrealistic dream because the Portuguese didn't love their black subjects (Subditos) and they were unwilling to share political, economic and social power with them.

Portugal, backed by its NATO allies, used her resources to pursue the most heinous colonial war and degradation of man in Africa. It ruthlessly subjugated the peoples of Angola, Mozambique and

Guinea Bissau. The nationalists put up heroic struggles in these territories. But even then, one would be right to say that the internal problem faced by Portugal for spending a great percentage of its resources on a futile colonial war was as important as the black nationalist struggles in explaining the attainment of independence by Angola, Mozambique and Guinea Bissau.

In Zimbabwe, the United Kingdom, which is the Metropolitan power, has acknowledged the colonial status of the territory despite the unilateral declaration of independence in November 1965, by the racist minority regime of Ian Smith. However, Britain has failed to take measures to re-assert its authority against the white minority racists. But as we noted in the case of South Africa, the oppressed blacks would gain nothing by their half-hearted armed struggles or the deliberate resignation and silent martyrdom of the majority. Zimbabweans can only win meaningful freedom at the cost of blood and tears in bitter struggles. I remember telling a group of Zimbabwean nationalists at the OAU Conference in Rabat, Morocco, in 1972, that the black militants in that country could send the white racists packing overnight if they organised an underground movement based on unity, discipline and oath-taking to get all black cooks and stewards to poison as many of their white masters as possible on an appointed date.

The white settlers in Zimbabwe and South Africa could not survive for a few weeks much less enjoy their great luxury without the exploitation of the labour of a timid majority black population. Words and words from the United Nations which are not followed by positive action are irrelevant.

But the black man is not only down in the colonial and racist territories. He is the underdog even in the new nations. Black states have only attained nominal independence or client freedom. For these new nations are easily manipulated by the former

Metropolitan powers which consciously ensure that they are ruled by a corrupt and mediocre leadership which has no vision of any kind. Good black leaders like Kwame Nkrumah, Murtala Muhammed, Sekou Toure and Julius Nyerere are either destroyed or incapacitated through imperialists machinations. The result is that the whites in America and Europe continue to have a crucial say in the direction of the political and neo-colonial economic systems of these states.

Expatriate whites are in the main, the security, diplomatic and economic experts and advisers to many of these new nations and the so-called experts manipulate the affairs of the black nations to suit their countries' vital interests. Countries like Nigeria, since July, 1975, Ghana, Guinea, Tanzania and Guyana which are not so directed are few. Imperialism also uses reactionary black leaders to destroy outstanding black leaders who possess greater heart and foresight. This explains the outsting, humiliation and the disgraceful death in the exile of Ghana's immortal Kwame Nkrumah.

*Black Man's Dilemma*

## CHAPTER SIX

# REVISED EDITION

# THE WORLD'S UNDERDOG

## AN UPDATE

The most important development on my submission in this chapter since 1976 was the transformation of the apartheid South Africa into a multi - racial nation with black African majority in control of the government.

By the time I wrote in 1976, South Africa was a racist country which operated repressive and segregated laws against the blacks, Indians and coloured peoples. The country was then sitting on a keg of gunpowder. The white racists were defiant of world opinion, pleas, economic and military sanctions and armed struggles by the blacks. The irrationality, obduracy and intransigence of the then racist President, Pieter Botha exacerbated me to the extent that I recommended, in the first edition of Black Man's Dilemma, mass rebellion of black cooks and stewards against their white South African masters, even if this would entail their poisoning some of them. I then felt that a desperate situation like the one faced by the oppressed and dehumanised blacks faced deserved an equally desperate solution.

However, the suggestion earned me serious anger and reprimand among some readers of the first edition of Black Man's Dilemma. One of such unhappy people was, unfortunately, a long standing admirer of my newspaper columns and articles, who sent a three - page sharp criticism of the suggestion on poison. Also critical of the idea is Engineer Reginald Dickson, who used extracts from Black Man's Dilemma in his book - AFRICA AMBIT. I made what some readers regard as an extreme suggestion in 1976 because I found the then racists' defiance and hard stance very nauseating. I also felt that losing some white settlers in such unfortunate circumstances would prompt a great majority of South African racists to see reason. And afterall, my suggestion would have resulted in a less tragic occurrence than an unprecedented blood bath and massacre of millions of both black and white South Africans which would have eventually taken place in the then racist enclave.

Fortunately for the whole world, Africa and South Africans, while Pieter Botha was stiff-necked, unreasonable and adamant, a new far-sighted and wise white leader, Frederik de Klerk, emerged in South Africa.

De Klerk met black race's greatest hero. Nelson Mandela, in Prison where the racists had kept him for twenty seven years. Mandela, the symbol and architect of black South Africa's principled struggles for freedom and against slavery in their God - given land, chose to remain and die in prison rather than obtain conditional release on racists' terms. But unlike the previous white racists' leaders, De Klerk released Mandela from prison unconditionally on February 11, 1990.

On his release, the obnoxious apartheid laws were repealed and the long entrenched racial barriers were removed, leading to multi-racial politics in South Africa. African homelands were abolished while the African National Congress (ANC) which fought against apartheid system from outside the country became a lawful and recognised organisation. The ANC and the white minority National Party agreed on basic principles for a new constitution under which every race in the country became enfranchised.

The election conducted under the new constitution in April 1994 was won by the African National Congress with 62.2 percent of the total votes cast, while the National Party came second with 20.4 percent. Mandela thus became the first President of a multi-racial South Africa. He stepped down in June, 1999 as President after spending five years in office. He was succeeded by President Thabo Mbeki in 1999.

Nelson Mandela is a great pride to the black race. He is one of history's magnificent heroes. He is in the rank of other great black Africans like Ahmed Sekou Toure of Guinea, Kwame Nkrumah of Ghana, Nwalimu Julius Nyerere of Tanzania and Sedar Senghor of Senegal.

Mandela was a man of uncompromising integrity, wisdom and unparalleled courage. The 27 years he spent in solitary confinement at the Robben Island prison could not break his soul. He rejected all entreaties to compromise on the side of slavery and servitude for his race and his black country men and women.

*Black Man's Dilemma*

CHAPTER SEVEN

## *1976 EDITION*

## *THE MYTH OF WHITE SUPERIORITY*

THE origin of racism or racial myths was quite varied. It is believed that the English language itself contributes to racism. It identifies "black" with evil and debasement and "white" with the good and pure. This has conditioned the way the whites perceive the black man. There have always been references to "black nights", "foul Aethiops" and "black devils". The whites also refer to the legend of Ham and the curse of Cain. This explains why when the whites first came in contact with the black man, they thought of him as a sinful, cursed, inferior and beast-like human being.

Slavery also contributed to the development of racial myths. For although the first African Negroes were landed in the New World about 1510, trade in black slaves had been active, although limited to the Mediterranean, by 1450. Slavery and the raid on the black population were even sanctioned by the Catholic Church. A Bull of Pope Nicholas V authorised the Portuguese "to attack, subject and reduce to perpetual slavery the Saracens, Pagans and other enemies of Christ southward from Capes Bajador and Non, including all the coast of Guinea". The Pope, however, stipulated a condition that all those captured must be converted to Christianity. Slave owners and dealers also justified their activities by the argument that blacks were incapable of moral feelings, that they were sub-human. Hence, they contended that there was justification to treat Negroes as sub-humans.

In short, racial myths on the existence of superior Caucasian race and the inferior black and other races, developed as a means to justify slavery as well as the attempt of Europeans to exploit overseas territories. Racial prejudices were manifested in the economic and imperial policies of colonialism. The servile status of the black slaves led to the black race being classified as unintelligent and immoral. It was a racial prejudice born of a relationship of clear exploitation. The whites regarded black men and women who had been deprived of their natural background by colonisation or slavery as irresponsible. This view of the blacks was further strengthened by the fact that slaves or colonial subjects who were forced to perform specific tasks by their masters deliberately showed little or no interest in their jobs.

However, racial prejudice was not confined to the New World. West Indian planters who returned to Europe brought their black slaves and servants back home. Also, some of the captured slaves were sometimes landed at European ports, especially in England, where they were publicly auctioned. All these gave the European populations their view of black men as peoples in servile and inferior position compared with their race.

Another source of racial myths was the ostensibly scientific investigation and speculation which was at its peak in the 19th and early 20th Centuries. At this period, mental capacities of the black man and white man were measured on the basis of facial angle, shape of skull and cranial capacity. The habit of looking down on the black and other coloured races which emerged was further reinforced by the keen interest in evolution and man's relationship to other members of the animal kingdom. For instance, in a paper read to the Manchester Philosophical Society at the close of the 18th Century entitled: *"An Account of the Regular Gradations in Man, and in Different Animals and Vegetables, and from the Former to the Latter"*, a submission, which was not convincingly substantiated, was made - that "the Negro seems to approach nearer to the brute creation than any other of the human species". The theories of Charles Darwin and Herbert Spencer were also misused while biology was similarly misinterpreted. All this gave rise to the view that the Negros were in a less advanced evolutionary position than the whites and were, therefore, mentally inferior.

But the racial prejudice was not confined to black peoples. It was manifested wherever the Western Europeans visited or whenever they settled among simpler peoples who occupied social and economic positions that were believed to be inferior to that of the white men. This was more prominent when these other peoples behave in a way or are used to customs which the Europeans do not understand and are therefore dismissed as unreasonable. The fact that these simpler peoples didn't have elaborate systems of governments or cities with great architectural monuments or couldn't make modern railways, cars or radiograms further strengthened the views of Europeans that the Negroes and other strange peoples were inferior.

This racial contempt and pride of the Western Europeans was also strong in Asia in general and India in particular. For instance, T. B. Macaulay, who was once the Law Member of the Governor General's Council in Calcutta, a writer and a member of the House of Lords, wrote as follows on the Bengalis, in the EDINBURGH REVIEW of October 1841:

*"The physical organisation of the Bengalee is feeble even to effeminacy. He lives in a constant vapour bath. His pursuits are sedentary, his limbs delicate, his movements languid... Courage, independence, veracity are qualities to which his constitution and his situation are equally unfavourable. His mind is weak even to helplessness for purposes of manly resistance; but.... what the horns are to the buffalo, what the paw is to the bee....deceit is to the Bengalee. Large promises, smooth excuses, elaborate tissues of circumstantial falsehood, chicanery, perjury, forgery are his weapons."*

Besides, for centuries, extreme and adverse views have been expressed on the assumed inferiority of the black man. Some of these were borne out of frustrations and grievances. Some were rooted in prejudices against the blacks. Demagogues expressed some of these views in frenzied outburst of emotion and invariably to sustain a system based on the exploitation of the black race.

In 1772, the Reverend Thomas Thompson published a monograph titled: *"THE TRADE IN NEGRO SLAVES ON THE AFRICAN COAST IN ACCORDANCE WITH HUMANE PRINCIPLES AND WITH THE LAWS OF REVEALED RELIGION'*. Also in 1852, the Reverend Josiah Priest gave a theological basis for slave trade in his work" A *BIBLE DEFENCE OF SLAVERY"*. And in 1900, C. Carroll published his work: *"THE NEGRO AS A BEAST OR IN THE IMAGE OF GOD"*. His work includes a chapter on *"Biblical and Scientific proofs that the Negro is not a member of the Human Race"*. In this chapter, C. Carroll claims that "all scientific research confirms the black man's "typically simian nature". So a basis was found in Christianity for racism against the Negroes. Evangelical Christian missionaries conveyed to their supporters in Europe a picture of inhabitants of Africa as dark and degraded. They, however, claimed that the inferiority of the Heathen could be eradicated. They could be transformed and saved.

This, without doubt, was a perversion of Christianity. For Christianity was anti-racism at the beginning. For instance, Saint Paul proclaims that: "THERE IS NEITHER JEW NOR GREEK, THERE IS NEITHER BOND NOR FREE FOR YE ALL ARE ONE IN CHRIST JESUS". Those who advanced racism and discrimination against the black race through Christian teachings also ignored the fact that one of the three Magi (the wise men) was a black man. And though they were not black, Mary, the mother of Jesus Christ and the 12 apostles of Jesus were believed to be Semitic.

There were other negative but clearly extreme views about the black man's inferiority, especially in the United States of America. From the 1890's, inflammatory works like Charles Carroll's "Negro a Beast", mentioned above (1900) and "The clansman" by Thomas Dixon (1905) were published. In Dixon's work the negroes were vilified and portrayed as "HALF CHILD, HALF ANIMAL, THE SPORT OF IMPULSE, WHIM AND CONCEIT.... A BEING LEFT TO HIS OWN WILL, ROAMS AT NIGHT AND SLEEPS IN THE DAY, WHOSE SPEECH KNOWS NO WORDS OF LOVE, WHOSE PASSIONS, ONCE AROUSED, ARE AS THE FURY OF THE TIGER". There are other demagogues like Dixon in the United States who believed that "the black man is not a man". That "his body is black, his language is black" and that "his soul must be black too". The average white man in America, therefore, sees the black man as a symbol of ugliness and evil and this notion of inferiority is put into practice in the white man's daily dealings with the black Americans. And strangely enough, both the white leaders and followers share this contempt for the blacks. For instance, the late

Field Marshal Smuts was reported to have said in an address in New York: "THE NEGRO IS THE MOST PATIENT OF ALL ANIMALS NEXT TO THE ASS". Smuts later explained to his audience that his remark had not been intended to be an insult. He was merely praising the virtues of the black man!

However, the extreme views on the debased nature of the black man are not confined to Europe and America. In Nicol Davidson's *"AFRICA- A SUBJECTIVE VIEW"*. Dr. Albert Schweitzer was quoted as having said: "My general rule is never to trust a black man". (And in his work: The African Image), Ezekiel Mphalele quoted a former Prime Minister of Southern Rhodesia as having once said: "Africans, until they are very much advanced, are all liars".

These racial myths and black inferiority arguments are charged with a lot of emotional force. Hence, it is so difficult to objectively discuss their importance in relation to social problems. Invariably racial myths and prejudice and the idea of superiority of races constitute a way of making a scape-goat of people who threaten the economic and social position or the cohesion of a group of people. Hence, the argument that the black man is biologically inferior to the white man and that he is unfit to live as a member of a white civilisation explains the legal and social discrimination against the black peoples of South Africa and in the deep South of the United States of America. It also explains why Australia has prohibited the immigration of coloured peoples.

The myths, which are sometimes manifested in form of pathological phobias are widely condemned as exaggerated prejudices of the social environment. For example, Professor Juan Comas, argues in his work; *"RACIAL MYTHS"* that; "To maintain that a man is an inferior human being because he is black is as ridiculous as contending that a white horse will necessarily be faster than a black horse". And the great harm which colour prejudice does to human relations throughout the world has been of serious concern to international organisations. This concern is reflected in the introductory clauses of the United Nations International Convention on the Elimination of All Forms of Racial Discrimination. The convention proclaims human dignity in freedom and equality, morally and legally. It rejects "any doctrine of superiority based on racial differentiation as scientifically false, morally condemnable, socially unjust and dangerous".

And in his address before the Algerian National Assembly on February 4, 1964, the late Secretary-General of the United Nations Organisation, U Thant, made the following condemnation of racial myths and discrimination:

*The proponents of racial discrimination have historically been the most emotionally backward and most spiritually bankrupt members of the human race. Their sickness really arises from a sense of fear and insecurity rather than from a superior pride...There is the clear prospect that racial conflict, if we cannot curb, and finally eliminate it, will grow into a destructive monster compared to which the religious or ideological conflicts of the past and present will seem family quarrels. Such a conflict will eat away the possibilities for good of all that mankind has hitherto achieved and reduce man to the lowest and most bestial level of intolerance and hatred. This, for the sake of all our children, whatever their race or colour, must not be permitted to happen.*

These are all unfavourable reactions to racial myths and prejudices. They constitute an awareness of the dangers which the myths constitute to equality of human-kind and harmonious relations between peoples. But the most intractable phenomenon which has continued to emphasise differences between categories and groups of mankind is the body of scientific and pseudo-scientific theory which denies the fact that differences among mankind are attributable to different conditions under which they are nurtured.

A. de Gobineau was one of the first well known racist theorists. He emphasised the inequality of the human races. This inequality was qualitative and not quantitative. Gobineau's conclusion is that the major races of man – the yellow, the black and the white – are different in their special aptitudes and not in absolute value. Gobineau confused the idea of race in purely biological sense with the sociological and psychological circumstances which produce human civilisations. From this initial error, he justified all forms of discrimination and exploitation. An important fact was ignored. That the different contributions of various races can, to a great extent, be explained by different historical, sociological and geographical circumstances.

Many other scientists have advanced arguments in support of the superiority of one race over another. Like the German scientists who argued that people of Northern Europe excelled the rest of mankind in intellect, morality and character. Or the Italian scientists who canvassed the view of the racial superiority of the Mediterranean peoples, who, according to them, were responsible for most of the great contributions to Western civilisation.

And earlier, the idea that some races are genetically inferior to others, which was a pronounced element of the Victorian thought, has been given scientific explanation. For instance, Francis Galton, a psychologist widely accepted as the founding father of intelligence tests, believed in the inferiority of the Negroes. In his book- *"HEREDITARY GENIUS"* - he expressed a "most unqualified objection" to "pretension of natural equality". His contempt for the Negroes is borne out by his view that "The mistakes that the Negroes made in their own matters are so childish, stupid and simpletonlike, as frequently to make me ashamed of my own species". Many other scientists shared Dalton's extreme views. They've supported the view that some ethnic groups are superior and others inferior.

Over the years, scientists also developed the psychological tests. This is a device to measure innate differences in ability. Various racial groups are given a series of problems to solve and their performance is used as an indicator of their ability. The French psychologist, Alfred Binet, developed the first series of intelligence tests in 1905. Alfred Binet, however, warned that his method could be meaningfully used to determine innate differences in ability if the persons or groups of persons to whom the tests are administered have similar culture, education and opportunities.

But intelligence tests are not perfect instruments for the measurement of native differences in ability. The cultural and social background may affect an individual's test performance. The person's attitude to the person administering the test, his education, his experience and his state of mind are a few of the factors which may affect the successful solution of the problems presented by the tests. The cultural background of an individual may, to a great extent, determine his attitude to the test, in a way that will appreciably affect what marks the scores at the test. A good or poor mastery of the language of communication can also affect the scores in the intelligence tests.

Also, psychologists who used intelligence tests in the early 1960s realise that a black man scores higher on tests administered by a fellow black. That he scored less when a white man tested him because being tested by a white man produced a stress which resulted in lower scores. This reveals how stress affects behaviour and intelligence. But it had been noted that stress improves performance in simple tasks but hampers it, some times seriously, in difficult tasks. This view further strengthens the argument that in the case of white and black Americans, white Americans usually score about 15 points more than blacks and black Americans do better on simple tasks, such as rote memory, than on more complex tasks like verbal reasoning.

Intelligence tests have also shown that black Americans and American Indians, whether they are adults or children, on the average obtain scores that are inferior to those obtained by white Americans. This is despite the fact that individual black Americans and American Indians sometimes obtain test scores that are superior to those obtained by individual whites. Furthermore, black Americans as a group sometimes do better in intelligence test scores than groups of white Americans

For instance, experiments have shown that in rural southern part of the United States where the whites enjoy better educational facilities in a segregated system, white Americans perform better than black Americans. But in some northern cities where the white and black live in similar environments, there is no major difference between the tests scores of the black and white Americans. Also, there have been very wide differences in scores at Intelligence Quotient tests even within the same racial groups, depending on the opportunities and environment. For instance, while intelligence tests in a big city like Los Angeles in California have revealed that black American children have Intelligence Quotient of 105, in the small rural area of the southern state of Tennessee, black children obtained Intelligence Quotient of only 58, in a situation, where a national average of Intelligence Quotient of 100 is to be expected for white Americans

During the First World War, when psychological tests were given to army recruits of all races in the United States, black Americans from some northern states where educational and economic opportunities are superior, obtained higher intelligence test results than white Americans from some southern states. But black Americans from the southern states where they faced serious educational and economic problems, obtained lower scores than the black from the northern states, where better conditions existed.

Also a study of black and white children by Dr.. B. Passamanick at New Haven in Connecticut in 1946 confirmed the significance of environment and nourishment in infant tests. In his work published in the Journal of Genetic Psychology, Dr. Passamanick discovered that there were no differences in mental and physical developments of black and white children. Both during pregnancy and after the birth of the children tested the black and white mothers had equal opportunity in terms of diet and general standard of living to give proper care to their children. On the other hand, in baby tests where black parents and children live in poorer economic conditions, inadequate nourishment and poor housing compared with the whites, test results have shown that black children have poorer physical and mental development.

One main conclusion that can be drawn from all the research and intelligence tests is that the range of mental groups is the same among all races. That race as a factor does not determine a person's level of intelligence. That environmental influences like education, social and economic status are as dominant as inherited mental capacity in the determination of a person's level of intelligence. Some psychologists and scientists have even argued that environmental opportunities are far more important factors in the development of man's intelligence than the innate capacity.

However, experts have not denied the fact that inherited mental ability provided an important explanation for psychological differences among human beings. People as individuals and families have different mental capacities. Some have inherited inferior mental capacity while some possess superior mental capacity. Furthermore, each of the major races- the Caucasian, Mongolian and Negroid - contain individuals who have inherited superior mental ability and those who are just averagely endowed. It has been established that how frequently various levels of inherited ability occur among people is the same for all races.

It means there is no genetical intellectual superiority of the white or yellow peoples over the black peoples. And as it has already been indicated, black peoples have proved superior to the whites in many areas of human endeavours. Besides, when white and black children live in an environment that is inferior economically, educationally and socially, they both grow up to have a mental level that is low compared with children of the same age in better environment.

But even then, it is unrealistic to deny the fact that there are sharp differences in the attainment of various races and cultures. There is, for instance, abundant evidence, like those mentioned in chapter three, that the Caucasian (white) and Mongolian (yellow) races have made significant contributions to civilisation. They have changed and improved their physical environment. Individuals among the white and yellow races have made great inventions and discoveries. They have sought and found solutions to critical problems, especially in areas where such solutions would lead to better standard of living for their peoples. They have devised easier and quicker means of contacting the rest of the world. But as shown in chapters four and five, the black race has not initiated and sustained the type of superior economic, educational and social opportunities which have existed among the white and yellow races for centuries.

This leads to an all-important point. If as psychologists and scientists have argued, the influence of environment is very important in determining the level of Intelligence Quotient which an individual attains, it is strange indeed that the black race has not, for centuries, appreciated the need to improve his physical environment and make it modern and better adapted to meet his basic needs. And even if our race has all along appreciated this need, it is obvious that we have been incapable of drastically changing our environment to make it suitable for superior mental growth.

It is a vicious circle. Environment is a crucial factor in the moulding of intelligence. But our race has failed to do something positive about its environment, apart from the mundane improvement on shelter, farming and clothing, without which we cannot even survive as a race. Besides, the black man has not been able to embark on a critical self-examination that can lead him to abandon all out-moded institutions, values and attitudes to life which have for centuries proved inimical to his progress. The result is that Africa, our home, which strangely enough is believed to be the birthplace of man, is inferior to other continents which are predominantly occupied by the Caucasian (white) and Mongolian (yellow) races. For if the truth be known, we are quite inferior to other races in terms of standard of living, architecture, education and general economic development.

Our inferiority is also manifested in the glaring failure to apply technology to improve things that can make life more comfortable for us. We were for centuries using our hand fan made of either feathers, leather or straw. Yet, our natural home – Africa- is a very hot continent. The hot climate should have spurred us to invent electric-fan as the cold climate spurred the whites to invent heaters. But the black man did not respond to a felt need. He did not invent electric fan until the white man brought one. And when the white man felt that the eletric fan was not enough for the scorching heat of the tropics, he brought the air conditioner. If the white man is interested in one of the basic foods in parts of Africa - pounded yam- he would not use our centuries old method of preparing it. He would device a simple machine with which pounded yam could be prepared far more easily and neatly. And we will gladly buy and use it. There are several other things which the white man has invented and the yellows improved upon. These are things that make life more comfortable for them and the black race - electric iron, electricity, pipe-borne water, electrical appliances, radio and television sets, motor cars, etc. On the other hand, the black man is greedy in his enjoyment of modern appliances and goods which the other races had for centuries worked hard to invent and which their scientists, engineers and technicians are still today toiling day and night to improve upon. We remain the poor immitators of the Caucasian and Mongolian races. We are copy-cats.

Many reasons have been given by my fellow blacks as the causes of our relative backwardness in comparison with the other races. Some argue that our colonial experience and the crippling effect of the slave trade were major explanations for our very little contribution to civilisation. It is true that slavery had a devastating effect on our development and many of Africa's finest peoples were forcibly taken to the New World. But the slave trade ended several years ago. We should have made desperate efforts to get out of its crippling effects by now. Ours was also not the first race to be enslaved or colonised in history. They should not constitute a permanent hindrance to our progress. Other blacks have blamed our relative backwardness on the unusual kindness of nature to the black man. That banana tree, plantain, palm trees, vegetables and all other food crops grow widely and profusely in the tropics. Unlike the cold winter climate which can lead to death if the whites have no heating system, the heat of Africa cannot cause death. This explanation is unconvincing because the scorching heat of different parts of black Africa should have spurred us to invent air-conditioners. The unusually hot ground of the tropics should have encouraged the use of sandals and shoes and prevent a situation in which more than 50 per cent of the population, until recently when cheap rubber sandals are produced in Africa, went about bare-footed in the modern nations of Africa.

Africa's isolation from Europe because of the Sahara desert and the all pervading inhibitions to progress which neo-colonialism has constituted to the new nations of Africa since their attainment of independence, are other explanations usually given for our relative backwardness. But China had the worst form of neo-colonialism quite apart from the civil strife that engulfed the giant nation for centuries. The Chinese were treated as subhumans by foreign powers who shared the land of China among themselves and had complete control of the country's economy for many years. However, the Chinese turned this humiliation into a source of strength. They defeated the neo-colonialists, fully mobilised themselves and squarely faced the challenge of nation building until China became a super-power within two decades.

The foregoing problems do not constitute convincing explanations for our relative backwardness. For one thing, slavery, colonialism, neo-colonialism, isolation and other problems are not peculiar to the black race. For instance, Mongolian nations like China and Japan which in the past faced more daunting problems had succeeded in calling forth their strength and they eventually made a break-through to modernity. The question that is all-important for us is why has the black race always remained behind other racial groups in attainments? I believe that although we are as intelligent as the other races, our centuries of failure to improve upon our physical and social environment, the dehumanising effect of colonialism, slavery and isolation, and the firm grips which the white neo-colonialists have on the new nations of Africa have all combined to condition our intellect and give us a perverted life outlook. The result is that our identity has always remained that of an underdog. As black peoples we are always pitied or at best merely tolerated like all beggars. We are not creative. We are not original. And for the black man to make any meaningful progress and win the respect of the other races, he must accept the incontestable fact that he is and has always been behind the rest of the world. He should then find out why and do something drastic about his backwardness. Countries like Tanzania, Guinea, Guyana and Nigeria since July 1976, which have accepted the need for originality and self-reliance in their quest for rapid development, should become more desperate to become modern nations, with highly developed technology. Other black nations should also bid farewell to their lethargy and make today and tomorrow so great for the black man that his yesterday's and today's backwadness will soon become a thing of the past. But such a leap forward requires a mental revolution on the part of all the blacks in the world. This is the message of this book.

## CHAPTER SEVEN

# REVISED EDITION
# THE MYTH OF WHITE SUPERIORITY
## AN UPDATE

My major submissions in the first edition remain the same for the 2002 edition and they are that:

All research and intelligence tests have reached the conclusion that the range of mental groups is the same among all races.

Race as a factor does not determine a person's level of intelligence.

Environmental influences like educational, economic and social opportunities are as important as inherited mental capacity in determining a person's level of intelligence.

The three major races of the world, the black, the white and yellow, all contain individuals who possess superior mental ability as well as those who are averagely endowed.

Over the years, racial myths and prejudices have been expressed, mainly by members of a race which sought to justify its economic, political and social subjugation of another race. Examples were the white racists of the deep South of the United States and the white racists of Apartheid South Africa in their treatment of the black population.

Racism was also used to justify colonialism and slavery by European imperialists and the Catholic Church and missionaries who portrayed Africans as barbaric and degraded peoples who should be enslaved and converted to Christianity.

There are sharp differences in the attainment of the black, white and yellow races, but the black race has not made any significant contributions to civilisation, which is mankind's common inheritance.

The black race has done very little to change and improve its physical environment. The race's standard of living has remained low while its general level of economic development has remained poor for several years.

Finally, if the blacks throughout the world accept the main recommendations in this book and embark on a critical self-examination of their past, present and future, with independent black countries of Africa achieving a spectacular breakthrough to modernity by becoming nuclear, industrial and economic giants, it is then and only then can the black man's membership of the human family be put on the basis of genuine equality.

CHAPTER EIGHT

# 1976 EDITION
# THE BLACK AMERICANS

I HAVE great respect for the 23 million black Americans who form 11 per cent of the 206 million Americans. I respect and admire their resilience and the greatness of their souls. Three centuries of oppression had failed to completely break their souls. At least, in the way, the whites would want them totally dehumanised.

The African slaves transported to the Americas had maintained heroic struggles since 1518 when black slaves were first transported by the middle passage across the Atlantic to the Americas. And after 1619 when a Dutch ship which landed at Jamestown, Virginia, sold twenty blacks to the English colonists, American colonies regarded their black African slaves as property and treated them as such. Also from the 1660s American colonies passed laws which made it legal for the colonists to enslave the blacks and their descendants and treat them as chattels.

With the increasing interest in slaves as agricultural expansion gained momentum in the New World, whole tribes disappeared in Africa while whole regions were depopulated. And there is a

*Black Man's Dilemma*

belief that it was the able-bodied, the cleverest and the physically strong black Africans who were taken as slaves to the Americas. I share the view that the best of the blacks were taken out of Africa as slaves. For one thing, the prospective white slave buyers were likely to prefer tall, healthy and able-bodied young men and women to old people or the sick. They had the highest market value. For another, the fact that many black Americans are today tall, well built, pretty and handsome has given credence to this idea.

The vigorous blacks transported from Africa to America under the most humiliating conditions and physical ill-treatment showed heroic defiance. Some undertook hunger strikes. Some, in their desperation and rage, fought the crew and made futile attempts at insurrection. The human spirit in the African slaves resented the degradation to which they were subjected. For instance, slaves were usually brought on deck once daily and forced to dance as a way of removing their unmistakable grief. But some of the slaves seized this opportunity to jump over-board, uttering cries of triumph and heroic defiance as they cleared the ship and disappeared below the ocean.

And when the African slaves arrived in America they were separated and grouped in a manner that people of the same tribe could not live together. The aim of the slave owners was to prevent any form of communication between slaves, thereby preventing conspiracy or rebellion. Slaves were also prevented from learning how to read and write. Their masters and supervisors only taught them half-understood, garbled and wrongly pronounced English they needed for their daily labour on the plantations. But while their masters were amused at poor understanding of the language, the slave used their poorly mastered English as a source of great strength. They displayed remarkable wisdom and intelligence inspite of great odds. They devised the Negro spirituals in which they gave multiple meanings to the English language. To the undiscerning listeners Negro spirituals were a sign of deep spiritual commitment and yearning on the part of African slaves. It provides inspiration for hard work by slaves. The spirituals symbolised a kind of servile compliance and piety. But to the African slaves, the spirituals revealed their feeling of rebellion and dissent. Through the spirituals, the slaves communicated among themselves. They exchanged ideas about the best way of escape from the unrestricted tyranny of their white masters. They expressed hostile feelings against their masters and supervisors as well as their yearnings to go back to mother Africa. They were all men and women of great courage and endurance.

But what can we say of our African forefathers who were left behind on the continent? What can we say of the character of black Africans who were not captured as slaves and our fore-fathers who organised the sales of their fellow tribesmen and women to white strangers from an unknown world? To my mind, our forefathers were men who lacked greater heart and foresight. They were selfish and greedy. They were easily carried away by the shoddy and inferior goods – beads, hot drinks and colourful dresses which the white slave raiders brought. They could not appreciate the best or long term interests of their peoples or the great sufferings the peoples they sold would be exposed to. Or if they appreciated these, they were so selfish they put self before the best interests of their areas. They colluded with European slave traders and raiders for more than three centuries until the conscience of the European elite was pricked and they started the battle for the abolition of the slave trade. The whites won the battle. All this leads to one inescapable conclusion. The best black Africans were taken to the New World as slaves. The greedy, selfish, shortsighted blacks were left behind on the African continent. Those left behind were, however, not necessarily the weakest.

Yet, an intriguing question remains unanswered. America is a continent where all the races of the world are represented. Millions of the unemployed and the poorer classes of Europe also emigrated to America from the 17th Century to the beginning of this Century. Also, the Chinese and other members of the Mongolian race emigrated to America. Initially, the Chinese also functioned as slaves in America and they were like the blacks, an oppressed group in the New World. But unlike the black Africans who were consciously made to lose their past and who are dehumanised, the Chinese in America were allowed to preserve some of their traditions, customs and family life. The Italians and the Irish also fell within the category of America's oppressed groups. However, unlike the black Americans they had the support and protection of the Roman Catholic Church.

But even then, this is not all the answer for the black Americans have been unable to make it up the ladder on their own as the other ethnic groups have done in America. While the overwhelming odds they have always faced are appreciated, yet, if we accept the view that the most intelligent, the healthiest and those of strong physical appearance were carried as slaves to America from Africa, it is difficult to explain why a great majority of black Americans are so backward today in America. For instance, a great percentage of the black Americans live in abject poverty in the United States-the wold's richest country. About 33 percent of the black population are very poor.

In 1972 and 1974, I saw the grinding poverty in which black Americans lived in New York, Chigago, Washington, New Orleans, Los Angeles, Atlanta and several other cities. My close observation of the sordid squalour in which millions of poor black Americans lived in the rat-infested, or dope-infested slums of the cities I visited created serious doubt in my mind as to the validity of my long held idea that the most intelligent blacks were carried from Africa as slaves while the corrupt and selfish ones were left behind. After my two visits to the United States, persistently crossing my mind was the thought that while the black Americans had shown great resilience in the face of unprecedented oppression, many have not in recent years fully utilised the stimulus provided by the American Society to make the blacks great and respected. Before I left on my first visit to the United States in 1972, a fellow Nigerian told me that Harlem in New York City, where the black population is concentrated, is worse than Mushin, the dirty, low income area of Lagos in Nigeria. I then thought that view was probably an exaggeration. But I was wrong. For Harlem in New York City, like the South Bronx, Bedford-Stuyvesant and other black "ghettos" or slums in America, have streets full of huge refuse everywhere, broken windows, and poorly-lit roads where crime is rampant and life is insecure.

I visited and studied the situation in black Harlem of New York City for several hours in 1972 and 1974. I noticed that huge refuse piled up near almost every house. There were empty tins and refuse everywhere in the streets. Several of the windows and doors of the cockroaches-and rats-infested houses were broken. I saw sordid squalor. I saw abject poverty with the old men and women who were either scantily dressed or in tatters sitting idly on the steps of dirty houses in the black Harlem of New York.

Able-bodied young men and women, some of them half naked, sat in the middle of the roads. Some of them had clean-shaven heads, some were busy painting some drawings on bodies of their almost naked colleagues. Blacks were found in rowdy pubs. There was a great deal of loud music, a lot of smoke, terrible odour and incessant yelling. Young men and women live daily on shots of heroine. Several women who, together with their children have been deserted by their husbands, live on public welfare. This is a meagre government financial assistance that is hardly sufficient to keep them at even the poverty level. It is a welfare assistance to which stringent and humiliating conditions are attached. I learnt that several of the black Americans I found in the ghettos of New York, Chicago, Atlanta, New Orleans and other cities were among 5 million Americans who collect one form or the other of public welfare payments yearly.

I noticed a sense of rage, a deep and abiding anger among poverty-stricken Black Americans who live in the ghettos of the world's richest nation. In the Black Harlem of New York city, banks, apartment houses, bars, theatres, businesses, department stores, loans and savings companies are largely owned by whites who live outside the slum of Harlem but take their huge profits home. There are discriminatory job practices and very high rate of unemployment in these ghettos. The welfare system by which the state gives financial assistance to the needy is archaic and primitive. Housing conditions are very poor. Schools are inadequate and so are their curricula and outmoded techniques of teaching. The depressing conditions in the black ghettos of the United States explain the high rate of crime in these areas and the increasing urge among the black to inflict pain, suffering and economic loss on the whites and their fellow blacks. Sometimes they break into and loot shops which belong to the white economic exploiters. As they did in 1964.

On the high crime rate, America's National Commission on the Causes and Prevention of Violence discovered that while the blacks constitute 11 per cent of the United States population, they are involved in about three fifths of the arrests for murder and more than half of the victims were black. It is the same pattern for robbery, rape and aggravated assault. It is reported that in 1968 and 1972, blacks were arrested for 27.5 per cent of all crimes in the United States.

The poor and needy blacks are victims of a white-dominated and white-directed system that condemns millions of black families to abject poverty, high dope addiction and school drop out rates. It is revealing that in the early 1960s more than half of all blacks were below the poverty line. This figure fell to about 33 per cent of all blacks in 1969. In 1970, of the 4.9 million black American families, 1.4 million (or 29 per cent) were living below the poverty level. Of this number, 820,000 (or 57 per cent) were headed by females. And poor families headed by black females are known to be the poorest of the poor. Their average income is 1,492 dollars and this is below what is regarded as the poverty level in America. And between 1960 and 1970, the number of blacks living in poverty-stricken fatherless families increased from 2.75 million to 3.5 million. The picture is equally gloomy for the blacks in terms of unemployment.

In 1948, America's Bureau of Labour Statistics revealed that the jobless rate of non-white males (the Non-whites are mainly blacks although some are Puerto Ricans), between the ages of 14 and 19 was 7.6 per cent. But by 1965, the percentage of unemployment in this age group had risen to 22.6. On the other hand, the corresponding figures for the unemployed white male teen-agers were 8.3 per cent in 1948 and only 11.8 per cent in 1965. This cannot be attributed to the failure of blacks to have necessary education because in 1965, it was far easier for white high school drop-outs to get jobs than for the black high school graduates. In other words, unemployment rates were far higher in 1965 for the black high school graduates than for the whites who did not complete high school education.

Besides, the black American is a victim of overt and institutional racism. Open racism in an action like the stoning, burning and general harassment of black families who try to move into white neighbourhood. Institutional racism is more disguised. It is this that keeps the vast majority of black Americans in the terrible slums known as ghettos where for most of their lives they are helpless victims of exploitative white landlords, real estate agents and traders. In short, the white American culture makes it impossible for the great majority of the blacks to find an identity, a sense of worth and relate to other Americans. This has resulted in a black rage which makes it impossible for the vast majority of blacks to create and to love. It explains why black Americans are scarcely completely at home in a country where they have lived for about 350 years. It is understandable. For there is an American way of life, a national style of life which assumes that blacks are inferior, that they were born to be hewers of wood and drawers of water.

The newly-come whites are accepted and made to feel at home. They are made to feel it is right to despise, feel superior to and exploit the blacks.

But even then, an important fact must be admitted. Despite the overt and covert racism and unbridled exploitation to which black Americans have been subjected, black peoples in America have all along embarked on heroic struggles to free themselves from the chains of enslavement and to preserve their identity. They have done more. They have shown great ingenuity in making the best use of their cruel environment to bring out great achievements in music, sports, religion and other areas of human endeavours. But black Americans can achieve a lot more to further the interest of the black race. For instance, black American youths could vigorously pursue scientific and technological studies and use their high skills for the benefit of black states throughout the world.

Many black Americans have struggled and sacrificed under great stress and strain and they have succeeded in increasing the number of their fellow blacks who have gained better economic and social status. For as far back as 1787, the Free African Society of Newport has been formed by freed slaves to promote group cohesion and repatriation to Africa. There were at the same period many similar societies in the North Eastern part of the United States. Those who believed that the ultimate hope of black Americans was a return to Africa included Paul Cuffee, a rich ship-owner, who transported at his own expense, a group of 38 blacks to Sierra-Leone in 1815. Other efforts were made. In 1852, Martin R. Delany, a black physician and editor of a weekly newspaper stated that he was convinced that people of African descent would never receive redress in America for the injustices they had suffered at the hands of the whites. In 1858, he led an expedition of black Americans who wanted to settle in Africa and signed treaties with many African traditional rulers. Also in 1858, Benjamin Coates and other leading black Americans formed the African Civilisation Society with the main aim of fostering social and economic ties between Africa and America.

But the urge to emigrate died down with the emancipation and the granting of citizenship rights to the blacks. In 1863, President Abraham Lincoln signed the Emancipation Proclamation freeing the slaves. Lincoln's Proclamation was quickly followed by the adoption of the thirteenth, fourteenth and fifteenth amendments to the American Constitution. The amendments outlawed slavery and gave citizenship rights to all former slaves. They guaranteed the slaves equal protection before the law and gave them the right to vote. With the emancipation, the blacks had high hopes that their conditions would improve. But in the 1870s, an end was put to their optimism. Emancipation was a farce, a mockery. The new citizenship rights conferred on the blacks were manipulated and subjected to the vicious whims of the white Americans. Hence, emigration efforts were intensified in the 20th Century and positive political action on the part of the blacks was manifested in different forms.

Black protest movement gained added momentum at the beginning of the century. In 1911, a group of black and some white Americans were anxious to protect the interests of the new rural migrant Negroes in industrial urban areas. They formed the National Urban League. The Organisation achieved much in the struggle of the black man for a respectable place in American Society. And in 1910, the National Association for the Advancement of Coloured People (NAACP) was founded. Among its several stated aims was its plan to challenge the legal basis of segregation. It therefore set up the Legal Redress Committee which achieved a lot. It brought up cases in the Federal Supreme Court on housing discrimination and denial of blacks' constitutional rights. Forty three of the 47 cases it argued between 1940 and 1963 were successful.

In 1963, a mammoth crowd of 200,000 Americans, mainly blacks but with some whites, marched on the Lincoln Memorial in Washington D.C. The aim was to emphasise the sad situation in the United States which still allowed widespread discrimination and injustice, especially against the blacks, after 100 years of the proclamation of emancipation of the American slaves. The march prompted some positive action from the government on civil rights. For instance, the constitution was amended to allow the abolition of the poll tax in state elections. Before 1965, payment of the poll tax had been used as a device to deny the blacks of their right to vote and be voted for. Also, the Civil Rights Acts of 1964 disallows discrimination in the use of public facilities and in employment, especially if the college, university, state, firm or municipal authority concerned enjoys any form of federal grant. But in so far as all states and many organisations enjoy enormous federal grants either directly or indirectly, the law has prompted considerable integration in colleges, universities and other institutions.

However, many black Americans believe that integration has

achieved very little. It has also raised deep psychological problems. Integration is regarded as a despicable and unrealistic goal. Those who hold this view quarrel with the basic idea of integration which is that in order to have a decent education or house, black Americans must move into white areas or send their children to white schools. This automatically reinforces the idea that white is superior to the black and that black is by definition and reality inferior. Hence, integration is seen as a device to maintain white supremacy. It is also believed that undue attention is focused by Americans on the few black children who get admitted into white schools while the problem of 94 per cent blacks who are left in the poorly-equipped and poorly-staffed black schools are neglected. Also ignored is the grinding poverty of the great majority of black Americans in a country of immense opportunities which the blacks have helped to build in a manner that is far more than the contribution of any other race. Furthermore, to many black Americans, integration means that black Americans must give up their identity as Negroes. They must deny their black heritage.

But despite the attitude of the militant black Americans to integration, it has made considerable progress. Besides, the black middle class have sought for and seized many opportunities. They have made considerable progress. Many black Americans have been integrated into the public sector. For example althouh the blacks form 11 per cent of the United States population, they hold 15 per cent of all full-time jobs with the U.S. Federal Government. In 1970, 39 per cent of all professionals in the United States were employed by Federal, State and Local Governments. And 60 per cent of all such posts were held by black American professionals. There are other achievements. By 1974, it was known that the United States Army had 12 black generals. There was a black American Admiral in the Navy and three Generals in the Air Force. Also, black Americans constituted about 13 per cent of American soldiers by 1974. Although black American progress is often exaggerated by the white propagandists of black success, yet, black efforts are real and in many directions.

For it was a sad story of complete black rejection and dehumanisation by the American whites a few decades ago. Like in the early 1900's, when the United States Press strongly criticised President Theodore Roosevelt for the lunch he had with the black American educationist, Booker T. Washington. But as against this, blacks dine today at the White House. During his first three years as US President, Richard Nixon nominated seven black Ambassadors. They include the first black ambassador to Nigeria, John Reinhardt.

In general terms, black Americans have made a lot of progress although the progress is comparatively not much when considered in the context of the phenomenal technological, scientific, educational and economic progress which the United States had made since it was founded and the poverty and suffering of the masses of black Americans today. One aspect of general black progress which is usually emphasised is that the black enrolment of college graduates in the United States is far greater than that for the entire continent of Africa. Also, it is claimed that American blacks now have a total income which exceeds 38,700 million dollars, a figure that is far greater than the budgets of many independent nations. This figure indicated an increase of 5,000 million dollars in the income of black Americans within a ten-year-period. But this figure becomes quite insignificant when it is related to the far higher growth in the economic strength of white Americans over the years.

There are a number of achievements in education. Up to 1860 only 28 blacks had graduated from college. By 1900, the number had risen to 2,500. Actual enrolment of blacks in colleges rose from 700 to 800 in 1860 to 470,000 in 1970, (including part time students)

But for more than two centuries (1619 to 1860), very little educational opportunity was allowed the few freed black slaves and there was none at all for the black slaves. Even then, many blacks struggled, sometimes with the assistance of the Church and philanthropists, to obtain good education. The progress was slow initially for by 1872 only seven black colleges were in existence and the rest were at best just secondary schools and by 1895, there were only 1,100 graduates of black colleges. In 1881, Booker T. Washington founded Tuskegee Institute. He encouraged industrial education by which the blacks were to acquire skills in crafts and liberal arts. His idea of what the black aspirations should be is summed up in the following famous statement he made at Atlanta in 1895:

> "It is at the bottom of life we must begin, and not at the top. No race can prosper till it learns that there is as much dignity in tilling a field as in writing a poem... The wisest among my race understand that agitation of questions of social equality is the extremest folly."

Unfortunately, the southern racists, in the United States perverted the doctrine of Booker T. Washington and used his idea of industrial education to perpetuate the southern racial caste system, thereby keeping the southern blacks the hewers of wood and drawers of water they had been since African slaves were transported to America in the 16th Century. Industrial education for the blacks was not used to prepare the blacks for their new roles in an economy undergoing fast changes in modernisation. Rather, it was used in the southern States as a devise to train the black Americans in pre-industrial skills - simple crafts, gardening etc. which were not of much worth to a fast changing industrial economy. A strong critic of Booker. T. Washington was the black historian, Dr. W.E.B. Du Bois. He argued that only with a strong liberal arts education- one that was equal to that given to the white

Americans - could black Americans hope to achieve economic and social equality with the whites. He argues that the United States, especially the white racists dominated south, did not need from the black Americans a mere labouring class but an intelligent black elite. In 1903, Du Bois said in his book: "Souls of Black Folk", that Washington's Tuskegee and other similar institutions were truly "centres of that underground and silent intrigue which is determined to perpetuate the American Negro as a docile peasant". He argued that Washington's type of industrial education merely taught the blacks to be good subordinates. Du Bois accused Washington of accepting, by his doctrines, "the alleged inferiority of the Negro".

The Legal Redress Committee which had since 1915 filed actions in the United States Supreme Court to fight discrimination also achieved much in the field of education. For instance, in Brown versus Board of Education in 1954, the "Separate but equal doctrine", which was established in Plessy versus Ferguson case in 1896 and which supported segregation, was abolished. With the forceful plea of Thurgood Marshall, a black American Lawyer, and now a Supreme Court Justice, the Court handed down its far-reaching and unanimous decision on segregation in education on May 17, 1954. The Supreme Court held that there were intangible factors involved in the separation of children by race. That segregation of black American children has a detrimental effect on them. The court also contended that such segregation "generates a feeling of inferiority as to the status of black children in the community that may affect their hearts and minds in a way never likely to be undone". It argued that the doctrine of "separate but equal" has no place in the field of public education and that separate education facilities are inherently unequal.

In 1950, in McLaurin versus Oklahoma State Regents case, the Supreme Court also ruled in favour of a post-graduate student,

McLaurin, who was being made to use segregated facilities for his post-graduate work at the University of Oklahoma. Black American youths also displayed great courage in a bid to ensure that the new benefits conferred by law were made use of. One confrontation between the Federal authorities and a State Government was in Little Rock where President D. Eisenhower called out Federal troops to integrate the schools. And President John Kennedy was compelled to Federalise Alabama National Guard when a defiant Governor George Wallace was using his guards to prevent three black American students from enrolling at the University of Alabama. At the University of Mississippi, Federal Government Marshals were asked to guard the first black American student, James Meredith, day and night for a whole year.

There was progress in other directions. In technology, science, sports and music, black Americans have, for several years shown indisputable excellence and creativity. For instance, a black American, Granville Woods who lived from 1856-1910, received more than 35 patents for his several inventions. He is known to have invented a steam - boiler furnace, an incubator, automatic air breaks and many other devices. Some of his inventions were sold to American Bell Telephone, Westinghouse Air Break Co. and General Electric. He invented railway telegraph which helped to stop accidents between moving trains.

Many others invented mechanical and electrical devices. Elijah McCoy invented the first self-lubricating industrial machine in America. This gave a big boost to industrialisation. In 1893., Daniel Hale Williams (1858-1931) was acclaimed as the first American doctor to operate on the human heart while Granville T. Woods also improved the telephone system invented by a white man, Alexander Graham Bell. A black engineer, Benjamin Baneker designed the Street system of Washington.

In music, there were great names like Marian Anderson of whom the great conductor Arturo Toscanini said: "a voice like hers was heard only once in a century", and Louis Amstrong (Satchmo).In sports were outstanding men like Joe Loius who won the world heavy weight crown and successfully defended it 25 times from 1934 to 1949; Jesse Owens, the black American track star who won the 100-and 200- meter events and the broad jump and who was also on the winning 400 meter relay team at the Olympic Games. There is also the legend of our time, world heavyweight boxing champion, Mohammed Alli.

In civil rights, outstanding black Americans vary from the extreme militant, Malcolm X to Elijah Mohammed, Martin Luther King and Thurgood Marshall, a black Judge of the Supreme Court. In education, we have mentioned men of profound intellect like Booker T. Washington and W.E.B. DuBois (1868-1963).

Another significant and positive development in Black American history is the growth of the black power concept. Stokely Carmichael and Charles V. Hamilton clearly explain the concept in their book:

> "BLACK POWER: The Politics of Liberation in America".
>
> Black Power is a call for black people in this country (U.S.A) to unite, to recognise their heritage, to build a sense of community. It is a call for black people to begin to define their own goals, to lead their own organisations and to support those organisations. It is a call to reject the racist institutions and values of this society."

Viewing black power as a concept that encourages black

Americans to participate fully in the affairs of their country, a concept that seeks to restore the black man's self-pride, Carmicheal and Hamilton also give this succinct explanation:

*"The goal of black self-determination and black self-identity - Black Power- is full participation in the decision-making processes affecting the lives of black people, and recognition of the virtues in themselves as black people. The black people of this country have not lynched whites, bombed their churches, murdered their children and manipulated laws and institutions to maintain oppression. White racists have".*

The reactions to the black power concept have varied widely. But it has led to one healthy development. It has, to a large extent, removed the inferiority complex and self-hatred from which the black Americans had suffered for about 300 years. More and more blacks are becoming proud of their race and heritage. They now resent skin bleaching and hair straightening which come from the strong desire to be like the whites. The black power concept emphasises a history and a tradition which black Americans are proud of. Blacks are now proud of their home, Africa. They wear "danshikis" and African hair styles. Some accept and practise the tenets of Islam. They extol black, the natural hair styles, the glories of African past and the potentials of an African future.

But the all important question is: How important is the black power concept as a solution to the overwhelming problems which black Americans face? I agree with the view that the black power emotion is healthy and desirable for a people who have been ruthlessly oppressed by the whites since they were forcibly brought to the New World more than 300 years ago. It is desirable that the blacks who were robbed of their language and culture, the blacks who were not allowed to become Americans and were at the same time forbidden to be Africans, should reach out for their past and regain their worth as human beings. This the black Americans have done through the black power idea.

But the black power emotion is not enough. The reality of the situation in the United States is that black Americans are, by and large, still backward and helpless. Grinding poverty is their lot. Their present day achievements are glaringly insignificant and inferior compared with that of other American racial and ethnic groups. They are still the under-dogs in a country of vast opportunities where all the races of the world are represented.

It all means that Black Americans must compel their acceptance as equals by fellow Americans. They cannot achieve this through the present misplaced emphasis on black studies and the chanting of black power slogans. The blacks must have massive and consciously organised struggles to break out of their present limitations. And this they can do only through education. For only education can offer a significant and lasting solution to the black man's dilemma in America. The blacks should aggressively seize the vast opportunities which America offers in higher education and turn out black giants in science, technology and other professions. With the acquisition of the right type of high level skills in science and technology, the blacks could force their way into America's skilled labour markets.

They could even do more. They could ably face their grave responsibility to mother Africa. For one thing, the wide economic, political and social gap which exists between the black and white Americans is just an insignificant reflection of the far wider gap that exists between Africa and the black world on one hand and the white world on the other. And if thousands of black Americans are able to attain eminence in science, technology, management and the professions, they can join the new nations of Africa to turn black Africa into a modern, industrial and highly developed homeland. This, to my mind, are some of the several ways black Americans can help to ensure that the black race makes it like the other races of the world.

*Black Man's Dilemma*

CHAPTER EIGHT

# *REVISED EDITION*
# *THE BLACK AMERICANS*
## AN UPDATE

In his two part review of Black Man's Dilemma, 1976 edition, in THE NIGERIAN TRIBUNE in 1982, the late Nigerian radical educationist, columnist and dogged fighter for human rights, Dr. Tai Solarin sharply disagreed with me about the quality of black men and women transported to the new world, especially the United States, during the period of slave trade.

Dr. Tai Solarin disagreed with my view that some of the best of the blacks were taken out of Africa as slaves. In the first edition, I agreed with historians who said that white slave traders would naturally prefer able-bodied, tall, healthy and intelligent young men and women to the sick, aged and dull looking blacks for shipment to the Americas. One reason that strengthened my belief that the best blacks were taken as slaves was my observation during several visits to the United States that many black Americans, descendants of black slaves, are today very tall, well built and good looking. Also, many of the people captured as slaves displayed heroic defiance and resilience while being shipped to the new world and as slaves working on their masters' plantations.

However, Dr. Tai Solarin, who was my close senior friend, in the first of his two part review of the first edition of Black Man's Dilemma, published in the NIGERIAN TRIBUNE of January 11, 1982, expressed the view that:

*"Any time there was a raid, it was the most intelligent who would be alert and would know how to melt miraculously away. A subdued whistle, a gesture from a neighbour, a quick clap of the hands and the most intelligent has evaporated. By and large, it was the stupid and slow of foot that got quickly roped off and carried away".*

*"Of course, a few intelligent ones would be unlucky to fall prey to the slave traders. It was some of these very intelligent ones who felt too proud to be caught as slaves who leapt overboard mid Atlantic. The unintelligent capitulated unconditionally. And anybody who sees the pictures of the slaves would easily agree they always looked stupid, because they were unintelligent".* His full contribution is in Appendix I.

The foregoing is part of the views of Dr. Tai Solarin, on the black Africans transported as slaves to North America. I disagree with Dr. Solarin's view that the unintelligent black Africans were shipped as slaves to North America. I hold firmly to my belief that black slave raiders and traders, including black traditional rulers who vigorously supported the slave trade, were selfish, greedy, wicked, inconsiderate and short-sighted. They were Africans of dubious character.

This view is further buttressed by the complete mess, which the black Africans left behind by the captured slaves, have made of the African continent throughout the period of slave trade, during colonial period and since the attainment of independence. I believe that black Americans and the large population of blacks in Brazil and generally in diaspora, are by every available evidence, better human beings than their kith and kin they left on the African continent.

Besides, after the publication of the first edition of this book, I had made several other visits to different parts of the United States during which I observed remarkable improvement in the standard of living and general life outlook of millions of Afro-Americans.

In all the black ghettos of large cities like New York, Washington, Atlanta, Los Angeles, New Orleans and Chicago, I observed a remarkable improvement in environmental sanitation, health, educational facilities and mode of dressing.

In the last ten years, I have made a special study of black Harlem in New York, where earlier between 1972 and 1974, I had found misery, grinding poverty, squalor, drug addiction, excessive alcohol and idleness as a way of life. In Harlem I found a lot of progress as shown by many decent buildings, nicely dressed people and several enterprising and well-educated business men and women.

In the large American society, black Americans have, since I first published this book in 1976, made tremendous progress in educational attainments and all areas of human endeavours. Thousands of Afro-Americans have made it to the top in the professions, corporate businesses, technological innovations, academics, religious and social organisations.

In the bar and bench, in the executive and legislative arms of government, churches, print and electronic media, sports, human rights groups and as heads of their own big and medium enterprises, so many outstanding Afro-Americans are now at the commanding heights of life in the United States. There are several thousands of highly educated and outstanding men and women, whose achievements have become a source of pride to mother Africa.

Of greater significance is that successful and articulate Afro-Americans have today rightly shown keen interest and taken positive steps in the affairs of black African countries.

For instance, great Afro-American achievers like Andrew Young, former United States Ambassador to the United Nations, Randle Robinson, chairman of TRANSAFRICA, A US-based Human Rights Group, Reverend Jesse Jackson, United States envoy for the Promotion of Democracy in Africa and many others, joined forces with exiled Nigerians during the tyrannical rule of the late Nigerian dictator, General Sani Abacha. They all put up a stiff fight against the Nigerian dictator, who, despite his glaring mental, moral and educational inadequacies as well as his unparalleled greed and dishonesty, wanted to become Nigeria's life President through a bogus political programme.

America's Randle Robinson boldly and persistently challenged the right of Abacha to personally participate in a transition programme he was supposed to have supervised to usher in democratic governance. He pointed out to Abacha that his plan on democracy, while M.K.O. Abiola, who won a free and fair election in Nigeria was kept in prison by him, was completely unacceptable to Nigerians and the international community. He described Abacha's political parties as government agents and not parties. He also made the important point that Abacha, who had participated in all the coup d'etats in Nigeria, could not bring about democratic rule.

That a lot of progress has been made in the positive interest and concern shown by eminent black Americans in the affairs of the continent is a very good development for the black race. Also, that several thousands of black Americans have become giants in science, industries, technology, the professions, management, politics, government and corporate businesses since Black Man's Dilemma was first published, has become a source of great joy to the author and millions of black peoples worldwide.

But that should not be the end of the story. Successful black Americans should do more. They must bring their skill, technology, management and wealth to Africa for its rapid development. They should invest heavily in Africa in a determined effort to turn the continent into a prosperous and highly developed homeland.

Above all, leading black Americans should frontally fight the excesses of a large majority of African presidents, prime ministers, heads of states and their ministers. They must expose and fight relentlessly African leaders who savagely loot their countries' treasuries and put Africa's stolen hard currencies in richer countries of Europe, America and Asia, thereby keeping their peoples in abject poverty. Black Americans must also open a completely new page in African history. On this new page, they must write a resolution. They must resolve that never again would they and the American government tolerate any seizure of political power by self-serving military in any black African country.

*Black Man's Dilemma*

CHAPTER NINE

# 1976 EDITION
# POST-INDEPENDECE HELPLESSNESS AND NEW HOPES

INDEPENDENT black African states are not yet free. This is despite the attainment of political independence by Ghana in 1957, Guinea in 1958, Nigeria in 1960 and by several others since 1960. Independence for these states has not meant the mental and economic liberation of the black man. Political freedom has been considered by many of them as an end in itself. A peaceful and beneficial revolution which the masses of the newly independent black nations hope for has never really occurred. Independence has brought only moral compensation to the colonised and dehumanised black Africans. It has established their dignity. But the black states of Africa and the black-dominated ones in the Caribbean are "masked colonies". They merely enjoy what Ghana's immortal Kwame Nkrumah called "fake independence".

The first evidence of post-independence helplessness is the complete lack of mental revolution in the black states. Admittedly, the attainment of independence indicated a kind of mental emancipation on the part of the colonised Africans. But political freedom should be the beginning of the bigger struggle for economic and cultural liberation. The few exceptions are Guinea,

*Black Man's Dilemma*

Kwame Nkrumah's Ghana, Tanzania, Nigeria since July 29, 1975, Angola, Mozambique and Forbes Burham's Guyana in South America. In some of the new states local cultural originality is dead and buried. It is replaced by the culture of the Mother country. In many places the colonial powers consciously killed the indigenes' self-respect. For instance, Portugal introduced the policy of assimilation in its former African colonies of Angola and Mozambique. She supressed all independent groups. The assimilated black - i.e. the assimilado - was asked to reject as intrinsically inferior his entire black heritage and association. If an African measured up to certain Western standards, he could legally become a "white" man. He became an assimilado after he might have been judged to have thoroughly adopted Portuguese language, dress and customs. He should also have achieved a passport to travel overseas, mainly to Portugal and Brazil. He was accepted socially by the whites in the night clubs and restaurants. He was even encouraged to marry a Portuguese woman. The assimilado was entitled to better jobs and housing. The French also encouraged the growth of black French men known as evolue. This was a French black elite group who were exposed to and have absorbed French "civilisation". Like the assimilados, they had the type of rights and privileges enjoyed by the white French men in the colonies and France. The British achieved their own mental colonisation of the subjected black Africans in more subtle ways. However, the blacks have an illusion of a cultural rediscovery. There are lots of "black and proud" slogans and a profuse display of ritual and bare-breasted dancers during national and international festival shows. But the black rediscovery is a farce because it doesn't touch the reality of the black man's past and present. It's also not a source of strength for the future. In short, the mental and psychological liberation of the black man has not started in many of the new states of Africa and the Caribbean. This partly explains why the black man's backwardness has been so persistent and recurrent.

Politically and diplomatically, black Africa is still regarded as a booty, a bone of contention or a pawn in the power struggles of the big powers. Economically, the independence of the new black states is more nominal than real. It is neo-colonialism through and through. The former colonial masters still decisively arbitrate on the pace and course of their economic development. They still very much direct the show. But in a sense this is understandable. Colonialism created miserable conditions which led to periodic famine, chronic malnutrition and health hazards for the people of Africa. The level of oppression of black Africans by colonialism was succinctly put in the Arusha Declaration as follows:

> *"WE HAVE BEEN OPPRESSED A GREAT DEAL, WE HAVE BEEN EXPLOITED A GREAT DEAL, AND WE HAVE BEEN DISREGARDED A GREAT DEAL".*

The oppression and exploitation of the Africans were manifested in different other ways. Roads and railways were built in colonial Africa only if they would promote import and export activities of the colonial powers, where exports were not available roads and railways were not built. The only exception was when they were needed to make the movement of troops and the conquest and harassment of the colonial peoples easier. Industrialisation was consciously discouraged in colonial Africa so that high level skills would not be generated. Scientific techniques and skills multiplied in the Mother Countries - the United Kingdom, Portugal, Spain and France - where goods were produced for the colonial territories.

But that was not all. Facilities like schools and hospitals built by the colonialists were very few. For instance, Ibadan, which is the most thickly populated city in Africa south of the Sahara had only 50 white expatriate officials and businessmen before the 1939-1944 War. But the British colonial government maintained only 34 hospital beds for the then more than 500,000 blacks while in the beautiful surroundings known as government reservations in the same city, the colonial government built a segregated, lavishly furnished hospital with 11 beds for the 50 Europeans. The picture was equally gloomy for Nigeria as a whole. While in the 1930s the colonial Nigeria, with a population of about 40 million, had only 52 hospitals which were mainly old and ill-equipped, the 4,000 whites in the country had 12 modern, well furnished and staffed hospitals. Colonial banks and insurance companies decided as an act of deliberate policy to discourage the granting of loans to black natives while loans were freely granted to the capitalist firms and white settlers. The colonial central banks and currency boards invested the huge funds earned from the exported African produce like cocoa, cotton and groundnuts in France, Belgium and Britain. The funds were not invested in the colonial territories which earned them.

The sum total of colonial exploitation, oppression and neglect is the primitive means of production which are now available in the new states of Africa and the Caribbean, their high mortality rate, and their lack of modern hygiene and medical precautions. In frastructure is absent. It's a world of grinding poverty, a land without doctors, without seasoned administrators and without engineers. The hungry black masses, despite the few reforms at the top, the fancy-dress parade, the flag waving and the blare of trumpets for the leaders, are still living in the Middle Ages. They are endlessly marking time.

The masses live in filthy environment. There is the primitive latrine system which allows night soil men to mix freely with citizens in broad daylight. There are no public toilets even in the modern elite areas. So after a decade or two of independence people still urinate and excrete by the sides of modern highways. Drainage is poor and sewage is out-dated. Uncollected refuse pile up and in many cities of Africa, refuse constitute, a hindrance to the free flow of fraffic. Besides, the destitutes, the lepers, the blind, the lame and lunatics roam the streets in many of the new nations of Africa. Millions of the people walk about bare-footed. They are poorly fed and clothed.

Many of the new states are still under the direct economic bondage of Western imperialists. They lack a modernising elite who can face their countries' complex problems squarely and destroy the facile glamour which the liberal white scholars of Europe and America have built around economic growth in the New World. The result is that the richer countries are becoming richer. They are recording a faster rate of economic development so that the gap between us is daily widening. While wages are low, costs of living in our poor nations are far higher than in the richer nations of the world. The poor people in the former colonies of Africa and the Caribbean cannot afford to eat food that is as rich as the type given to cattle in some economically advanced countries. Housing, clothing and transportation are far more expensive in the new nations than in the former Metropolises which today still continue with the unbridled neo-colonial exploitation of their former territories. And distressingly, the elite and the masses of the black nations have been exposed to the high standard of living and luxury which the highly developed nations of the world enjoy. But we as the world's poor blacks have not accepted the type of discipline, the type of self-denial, the type of strong determination to make their societies better than they found it, which have all combined to make some of the world's rich nations rich.

Besides, some of the new African states have been still-born since birth. They are so heavily dependent on the mother country that if the foreign aids were withdrawn the state machinery would collapse at once. They are practically defenceless and incredibly weak. The mother countries had ensured that these states would remain very weak. And France is the most guilty of these mother countries. France today constitutes the most stupendous menace to the new states of Africa. America comes second. France has ensured that, apart from Guinea, all its former territories in Africa remain "client" states which are still linked to it to an extent that makes a mockery of their independence and draws a wedge between them and their more independent neighbours. South Africa, the United States, Portugal, Spain, France and Britain are all enemies of black nations. They strengthen the racist South Africa which is one of the biggest threats to Africa. But France has today emerged as Africa's enemy number one. It has concluded an agreement to give nuclear device to the racist government of South Africa, the strong protests of black nations and the rest of the world notwithstanding.

France played a wicked role in Nigeria's civil war. She was interested in our country's disintegration. Inspite of her sad experience and the humiliating defeat she suffered at Die Bien Phu in 1954, a defeat that forced her out of Indo China, France still refused to accept independence as a legitimate goal for her colonial territories. In Algeria, she succumbed to the wishes of the people only after Algerians had put in seven years of violent insurrection which began in 1954 and which she ruthlessly but fruitlessy suppressed. France did more. She organised brutal killings of Africans in Morocco and Bizerta in Tunisia. She was a partner in the widely condemned Suez Canal aggression of 1956. She stubbornly exploded atomic bombs in the Algerian Sahara despite the strong condemnation of Nigeria and other African countries. Treachery, wickedness and insincerity run like scarlet thread through the entire colonial history and policy of France. But the other colonial masters are also still bent on directing the show in Africa while the new arch imperialist, the United States, has arrogated to herself the right to think and decide for the nations and peoples of Africa.

## Post-Independence Helplessness and New Hopes

Since the attainment of independence black nations have been sinking more deeply into economic backwardness. It is sad indeed that their economies are yearly exposed to the ruthless plunder brought about by investments by the richer nations. Foreign investors made enormous profits yearly from the neo-colonial economies of the new nations. The major investments are designed to accelerate production of raw materials, minerals and semi-processed produce for the advanced economies of Europe and America. Our economies are only responsive to what the world market is ready to sell and buy and not to the internal development needs of our countries. The much sought foreign investments do not contribute much to the development of a sound technical and material base for our economies. The economy is permanently hampered by the inadequate growth in exported goods, the exploitative nature and strings of foreign aid and high population growth rate. It's a vicious circle of poverty and our young nations continue to remain underdeveloped and poorer. We have not learnt to look inward and build self-reliant economies.

Grandiose development plans are prepared and launched regularly with noise and fanfare. But ours has been the sad story of growth without development. The more money that is made from increased export of cocoa, rubber, cotton, groundnut or petroleum the more is spent on the importation of luxurious and essential consumer goods while the huge profits go to the former colonial powers-the Metropolises. The economy is not self-sustained. It does not meet domestic goals. It is entirely dependent on the vagries of the world market and manipulations of the international monopoly syndicates. Black Africans have also proved that our race excels all other races in its love of conspicuous consumptiom, grandeur and luxury. And our productivity is at the same time the lowest in the world. The masses are not mobilised because black leadership has uncritically accepted the trial and error approach to economic development of the West. They cite Great Britain and her long and costly journey to industrialisation which lasted about 400 years. Black intelligentsia is not interested in the total planning, total regimentation, total mobilisation and self-reliance through which one-time backward, exploited and confused nations like China and the Soviet Union became world powers within a few decades.

The black man needs a mental revolution. Without this he can never fully realise the need to be original and to assume full responsibility for his own progress. He must develop a new and original ideology that's not a poor copy of either the capitalist or communist approach to economic development. He can borrow from the East or the West but he must evolve in his own way, taking account of his own cultural heritage and the reality of his situation. We have been suddenly propelled into a civilisation different from our own. We must therefore find a way of combining foreign methods and some of our tranditional institutions and values so as to forge a new basis for rapid economic development and a new civilisation. One important fact we can ignore only at our peril is that meaningful development cannot take place in black Africa as long as our production strategy is influenced by the demands of the world market which is determined by the pattern of production and consumption within the capitalist countries of Europe and America. We must reject the laws of supply and demand as far as they relate to the West dominated world market. This was what China did. We must satisfy our internal economic needs and encourage the invention of machinery and acquisition of technological skills because they are the real basis for meaningful economic development.

However, of all the factors which have kept the black race the world's underdog the mental laziness, greed and indiscretion of our middle class are the most crippling. Our middle class, professional, intellectual or political, are victims of spiritual penury.

*Post-Independence Helplessness and New Hopes*

Their pre-occupation is to be part of the racket. Black elite are not captains of industry. They are not engaged in meaningful production. They are not inventors. They are not visionary builders of a great nation. They are businessmen and middlemen, pure and simple. Black bourgeoisie in the free nations of Africa and the Caribbean are willing tools of neo-colonialism and capitalism. They are content to serve as the business agents of the Western bourgeoisie. They are so different from the bourgeoisie of Britain, Germany, France, Russia, China or Japan in that they are not inventors, pioneers or discoverers of new worlds and great ideas. They are just happy to be the middle man to Western enterprise. And the mind of the black intelligentsia is hardly different from that which is prevalent among the crowd. Since the attainment of independence, our highly educated elite have not accepted the challenge to think afresh, to examine new ways of doing things. They have not seen any different angle to modern technology. At best, they are copycats. The universities could not adapt science to the peculiar needs of our new nations. Their research works are irrelevant and only a few of them have any bearing on the crucial questions which our young states face. In short, black intelligentsia do not possess greater heart and foresight.

Worse still, many of the new political leaders of Africa and the Caribbean have no specific qualifications or experiences. They've also displayed glaring incompetence. They are cunning demagogues who, in order to survive at all, surround themselves with a tight security network. Opinions are muzzled. Elections are rigged. Honest expression of opinion is regarded as enmity while any disagreement with the all-powerful leader is an open rebellion against the state. Nobody can effectively spearhead the dissenting opinion. The security of the state is confused with the security of the president. The black political leaders are infected with the fatal malady to retain power for an unlimited period. Presidents, ministers and other political leaders surround themselves with an assortment of profiteers, upstarts and crooks, whose behaviour invariably bring national and international discredit to the image of the new black states.

The political leaders, as it happened in Nigeria, during the regime of General Yakubu Gowon from 1966 to July 29, 1975, were usually pre-occupied with filling their pockets as rapidly as possible. It does not matter whether their countries sink all the more deeply into stagnation. But in order to hide their countries' stagnation and helplessness, the selfish black leaders erect and boast about grandiose buildings in their capitals and spend a lot of money on prestige projects. For instance, it is a tragedy too deep for tears that General Yakubu Gowon's government built a multimillion naira stadium at the Race Course in Lagos just to provide the right venue to welcome the Queen of England. A special building was also being decorated for the august visitor by the time Gowon's government was overthrown. And all this happened in a country where more than half of the population go about bare-footed and where millions still feed on foods which many Europeans would hesitate to give to a cat or dog. The ousted Nigerian leader and his group of extremely corrupt sycophants were fully aware that in Lagos where they were spending millions of naira to welcome the Queen of England, there were no public toilets, there was a permanent traffic jam and electric power failure, with grossly inadequate health and educational facilities.

But while Nigeria and other black countries drifted without any conscious direction, the former colonial power retained control mentally and institutionally. It all means that for the black nations to make it politically and economically, there must be a revolution. The leaders must be liberated in order to be in a position to truly liberate their countries from the neo-colonial yoke. The indiscriminate exploitation of the masses and wide-spread corruption among political leaders must also come to an end. Poor countries like ours with a national malaise, economic rut and outdated institutions and beliefs to overhaul must have leaders who will be devoted to frugal living and service to their countrymen. One can only hope that with the aid of time and experience black countries will be able to produce their own special category of intelligentsia, a middle class with greater foresight, men of action and vision.

## NIGERIA, AN EXAMPLE IN POST-INDEPENDENCE CONFUSION AND HELPLESSNESS

From the attainment of independence in 1960 to the birth of the Murtala Muhammed regime on July 29, 1975, many of the leaders who ruled Nigeria did not hide the fact that ours was a neo-colonial state. That ours was nominal or masked independence. Nigeria became a recognised agent of Western imperialism. And as the years unfolded, successive governments made unequivocal declarations of their intention to strengthen their neo-colonial economic relationship with the Western countries. So the unbridled exploitation of black man's most thickly populated nation continued.

Nigeria's chronicle from 1960 to 1975 reveals much confusion, helplessness and a clear betrayal of the black race. My country has a fifth of Africa's population, and more than half of the population of West Africa's sub-region. The country takes 5 per cent of Africa's land area. By virtue of her size and population, Nigeria should be a fountain of inspiration to the smaller states of Africa. She should be a spring of enthusiasm for the territories still struggling for freedom. But my country was neither. And what a tragedy it was that for many years after independence, we threw all our influence, respect and goodwill away, we lost our leadership right and role in Africa and betrayed the aspirations of black peoples throughout the world.

We started wrongly by the open admission of our leaders that it was their intention to keep Nigeria a semi-colonial appendage of the United Kingdom. Nigeria was to sign the Anglo-Nigeria Defence pact. This was eventually abrogated. Thanks to the vigilance and protests of our Press and undergraduates. We were so dependent on the Western imperialists that we planned that about 50 per cent of the funds for our First National Plan (1962-1968) would come from foreign loans and grants and mainly from the West. Ours was the worst example of growth without development in Africa, a hotch-potch of traditionally and neo-colonially oriented economy. Whatever economic growth rate was recorded did not lead to any remarkable rise in the standard of living of the massess. Corruption, greed and disunity became the most dominant features of our national life. There was a lot of conspicuous consumption as politicians flaunted their newly acquired wealth in the midst of their povery-striken country men and women. To our great misfortune, the rulers became helpless victims of self-defeating rivalries in unnecessry pomp and pageantry.

But it was in politics that the country faced the biggest confusion. There was a big struggle for ethnic ascendancy. The white man consciously encouraged ethnic chauvinism during the colonial days and a few of the leaders who sought to forge a new national loyalty after independence did not succeed. While the national drift and the disruptive effects of tribal nationalism daily became apparent, the Western imperialists, our so-called friends, covered their contempt and pity under spurious slogans. Nigerian leaders were described as coolheaded moderates while our country was a show-case of democracy in Africa. Nigeria was a fountain of civil liberties. Even then our sense of crisis accumulated. The 1962 census count whose figures were described as "worse than useless" by the then Eastern Nigeria government sparked off a chain of reactions. There were charges and counter-charges of inflated

## Post-Independence Helplessness and New Hopes

figures and attempts to drag the Federal Government to court. This was followed by the feud within the Action Group, which was the ruling party in the former Western Region, and the declaration of a state of emergency. Later came the treason trials and the imprisonment of the Action Group leader and his key lieutenants.

By December 1965, we were in a very serious crisis. For shortly after the October 11, 1965 elections into the Western House of Assembly, allegations of rigging, gerrymandering, dumping and the election of candidates who scored minority votes were made and refuted. But the defeated took the laws into their hands. They did not go to court. Confusion became immense. There were disorders and lawlessness. There was a big stalemate. People were burnt alive. Houses were burnt or demolished in broad day light. It was an era of confused politics. But strangely enough, it was when the Western Region riots grew worse that Nigeria, then the leading Western imperialist agent in Africa, agreed to host the Commonwealth conference on Rhodesia in Lagos, Nigeria, with its confused politics at home, once again betrayed the new nations of Africa. The Lagos Conference gave Great Britain a diplomatic support on its handling of the Southern Rhodesia (Zimbabwean) situation. Nigeria therefore helped Britain to render the OAU's condemnation of the white minority regime in Zimbabwe and proposals quite meaningless.

It was under an atmosphere of a serious political confusion that some patriotic army officers made a bold attempt to put things in order. The first Nigerian coup detat of January 15, 1966 took place. Five majors staged the coup. They killed the federal Prime Minister, the Northern and Western premiers, a federal minister and nine army officers. However, the intention of the coup planners was betrayed. It was a one-sided coup for only one Ibo army officer was killed and the two Ibo premiers were saved. But in spite of all this, the government subsequently formed by Major-General Aguiyi Ironsi and the Governments formed by the four regional governors he appointed received nation-wide enthusiasm for one major reason. The citizens supported the regime because they hoped that it would evolve a coherent, deep-rooted and forward-looking philosophy that could save Nigeria. But with the arbitrary promulgation in April, 1966, of Decree 34, which replaced our federal system of government with a unitary one, the bogey of tribal domination once more became real. Widespread killing of Easterners followed in May, 1966, and another coup took place on July 29, 1966 when the then Head of State and the Governor of the Western State were killed. This brought Lt.-Col. Yakubu Gowon, then 34, to power as the head of the Federal Military Government. The new Head of State said there was no basis for Nigerian unity and it was the timely intervention of a number of senior federal civil servants that saved our country from immediate disintegration. Yet, the situation was very tense and all efforts made to reconcile the former Eastern Region to the rest of Nigeria at a meeting held in Aburi, Ghana , failed. On may 30, 1967, Lt Colonel Emeka Ojukwu, the then governor of the Eastern Region declared the secession of his region from the rest of Nigeria. The secessionist area was named the independent republic of Biafra. Fighting broke out in the early hours of July 6, 1967. All peace efforts failed and the war was fought until early 1970 when the rebels surrendered.

Although the war dragged on for too long while foreign manufacturers, their Nigerian collaborators and contractors exploited our nation's misfortune. Yet, many people praised Yakubu Gowon for his humane approach to the prosecution of the war and his "no victor no vanquished" policy at the end of the war. His attitude made our task of national reconciliation fairly easy.

*Post-Independence Helplessness and New Hopes*

At the end of the civil war, the nation started on another drift. The spirit of oneness re-kindled by the civil war had been lost. Public corruption was rife and Gowon displayed a clear weakness of character in that he completely trusted and accepted the wrong pieces of advice of an assortment of corrupt and selfish governors, commissioners, public officers and businessmen who were very close to him. Many of these close confidants indulged in excessive luxury, greed and graft. By 1972, Gowon's government had become glaringly inept. Our economy was ruthlessly exploited by foreign and indigenous business interests. There was crippling inflation. And General Gowon's government worsened the situation by approving fantastic wage increases for civil servants in form of Udoji awards, without any serious consideration for the repercusion on the private sector. The permanent secretaries based their recommendations mainly on selfish considerations. The awards led to widespread industrial unrests, greater inflationary pressure and a lot of hardship on a great majority of low-income workers. The ousted government wanted cheap popularity but got industrial chaos instead. It created a cement mess which clogged the ports. More than 400 ships, 185 of which carried cement, were at Apapa Port by the middle of 1975. Gowon's regime had ordered 20 million tons of cement at a total cost of N608 million. And Nigeria was paying N3,500 a day as demurrage on each vessel that could not off-load because of port congestion. Western imperialists who were the friends and closest advisers of the regime did a good business from this. Nigeria also suffered from perennial petrol shortage and acute traffic congestion. Before Gowon's regime was overthrown in July, 1975 Nigeria sat on the fence on major international issues. The government showed apathy in the affairs of the oppressed peoples of Southern Africa. In African affairs, I noticed at the OAU Conferences at Rabat in 1972, Addis Ababa in 1973, which I covered as a journalist, that Nigeria made vigorous declarations which were not backed by positive actions. And despite all the propaganda to prove the contrary, my country was between July 1966 and July 1975, an agent of Western imperialists. As the country drifted, Gowon showed an amazing ignorance of the hopeless situation in our country and the suffering and aspirations of the common men and women in the streets all because the mediocres or the intelligent but extremely dishonest governors, commissioners and others he put in crucial positions persistently deceived and flattered him. The few commissioners and permanent secretaries who were sincere and honest with Gowon had no decisive say. And even when it became so obvious that the government was no longer wanted, when the possible dates of coups were openly discussed in Lagos pubs, when Lagosians regularly shouted "thief" and "barawo" whenever our then Head of State passed, and when it required maximum security and a paralysed Lagos traffic to get him safely to and from the airport, Gowon's advisers prevented him from doing any hard and realistic thinking or take firm actions. The regime became thoroughly discredited and it dragged its feet on everything. Gowon could not create new states. He could no change the all-powerful governors and when the executed Governor Joseph Gomwalk was accused of corruption, impriopriety and abuse of office by Aper Aku, Gowon publicly declared that he had cleared Gomwalk of all wrong doings. He did this within a period of 48 hours and without telling the public the basis for the former governor's clearance. Above all, he revealed an inordinate ambition to rule Nigerian indefinitely when he broke the earlier promise made by the Military Government that it would handover power to civilians in 1976. The inordinate ambition was also revealed in the unguided utterance he made shortly before he was overthrown that by the time he ceased being Nigeria's ruler he would be too old to return to the barracks.

## NIGERIA'S NEW SITUATION

On July 29, 1975, the corrupt, confused, neo-colonialist regime of

## Post-Independence Helplessness and New Hopes

Yakubu Gowon which drifted without any conscious direction was swept away in a military coup. It was a neat bloodless coup. Nobody was arrested or detained. The ousted Yakubu Gowon and other self-exiled Nigerians were invited to come home and join in building a new nation. Gowon's salary and other entitlements were given to him. At the time of the coup, people were completely fed up with the ousted regime. It was therefore a great relief when General Murtala Ramat Muhammed and other military officers removed the Head of State and arrested the dangerous national drift. Their intervention gave Nigeria a new lease of life. Murtala Muhammed's government had a clear understanding of the complex, social, economic and political problems which our country faced and he succinctly explained these in his maiden speech of July 30, 1975, when among other things, he said:

> *"Events of the past few years have indicated that despite our great human and material resources, the government has not been able to fulfil the legitimate expectations of our people. Nigeria has been left to drift. This situation, if not arrested, would inevitably have resulted in chaos and even bloodshed."*

Muhammed's regime was one of action and determination. A sense of purpose and discipline was promptly infused into our public life. Over 10,000 public officers were removed from Federal, State and Local Government services in a nation-wide purge of the public service. There were some abuses and injustice in the exercise but a panel was set up to examine such abuses. But above all, both civilians, soldiers and policemen were purged. Those who lost their posts included secretaries to the military government, permanent secretaries, senior army, naval and police-officers, professors, judges and general managers of public-owned enterprises. People of all states and tribes were purged without any discrimination.

The regime firmly resolved to fight corruption. It set up assets, probes and confiscated the assets of former governors, soldiers, policemen and civil servants who had corruptly enriched themselves. An anti-corruption institution and a public complaints commission which would treat the issue of corruption and other malpractices on a continuing basis were set up. In picking public officers to serve in the government, preference was given to strong men of sound character, integrity and proven ability. Unlike the ousted regime which put mediocres, psychophants and corrupt men in many key national positions, Muhammed's government appointed many patriotic citizens, whose feet the spies dogged during Gowon's era because they were critics or dissenters, into key national and state offices. His government embarked on a new vigorous policy on foreign affairs. Our bogus non-alignment policy which had since 1960, made us an agent of Western imperialism, was changed by General Muhammed to that of positive commitment to the liberation of Africa. He made an unequivocal declaration that Nigeria would no more remain a pawn in the power struggles of the world powers or be a puppet of the West. Our country gave massive financial, moral and diplomatic support to Angola during the country's imperialist engineered civil war, much to the annoyance of the United States of America.

We have also assisted Mozambique and other nationalist fighters in southern Africa. Nigeria is at last taking its rightful place in Africa and the world. She is doing so without any inhibitions and without apologies.

Our country's complex economic problems are now being tackled with vigour and the interests of the masses have remained the overriding consideration. There has been a better approach to price control and essential commodities are being imported in large quantities. The regime identified those responsible for importation of the 20 million tons of cement which blocked our main port and almost ruined our national economy. It off-loaded the ships and broke the backbone of port congestion. Besides, it has solved the perennial problem of petrol shortage which in Gowon's era made Nigeria a laughing stock to the rest of the world for though ours was one of the leading oil producing countries we were persistently short of oil for domestic use. A law was passed prescribing capital punishment for anyone who hinders the distribution of fuel. The regime was equally firm and decisive in all its other actions. It has embarked on massive investment on education and planned the execution of a bold national health scheme. A definite political programme which aims at handing over political power to civilians in 1979 had been drawn up. So far the the regime has kept every word of its promise on the plan. Other serious matters on which Gowon's regime dragged its feet and on which the new regime took prompt and far-reaching actions are the creation of seven new states, the cancellation of the last controversial census and the location of a new federal capital at Abuja. All this leads to a major conclusion. If the good people of our country are allowed to maintain the present tempo of progress, the black race can have a giant black nation it can be proud of in two decades from now.

## FEBRUARY 13, 1976 FOILED COUP AND LT. - GENERAL OBASANJO'S REGIME

On February 13, 1976, General Murtala Muhammed who led the new government with firmness and dedication from July 29, 1975, was assassinated by a group of dissident soldiers led by Lt.-Col. B. S. Dimka. The governor of Kwara State, Col. Ibrahim Taiwo was abducted and killed. The rebels also held the national radio station for a few hours. There was a massive reaction by the University students and the general public against the coup as soon as the first broadcast was made by rebel Dimka. The plotters were tried. Some were publicly executed while some were jailed.

*Black Man's Dilemma*

The deep appreciation of General Murtala Muhammed's short but effective rule was demonstrated by the Nigerian public when he was being mourned by the nation during and after his burial. He died a national hero.

That Lt.-Col. Dimka, Major-General I. Bisalla, Joseph Gomwalk and others planned the coup of February 13, 1976 at the time they did and with the motives that were later made public confirmed the main theme of this book that the black man is not only extremely selfish but he never puts the best interest of his community above individual selfish considerations. That Dimka and other plotters could think of overthrowing a regime that had done so much within so short a period, a regime that has, through its vigorous and imaginative domestic an foreign policies, given Nigerians and the blacks some pride, reveals how depraved and mentally enslaved the black man is. The plotters naively accused Murtala Muhammed's regime of being communist because it gave financial, diplomatic and moral support to Angola against the wishes of the United States, Britain and other imperialist nations. The rebels also sought to restore to power the thoroughly discredited Yakubu Gowon and his governors. It is sad indeed that a group of unpatriotic and selfish soldiers sought to restore to power a regime that was for nine years very deep in corruption, which made Nigeria an imperialist puppet, exposed our country's human and material resources to a free for all exploitation by Western neo-colonialists, a regime that has completely lost contact with the sufferings and aspirations of ordinary Nigerians.

It is however comforting that the efforts of Murtala Muhammed and his key lieutenants to turn Nigeria into a respectable nation that black peoples can be proud of could not be stopped. Instead, the plot was crushed promptly. But above all, Lt. - General Olusegun Obasanjo, a man of great dedication, intelligence and patriotism, who is fully aware of the responsibility which Nigeria;

because of her size, population and wealth owes the entire black race, has succeeded General Murtala Muhammed as Head of State. The Supreme Military Council, the Federal Executive Council and the Council of States have under his leadership, embarked on many positive actions. They have also sought original solutions to some of our country's problems. One of these is the "Operation Feed the Nation" campaign which is a new and imaginative idea. All segments of our society are being mobilised to produce food crops and vegetables so that we can become self-sufficient in domestic food requirements. It is through such bold efforts to achieve domestic self-sufficiency that we can break the back-bone of neo-colonialism. Nigerians will produce their own food as well as raw materials for our industries and spend our oil incomes to import expertise and capital goods from all over the world for rapid industrialisation. Lt.-General Obasanjo's regime has faithfully prosecuted the government's political programme and its plan to return power to a democratically elected government in October, 1979.

The government continues to be purposeful and dynamic in foreign affairs. And since Muhammed's death, the new regime has enunciated its foreign policy objective which has as its cardinal aims the promotion of self-reliance and rapid economic development in Africa and the rest of the developing world, the fostering of the necessary political and economic conditions that will ensure the sovereignty, independence and integrity of all African countries and the promotion and defence of justice and respect of human dignity, especially the dignity of the black man. Obasanjo's regime has embarked on an equally bold attack on inflationary pressures. It has stepped up the supply of essential goods, effected some restraint in the rate of public and private spending and exercised greater vigilance in the enforcement of price control measures. A brave plan has been announced to build 200,000 units of houses by 1980 while a more effective control of rents in all major urban centres has been embarked upon.

Significant also is the frontal attack by the government on our neo-colonialist economic structure. The Nigerian Enterprises Promotion Decree which was promulgated in February, 1972, by the discredited government of Yakubu Gowon and which took effect from April, 1974, has as its main aim the involvement of Nigerians in our country's major economic activities, which were hitherto dominated by foreigners. But unscrupulous foreign entrepreneurs in collusion with indigenous businessmen, some civilian commissioners, permanent secretaries and other highly placed public officers circumvented the decree and frustrated its major aims. The present government has taken a positive decision to rectify all the glaring anomalies in the second phase of the indigenisation programme which is to take off in April, 1977. It will give effective control of foreign-owned enterprises to as many Nigerians as possible in keeping with the regime's declared belief in egalitarian principle. Besides, all foreign banks had been made to give 60 per cent of their shares to Nigerians as from September, 1976. These are all far-reaching measures that have affected and would continue to adversely affect powerful foreign and domestic economic interests. These interests, especially the Western imperialist ones, could seek ways and means to undermine the people's confidence in the present progressive administration. And if this fails they might seek political control through their Nigerian puppets during elections and when the army hands over to civilians in 1979. Experience has shown that for any progressive step taken by any African nation, the imperialists are usually ready to make ten counter moves to frustrate it. Nigeria and its peoples need great vigilance.

*Post-Independence Helplessness and New Hopes*

## HOW NKRUMAH'S GHANA, TANZANIA AND GUYANA RAISED THE BLACK MAN'S STATUS

Among several black or black-dominated countries I had either visited in Africa and the Americas or whose affairs I had followed keenly since their attainment of independence, Nkrumah's Ghana, Guinea, Tanzania and Guyana have all given me some sense of pride as a black man amidst the post-independence confustion and helplessness of the black nations. For instance, before and since the attainment of independence by Ghana in 1957 and until he was ousted, vilified with a price put on his head by his countrymen, Kwame Nkrumah was the symbol and architect of revolutionary victory in Africa and the forward march of black man's history. Nkrumah, a dedicated Pan-Africanist and a man of vision and action, persistently declared that the independence of Ghana would be meaningless unless it was linked with the total liberation of the continent. The emergence of Ghana and Nkrumah philosophy of Africanism earned the black man a great deal of respect among the Caucasian and Mongolian races. For his outstanding accomplishments at home and in foreign affairs, Nkrumah had, before his overthrow while he was on a Vietnamese peace mission, become an increasingly important African voice in world affairs. By Nkrumah's policies, statements and actions, the black man was able to walk with his head erect in Alabama, Lusaka or Notting-hill. He forged a new identity for the black man, whose race, was, before the era of Nkrumaism, glaringly a race that was merely pitied or tolerated like beggars by the other races of the world. In Ghana, Nkrumah forged a new national loyalty, contained the disruptive effects of tribal nationalism, instilled discipline in the Ghanaians and fostered in them a great sense of pride in their black heritage.

He vigorously spread his philosophy that could assure the new states of Africa of economic independence through a massive mobilisation of their natural and manpower resources. He advocated the need for a revolution that can guarantee Africa of a most rapid break-through to modernity. He believed that this would entail socialist planning and regimentation so that the will of the remaining colonialists could be broken with neo-colonialism suffering a disastrous defeat. In Ghana, he practised what he preached by mobilising the resources of Ghana and the foreign loans he attracted for the construction of the Volta Dam project, beautiful roads and several industries. The Western imperialists were displeased with his socialist commitments and vigorous foreign policy. The West manipulated the world cocoa price and forced it to be on the downward trend. It then masterminded Nkrumah's overthrow. Happily though, General Ignatius Acheampong's government and the people of Ghana have now shown a remarkable appreciation of Nkrumah's contributions to the greatness of Ghana and Africa.

Sekou Toure's Guinea has also proved that with the right type of leadership, a black nation can survive and achieve a lot despite persistent imperialist plots. Toure possessed the discipline, the determination and foresight to foster the kind of African revolution to which Nkrumah dedicated his life. When I was in Guinea in May, 1972, I observed an element of charisma and resolute sincerity in Sekou Toure's pattern of leadership and in his mobilisation efforts. Discreet enquiries from Guineans and foreigners, even his foes, convinced me in 1972 that Ahmed Sekou Toure has amassed no personal wealth. I saw him driving his own citroen car in complete defiance of officials who pleaded that he should be driven by a chauffeur under the sacred principles of protocol. His ministers took a cue from him. They personally drove their own landrovers. President Toure constantly stopped his car, hugged children and youths who gave him thunderous ovation. Whenever he shouted the "long live the revolution" slogan, thousands of his countrymen and women re-echoed it in a

*Post-Independence Helplessness and New Hopes*

deafening unison.

It is this dedication and sincerity that enabled Guinea under the leadership of Sekou Toure to put to shame the firm resolution of the late French President, Charles de Gaule, to wreck the young nation that had the effrontery to say a capital "No" to his 1958 referendum thereby seizing independence from France overnight. Before their hurried departure from Guinea in 1958, French men deliberately damaged street lights, removed tables, files and even pins from all offices. They left the beer and soft drinks they could not carry away in poisoned state. But the highly disciplined Toure defeated events. It was the same leadership quality that enables Sekou Toure to successfully mobilise Guineans who rose like one man to ward off foreign invaders any time they showed up. He gave them the vigilance that has led to regular discovery of treacherous but highly placed Guineans who were alleged to have been paid by the imperialists to undermine the sovereignty of Guinea and destroy a country that has become one of the biggest obstacles to imperialist and neo-colonialist manoeuvres in Africa.

Also, through his famous Arusha declaration and the far-sighted policies that emanated from it, Dr. Julius Nyerere, the President of Tanzania has given his country a self-reliant economy. In Tanzania there is no real poverty or starvation although talking in terms of per capita income, the country is one of the world's 25 poorest countries, Tanzanians are encouraged to be self-sufficient in agricultural requirements and in their domestic needs for industrial products. The country thereby conserves its foreign exchange which is spent to foster rapid economic growth. The people and the land form the focal points of the economy. Dr. Nyerere is an African leader of vision and action.

I am also impressed by what I saw in Guyana, South America, in 1972. Although Guyana is a small country of less than a million people, yet its leader, Forbes Burnham, struck me as a man with original ideas who is prepared to borrow from the East and the West but synthesis and adapt only foreign ideas that suit his country's peculiar circumstances. Burham is firm and vigorous in his domestic and foreign policies. This, combined with his purposeful leadership, has turned the heterogeneous Guyana into a progressive black dominated nation the black man can be proud of.

CHAPTER NINE

# REVISED EDITION
# POST INDEPENDENCE HELPLESSNESS AND NEW HOPES
# AN UPDATE

## SOME AFRICAN COUNTRIES

**AFRICA IN PAINS**

Since 1976 when Black Man's Dilemma was published, the most devastating development that has saddened me most was the emergence of many political leaders, military and civilian, in black African countries.

What I perceived, while writing the first edition of this book, as black Africa's post-independence helplessness had been worsened beyond words with an assortment of incredibly callous leaders, who took control of their nominally independent countries. Some were very unintelligent and poorly educated. A few that were intelligent were greedy and dishonest, thereby making treasury looting and mind bogging corruption the cardinal policies of state and governance. The result was that they caused their country men and women to sink deeper into grinding poverty, squalor and serious human deprivation.

These visionless and wicked black African leaders looted the financial, mineral and other resources of their impoverished countries and transferred their ill-gotten fortunes to the economically developed countries of America, Europe and Asia. They had milked their countries dry and left seventy to eighty percent of their citizens living below poverty level. Many also engaged in grave human rights abuses in form of state organised murders, torture and imprisonment of perceived opponents and innocent citizens.

In their unbridled looting of national treasuries, corruption and reckless misuse of political power, the situation has become so bad since the death of great black leaders like Kwame Nkrumah, Julius Nyerere of Tanzania, Ahmed Sekou Toure of Guinea, Sedar Senghor of Senegal, and Muritala Muhammed of Nigeria. This very sad turn of events had made the new hope I cherished for black Africa in 1976 completely dimmed.

Some of the bad rulers, especially the late William R. Tolbert Jnr of Liberia, Mobutu Sese Seko of the former Zaire, now Democratic Republic of Congo and Sani Abacha of Nigeria, were so selfish and greedy that they turned the affairs and resources of their countries into that of their families, friends and sycophants. Those whose greed, tyranny, imbecility, bestiality, treasury looting and impoverishment of the masses were legendary and whose shameful records will be spotlighted briefly in this chapter include William R. Tolbert and Sergeant Samuel K. Doe of Liberia, the buffoon and tyrant of Uganda, Field Marshal Idi Amin, Mobutu Sese Seko of Democratic Republic of Congo, Kamuzu Banda of Malawi, Robert Mugabe of Zimbabwe, Jean Bedel Bokassa of Central African Republic, Gnassingbe Eyadema of Togo, Alhaji

Shehu Shagari, General Muhammed Buhari, General Ibrahim Babangida, General Abdulsalami Abubakar and General Sani Abacha of Nigeria.

## LIBERIA

### PRESIDENT WILLIAM R. TOLBERT JNR

Tolbert Jnr., an Americo-Liberian, who was assassinated in 1980 by Sergeant Samuel K. Doe, brought nepotism to an unparalleled level. He appointed his brother Stephen, as the Minister of Finance, while his brother, Frank, was President of the Senate. His daughter, Christine, was the Deputy Minister of Education.

He appointed his son, A.B. as the ambassador at large for Liberia while his four sons-in-law were Deputy Minister, Minister of Defence, Commissioner for Immigration and a Director of AIR LIBERIA. Other children, his three nephews, brothers-in-law and many other blood relations were appointed into other significant public positions.

### SERGEANT SAMUEL K. DOE

Unfortunately, however, Master-Sergeant Samuel K.Doe, a non-commissioned officer who seized power in 1980 after killing Tolbert and thirteen of his collaborators in government, was a barely literate nonentity, who committed a lot of atrocities before he was killed in a gruesome manner with his mutilated body put on display in Monrovia.

### SAMUEL DOE'S ATROCITIES AND MISDEEDS

* He executed his vice in the People's Redemption Council, Thomas Weh Syen and four others in1981.
* He sacked the Army Commander, Thomas Quiwonkpa, in 1983. He was accused of a plot.

* Quiwonkpa was brutally killed in 1985 when he attempted a coup detat. His dismembered body was put on display in Monrovia.
* Another colleague of Samuel Doe in the 1980 coup, Nicholas Ponder, was summarily executed in 1988. He was also accused of master-minding a coup.
* It was reported that Doe stole a huge amount of his country's foreign currencies and kept the stolen funds with some Nigerian government and business leaders.

## THE ROLE OF THE UNITED STATES

However, there was a most unfortunate aspect of Doe's violent and crude Government, which confirmed the fact that the United States and Western European Countries are enemies of black Africa. It is that the West would always support any black African leader, no matter his level of violence, corruption, crudity and human rights abuses, as long as he serves the Western nations' interests of keeping these countries in perpetual economic slavery. This explains why as hopeless, inept, violent, and crude as Samuel Doe's government was, the US Government under Ronald Reagan gave financial, economic and other forms of aid to Liberia.

## UGANDA

### FIELD-MARSHALL IDI AMIN

He was a ruthless tyrant and a buffoon who ruled Uganda for eight years(1971-1979). He was surpassed only by Sani Abacha of Nigeria in tyranny and wickedness among black African military dictators. He overthrew the democratic government of president Milton Obote on January 25, 1971 in a coup detat believed to be masterminded by Israel and Britain. He was driven out of power into exile in 1979.

## IDI AMIN'S ATROCITIES

* Dungeons full of corpses were discovered after his overthrow. Some estimates put the number of people he murdered at 200,000.
* On assumption of power he killed many Ugandan soldiers, especially those from the tribe of Milton Obote, the President he overthrew.
* In 1972, he murdered the Chief Justice, Mr. Benedicto Kiwanuka and the vice-chancellor of Makere University, Frank Kalimuzo.
* In 1977, he murdered an Anglican Archbishop, Janan Luwuum and two prominent cabinet ministers, Lt-Col. Oryema and Obot Ofunbi.
* He killed Michael Kawaiya Kaggawa, a millionaire. His body was thrown into a burning Mercedes car outside Kampala.
* He murdered Clement Kiggundu, a reverend father and editor of a Catholic newspaper, Munno.

## SOME ACTIONS THAT GLARINGLY REVEALED IDI AMIN'S BUFFOONERY

* In 1985, he promoted himself a Field Marshal over his hundreds of ill-equipped rag-tag army, which was decisively routed and humiliated by Tanzanian army and Ugandan rebels in 1979 when the triumphant troops entered Kampala.
* He forced the Makerere University, Kampala, to award him an honorary Doctor of Letters degree, D.Litt.
* He created a special order, the Conqueror of the British Empire, CBE, and awarded it to himself.
* He awarded himself Uganda's Military Cross, Distinguished

Service Order and the Victoria Cross. With his huge figure and height of 6ft 3ins, he enjoyed parading these fake medals at every opportunity.

## DEMOCRATIC REPUBLIC OF CONGO (FORMERLY ZAIRE)

### MOBUTU SESE SEKO

He was one of the most notorious dictators who ever ruled in black Africa. He almost completely ruined his country, one of the most richly endowed in the world. He died of prostrate cancer in exile in Morocco in September 1997 after serving for 32 years as President of Zaire (1964 to 1997). He fled Kinshasa, capital of the then Zaire, in 1997 after rebel forces, led by Laurent Kabila, over-ran the city.

Mobutu stole so much money from his country that modest estimates put his wealth at 7 billion US dollars. This amount is about 70 percent of his country's national debt. However, other reports put his assets at 10 billion US dollars. He was richer than his country. In Switzerland alone, his assets and funds were put about 4 billion US dollars.

He owned several mansions in France, Belgium, Switzerland, Portugal, Luxembourg, Spain and Italy. He also had investments and properties in South Africa, Chad, Ivory Coast and Senegal. Mobutu's looting of his country was so staggering and the ruin he brought to Zaire's economy was such that the country's currency was virtually worthless, while inflation was more than 9000 per cent by the time he was ousted from power. His country's economy was in shambles. Corruption became a way of life. The situation was so bad that Mobutu told Zaireans at a public rally "Go ahead and steal, but don't steal too much or you will get caught."

Mobutu diverted earnings and profits from sales of Zaire's rich gold, diamond and copper to his personal accounts. During the cold war period the Western World passed a lot of funds through him to UNITA, the Angolan organisation sponsored to destabilise the Marxist MPLA regime in Angola. He diverted a greater percentage of the aids passed through him into his personal account. He also took bribes from the western companies who exploited Zaire's rich mineral resources.

He was known for his treacherous role in the affairs of his country and Africa. He collaborated with American Central Intelligence Agency and fellow Congolese, Joseph Kasavubu, and Moise Tshombe in the abduction and murder of Patrice Lumumba. He was a friend of the then Apartheid Government in South Africa against the official position of the Organisation of African Unity(OAU) and the aspiration of the black majority of that country.

He was ruthless in his efforts to consolidate himself in power. He executed many politicians and forced many opposition leaders into exile. He forced a one-party state on his people and organised kangaroo elections where he scored 99.5 per cent of the votes.

### HE WAS A FRIEND OF THE WESTERN WORLD

Expectedly the Western World, especially France, Belgium, (Congo's former colonial master) and the United States strongly supported Mobutu, his repressive policies and the ruinous looting of his country's treasuries notwithstanding. As usual, the major consideration of the West was the freedom given to their countries' businesses to exploit Congo's mineral resources.

The complete lack of concern of the West for Africa's well-being was demonstrated by the condemnable statement made by the former US President, Ronald Reagan, who referred to Mobutu as "a voice of good sense and goodwill". As noted above, Reagan also backed the notorious and brainless President Samuel Doe of Liberia

## CENTRAL AFRICAN REPUBLIC (CAR)

### JEAN BEDEL BOKASSA

He was an absolute dictator who reigned in his country for fifteen years. He came to power by staging a coup d' etat which overthrew President David Dacko in December 1965. He followed the high handedness of the French colonial masters by imposing heavy taxation on the citizens. He rounded up unemployed city dwellers in Bangui and sent them to remote camps in the eastern part of the country.

He became notorious for personal violence and in 1969, Bokassa personally executed his right hand man, Col. Alexandre Banza, because of an unsubstantiated plot to overthrow him.

He promoted himself full general in 1970 and President for life in 1972. He brought an ominous innovation to execution of justice in 1972 when he ordered that convicted thieves must be punished by his soldiers by mutilation or death. Sitting on his marble throne, he personally administered justice to prisoners who lay on a slab of rough concrete opposite him. Most of them were murdered or mutilated and left to die.

Many of his political opponents were sent to Ngaraba prison where they were tortured to death.

He once made an elaborate search for a daughter he had fathered through a Vietnamese woman in the French Indo-China where he served with the French forces. Two women showed up claiming to be his daughters. He accepted one as his daughter and adopted

*Post-Independence Helplessness and New Hopes*

the second.

In 1977, he declared the Central African Republic an Empire with himself as Emperor Bokassa I. He planned to found a dynasty of Emperors through his many children. The ridiculous coronation cost his poor country about 14 million dollars.

The country paid for an intricately fashioned crown and imperial robes embroidered by twenty five Paris designers. A gilded eagle throne was made for him.

However, his tyranny, misrule and idiosyncracies came to a climax in 1979 when school children joined University students in protests against compulsory purchase of expensive school uniforms designed and produced by his family. Bokassa arrested the children, some of whom were under 10, put them in Ngaraba prison, where about 100 of them were murdered. It was alleged by sources close to Amnesty International that Bokassa personally participated in the murder of the children. The outrage was so great and this led to the French sponsored coup d'etat that ousted him from power while he was in Lybia in 1980. Bokassa was later tried and sentenced to death in absentia for complicity in murder, arbitrary arrests, official corruption and cannibalism.

He and six others, including his son-in-law, were sentenced to death for the murder of the school children. The six others were executed in 1981 while Bokassa was in exile. He later returned to his country, tried and sentenced to death for murder, theft and cannibalism.

HE ENJOYED FRANCE'S SUPPORT

As usual, the former colonial power, France, actively encouraged Bokassa's tyranny, eccentricity and squandermania. The French policy was to encourage and maintain clients to rule African countries which they regard as important. And the Central African Republic was very important to France because it has a large deposit of uranium, the exploitation of which France has always been interested.

## MALAWI
### HASTINGS KAMUZU BANDA

He was one of the longest serving African Presidents by the time he was forced out of power in the first-ever democtractic election held in his country. He served as President of Malawi for 30 years and had become so unpopular by the time he was defeated in the first multi-party election held on May 17, 1994.

Educated in South Africa, the United States and Britain, he qualified as a doctor and practised medicine in the U.K. and later Ghana for many years.

With the encouragement of Kwame Nkrumah of Ghana and some young nationalists in his country, he joined the independence movement and was elected President - General of the Nyasaland African Congress. The Congress later became Malawi Congress Party (MCP), with Banda still its President. When the Central African Federation was dissolved in 1963, Banda became the Prime Minister on February 1, 1963, with the country's attainment of internal self-government. Malawi attained full independence in July, 1964. He started well with the introduction of many agricultural and educational reforms in the country.

However, Hastings Kamuzu Banda soon became despotic with a strong personality cult built around him. He became the supreme leader and the symbol of his party's supremacy with the party demanding that every member must idolise him. He arbitrarily sacked his cabinet ministers including a co-nationalist leader, Orton Chirwa and two others in 1964. Their offence was the stiff opposition they gave to his decision to delay Africanisation of the public service, his collaboration with Portugal against the Organisation of African Unity (OAU) and his plan to move the capital to Zomba.

When Malawi became a Republic in July 1966, he became the country's executive President and in 1971 he became its Life-President. Trade Unions were rendered powerless and subservient to the party and there was a lot of religious intolerance which led to the ban placed on the Jehovah Witness sect. Banda worked against the interests of the OAU and the rest of Africa. He became a strong ally of the then much hated apartheid government of South Africa with which he co-operated fully economically and diplomatically. The apartheid Prime Minister, John Vorster was in Malawi on State visit in 1970 while Banda also paid state visits to the racist enclave in 1971.

He became very despotic and corrupt with his ownership of many business ventures and several properties in Malawi. He also resisted agitations for democractic reforms and an end to his life Presidency.

For years, he ignored the agitations of the exiled Malawi who were against his one-party dictatorship. However, he soon faced a big agitation within the country for a multi-party democracy. This was initially led by Chafuka Chihana, a trade unionist.

Internal and external pressures for political reforms mounted further until 1993 when he was forced to concede to a referendum. This led to constitutional changes which allowed multi-party democracy. Several new parties were formed in the country.

Banda became seriously ill by October, 1993 and he underwent a neuro-surgery operation in Johannesburg, South Africa. And to everybody's surprise, he returned to power in December of 1993. On May 17, 1994, the first multi-party elections in Malawi for 30 years were held. Banda and his Malawi Congress Party were defeated by the United Democratic Front led by Bakili Muluzi who became the new President. Banda retired from politics on September 24, 1994, although he retained the title of Life President of Malawi Congress Party (MCP).

## ZIMBABWE

### ROBERT MUGABE

When Robert Mugabe assumed office as Zimbabwe's first Prime Minister following his country's hard-worn independence in April 1980, he gave the picture of himself as a patriot who, along with other freedom fighters, put his life on the line in strenuous struggle for the independence of Zimbabwe.

Many of the African leaders described him as a social democrat appropriately chosen to extricate the people of the newly independent Zimbabwe from the exploitative claws of the white minority community. Mugabe was then seen as a leader who would lead his people to a new nation where social justice, freedom and rapid economic development would reign.

On the face value, Mugabe cut the picture of a man of great esteem. He ostensibly showed signs of being calm and sagacious. To demonstrate a semblance of his sagacity, he made a public proclamation to the effect that his government would embark on a policy of reconciliation so as to ensure peace in the country. This was hailed by all and sundry and Mugabe seemed to enjoy the support of people who were out for genuine peace and progress of the country. Even the white community from whom the reins of government was wrested by Mugabe had cause to describe Mugabe as a man who metamorphosed from "a blood thirsty terrorist" to a moderate and magnanimous statesman.

The honeymoon for Mugabe, however, did not last for more than twenty-one months before he unmasked himself as a man whose utterances are usually at variance with his real intentions and actions. For instead of reconciling the various communities, Mugabe began to tear them by the roots. He started to read meanings into people's actions. He began to perfect ways of perpetuating himself in power.

The first step he took was to eliminate people he suspected to be against his grand design to remain in office for life as the Prime Minister of Zimbabwe. People were indiscriminately arrested on trumped-up charges of treason.

The first person to be arraigned before a High Court in Salisbury was a Republican Front Member of Parliament, Wally Stuttaford, who was representing Ian Smith's Party in the Matabeleland Constituency. Stuttaford was accused of conspiring with others with the intention of illegally overthrowing the constitutionally elected government of Mugabe. Before people had time to ask for facts, Mugabe ordered the arrest of another Parliamentarian. His next victim was Sidney Malunga, Matabeleland North Member of Parliament for Joshua Nkomo's Patriotic Front (ZAPU). Malunga was held along with several other party members who Mugabe suspected of not being favourably disposed to his lust for perpetual stay in office as Prime Minister of Zimbabwe.

Ever since, there has been a whirlwind of suppression, intimidation, incarceration and even murder of hundreds of freedom-loving Zimbabweans on mere suspicion of refusal to support Mugabe's pertpetual stay in power.

The unfortunate aspect of Mugabe's ambition and misrule is that while he junkets from one world capital to another posing as an international statesman, the plight of the citizens of his country has continued to go from bad to worse year in year out.

Since Mugabe's assumption of office as Prime Minister in 1980, exploitation of the working population has been on the increase, despite his claim to socialist inclination. His lust for office and avowed desire to stay put in office for life has made him close his door against scientific and economic development which could have helped to bail out his country from backwardness which is easily discernible in Zimbabwe.

Mugabe still wants to sit tight in office despite the crying need for a change and despite the fact that the masses of the citizens of Zimbabwe remain among the poorest in the world. He recently, 2002, won another seriously disputed election.

## KENYA

### ARAP MOI

President Arap Moi of Kenya on October 7, 1991 became one of African leaders who would not voluntarily quit office for whatever reason while still alive. For on that day he manouevred the Kenyan Parliament to pass a Bill which granted him as President the right to remain in office for life. With a clause of the same Bill, all the opposing parties of the ruling Kenya African National Union (KANU) were banned, thereby making Kenya a one-party State. Having been bribed, about two-thirds of members of Parliament and 36 cabinet Ministers voted to pass the bill. Simultaneously, an organised rally was held at Narok, about 100 kilometres from Nairobi, the capital of Kenya, where members of KANU pledged their support for the passage of the controversial Bill.

## Post-Independence Helplessness and New Hopes

Shortly after the announcement of the passage of the Bill was made over Kenya National Radio and the former Vice President under Jomo Kenyatta, Odinga Odinga, described the Bill as a sign of madness, riots broke out in several towns. Aggrieved residents matched to district offices of the ruling KANU and set them ablaze with demand for democracy and an end to dictatorship.

In order to suppress the dissent, President Moi used the tactics of recruitment, removal, dismissal and intimidation to consolidate his hold on power. In the process, many of those who directly or indirectly contributed to the emergence of Arap Moi as President who did not buy the idea of his remaining in office for life were either politically or physically eliminated.

When Arap Moi discovered that there were within the rank and file of KANU, members who did not support his idea of staying in office for life, he threatened and warned that members suspected to be giving support to pro-democracy groups would be severely dealt with.

Within a few days after he gave his warning, President Moi ordered the arrest of Ahmed Salim Bamakriz for supporting a pro-democracy group.

Thus, since 1978 when he came to power following the death of former President, Jomo Kenyatta, the people of Kenya have been kept under the dictatorial regime of Arap Moi. For instance, since he transformed Kenya into a single party State in a determined effort to remain in office for life many democracts have been forced into exile while the economy of the country has continued to be on the downward trend.

With the clamour for true democracy gaining ascendancy in Kenya and throughout Africa, Arap Moi recently announced that he would hand over power to Jomo Kenyatta's son early in 2003. He has been sent out of power and Kenyatta, his nominee, was defeated.

## TOGO

### GNASSINGBE EYADEMA: THE LONGEST SERVING AFRICAN PRESIDENT

With the defeat of Hastings Kamuzu Banda of Malawi who by the time he was out of power in 1994 had served for 30 years as his country's President, President Gnassingbe Eyadema of Togo is today the longest serving sit-tight president in Africa. Eyadema has ruled his country for 35 years.

He recently sacked his prime minister, Gabriel, Agweyame Kodjo, and replaced him with one of his ministers, Koffi Sama.

Eyadema initially ruled Togo as a one-party State for 25 years but due to serious internal and external pressure and agitations, he allowed multi-party elections in 1993 and 1998. But the two elections were massively rigged and disputed. This prompted the European Union to sanction and suspend all aids to Togo. The suspension is yet to be lifted. He had twice postponed parliamentary elections due in April, 2000, but postponed till March 2001 and was yet postponed indefinitely. Eyadema had received widespread criticisms from within and outside his country for his appaling human rights record.

CHAPTER NINE

## *REVISED EDITION*

## *POST INDEPENDENCE HELPLESSNESS AND NEW HOPES: NIGERIA'S BETRAYAL OF BLACK HOPE*

### *AN UPDATE*

As a black man and a Nigerian, my heart bleeds as I write this chapter. It has bled before and since 1976 when I published the first edition of Black Man's Dilemma.

Nigeria's recurrent predicament, its non-performance, its retrogression and glaring failure have constituted a source of agony to this writer and millions of patriotic and thoughtful Nigerians as well as black peoples in diaspora.

It is very sad that my country is still crawling after about 42 years of independence. It has not even crossed the fence, while the rest of civilised humanity is right there on the moon. This is sad because Nigeria has all it takes, except good leadership, to become a virtually self-sufficient medium world power within twenty years of its independence. With one out of every five Africans South of the Sahara being a Nigerian and with one out of six blacks worldwide being a Nigerian, my country is the most thickly populated black country in the world.

Nigeria is also one of the richest countries on planet earth. Some researchers assert that with its known wealth and untapped resources, Nigeria is nearly as rich as the United States of America. Every type of mineral is found in Nigeria. It is a leading world producer of petroleum and its oil is among the best in the world. It has every source of energy in abundance. Its agricultural land is fertile. Above all, Nigeria has some of the world's most energetic, educated and creative population in Africa.

Unfortunately, since its independence in 1960, for every step Nigeria took forward, it took five steps backward. It has got the misfortune of having a great percentage of its leadership being very corrupt, selfish, excessively greedy, short-sighted, inept, wicked and visionless. The masses are among the most indisciplined peoples in the world. Mainly because the leadership has no example whatsoever to show the ordinary citizens in discipline, integrity and patriotism.

Since 1960, Nigeria has also lacked long-term strategic planning in everything – electricity supply, pipe borne water provision, agricultural transformation, road development, industrialisation, employment and education. It has pursued only superficial trial and error, fire – brigade approach to development. Only development policies and projects that allow self- enrichment and graft are favoured. Loans, grants and aids from international sources are stolen with impunity with the thieves hardly made accountable for their misdeeds.

The result is that Nigerians born about forty years ago, have not, throughout their adult life, experienced uninterrupted supply of electricity or a running tap water for just a week. They know only

## Post-Independence Helplessness and New Hopes

poorly constructed and dilapidated roads, a totally collapsed railway system with a lot of the rail lines sold as scraps by the government, an erratic telephone system that breaks down on weekly basis. Nigeria has not succeeded in running an effective airline. And the public transport system has always been unreliable and chaotic with its vibrant private sector initiative so exploitative.

Nigeria should be a giant and a source of pride to the world's black peoples. But it is neither. Rather, it is still tottering after 42 years of independence. In the following pages, I will examine the most important factor that has made Nigeria a failed project and a disgrace and source of sorrow to the black world.

Nigeria's greatest problem is the sustained and extraordinary looting of the country's treasury and unbridled corruption by military men and civilian politicians. Nigeria has recently been identified as the world's most corrupt country. And it occasionally shares this prime position in dishonour with Bangladesh.

And come centuries, Nigeria may remain decadent, poorer and deeper in its recurrent predicament unless the military and political leaders who have stolen its billions of dollars and British pounds are forced to return their loot and be punished for their heinous crimes against Nigerians.

In the following analysis of the super stealing and mind bogging corruption that have prevented Nigeria from realising its potentials, I have relied on the investigative reports of Nigeria's leading newspapers and news magazines, especially TELL, THE NEWS, NEWSWATCH AND THE WEEK, report of the Nigerian governments' panels and commissions on mismanagement of funds and abuse of office by public men and women, government gazettes and decrees, foreign newspapers and magazines, a special publication, AFRICA CONFIDENTIAL and a well researched book – NIGERIA: THE STOLEN BILLIONS- by a Nigerian revolutionary crusader and renowned author – A. Arthur Nwankwo.

## NIGERIA : 1960 TO 1979

This period has been fully analysed in chapter nine of the first edition of Black Man's Dilemma. It covers the government of Nigeria's first Prime Minister – Alhaji Abubakar Tafawa Balewa and the then regional governments, (1960 to January 1966), the short – lived military government of General Johnson Aguiyi-Ironsi (January – July 1966), the military government of General Yakubu Gowon (1966 to 1975) and the military government of General Murtala Muhammed and General Olusegun Obasanjo (1975 to 1979).

The major uproar on financial mismanagement during the Muhammed/Obasanjo era was the allegation that the sum of N2.8 billion belonging to the Nigeria National Petroleum Company (NNPC) was missing from its account. The disclosure was first made by a popular Nigerian newspaper – the PUNCH.

The allegation and controversy it generated dragged on and the second Republic Government of Alhaji Shehu Shagari instituted the Justice Ayo Irikefe panel on the missing N2.8 billion. Many witnesses testified but the fund could not be traced.

However, it was later alleged that the money was paid into the London branch of the defunct Bank of Credit and Commerce International. And that the staggering sum of 14 percent annual interest on the N2.8 billion was shared by some Nigerians while the principal sum was returned to the Nigerian Government account without the accrued interest.

*Post-Independence Helplessness and New Hopes*

## CIVILIAN GOVERNMENT OF ALHAJI SHEHU SHAGARI (OCTOBER 1, 1979 TO DECEMBER 31, 1983)

Alhaji Shehu Shagari was sworn in as President and Commander -in- Chief of the Armed Forces of the Federal Republic of Nigeria on October 1, 1979. Political power was handed over to him by the military government of General Olusegun Obasanjo. Shagari's government was overthrown in a military coup d'etat on December 31, 1983 after spending four years in office and shortly after his political party, the National Party of Nigeria, won a massively rigged and widely disputed elections.

EVIDENCE OF CORRUPTION, FINANCIAL MISMANAGEMENT AND TREASURY LOOTING UNDER SHAGARI'S NATIONAL PARTY OF NIGERIA GOVERNMENT

Nigeria earned N40.5 billion from 1979 to 1983 and Shagari's NPN government squardered it.

In 1979 when he was sworn in as President, Nigeria's external reserve was N2.3 billion. Shagari's government spent all the money and by the time he was overthrown in 1983, Nigeria had a huge external debt of N10.21 billion.

Nigerian rulers transferred the country's foreign exchange earnings outside the country under the disguise of importation of goods. The result was that goods worth N15.2 billion were not inspected by the inspection agency, the Societe Generale de Survelliance. In effect, the huge sum of money was just transferred and kept in foreign accounts by dishonest leaders.

There was massive inflation of the internal debts owed contractors by the government. A public enquiry revealed that out of about N7.2 billion allegedly owed to the contractors, only N300 million was actually owed. The balance of about N6.9 billion was claimed by fraudulent politicians and government officials.

Also, Brian Sledgemore, a British member of Parliament, gave details of how Nigerian leaders fraudulently transferred more than ₦6.billion from Nigeria through Johnson Mattey Bank using fictitious importation of goods as a cover for the monumental fraud.

Many public contracts for hospitals, roads and buildings for higher institutions were awarded at highly inflated costs and most of them were never executed. An example was the ₦100 million Bi-Water project in Niger State which was financed with foreign loan. The Awoniyi Judicial Commission revealed that only 25% of the foreign loan was spent on the project. The remaining 75% could not be accounted for. The belief is that it was shared by politicians and government officials.

## THE MILITARY GOVERNMENT OF GENERAL MUHAMMADU BUHARI AND GENERAL TUNDE IDIAGBON (DECEMBER 1983 TO AUGUST 1985)

Of all the military governments that ruled Nigeria, there was virtually no evidence that the Mohammed Buhari and his deputy, Tunde Idiagbon, perpetrated the type of unbridled corruption, treasury looting and the illegal siphoning of Nigeria's hard currencies to secret overseas accounts for which all other governments were notorious. However, one of its officials, the then Minister of Finance, Alhaji Abubakar Alhaji, was involved in a major financial scandal during one of the meetings of Organisation of Petroleum Exporting Countries (OPEC) in Vienna, Austria.

He was alleged to have withdrawn £500,000 in London. This money was stolen by a call girl who drugged him in his five-star hotel in Vienna. As a face-saving device for Nigeria, the money stolen was reduced and announced to be only £37,000 by the Nigerian delegation to OPEC meeting, also with a face-saving claim that the money belonged to the Nigerian government. The scandal earned Buhari's government a lot of embarrassment from the World Press.

The birth of Buhari's government further revealed the short-sightedness, insensitivity and complete lack of discretion of the Nigerian military leaders. To many Nigerians, it was so scandalous that the Army selected, after their coup de'tat, Mohammed Buhari as Head of State and Tunde Idiagbon as his deputy.

The two men were of a minority Nigerian tribe which is very powerful politically – the Fulanis. In a country with many big nationalities like the the Yorubas, Igbos, Hausas, Ijaws, Tivs, Kanuris, Efiks and several others, it was so unwise and inconsiderate to have appointed soldiers for the two leading positions in the country from one tribe, talk less of a minority tribe.

However, it was in the area of double standard and oppressive and repressive policies that the regime had been found very notorious. The government of Buhari / Idiagbon showed tribal bias when it put the overthrown President, Shehu Shagari, a Fulani, under house arrest but put his deputy, Alex Ekwueme, an Igbo, in detention.

The government demonstrated glaring inconsistencies. When the government advocated discipline and accountability in public life and started its War Against Indiscipline (WAI) campaign, many Nigerians jubilated over the new situation in their country. They believed that indiscipline was always one of their country's biggest problems. For years, Nigerians had envied Ghanaians for the disciplined way of life, which their immortal hero and leader, Kwame Nkrumah instilled in them and the aversion to unbridled corruption which the summary execution of their leaders by Jerry Rawlings forced on Ghanaians.

The government also compromised its war against indiscipline campaign because soldiers jumped the queues at public places and Buhari's second in command, the late Tunde Idiagbon, contrary to the government's regulation which forbade juveniles from the performance of yearly pilgrimage to Mecca, took his teenage son to Mecca.

The regime detained many corrupt civilian politicians under the State Security (Detention of Persons), Decree 2 of 1984 and many were tried, convicted for various offences. Some were made to refund their ill-gotten wealth while some were banned from holding public offices for seven to ten years. There were Central and Zonal tribunals which tried civilian politicians.

Unfortunately, while its efforts at curbing widespread corruption among leaders was appreciated, it put many innocent people in detention without trial, under very degrading and inhuman conditions in its bid to silence opposition. Fundamental human rights were assaulted and two prominent journalists, Messrs Tunde Thompson and Tony Irabor, were jailed for reporting the truth. A number of other journalists were also detained.

## THE MILITARY GOVERNMENT OF GENERAL IBRAHIM BADAMASI BABANGIDA (1985 TO 1993)

When General Ibrahim Badamasi Babangida came to power after a palace coup that overthrew the military government of Buhari/Idiagbon, there was a lot of hope and euphoria. For one thing, Babangida released many citizens who were unjustifiably detained by the ousted regime. For another, he promised the country far reaching economic reforms and lasting democracy. The euphoria was however, short – lived because his policies created a great deal of hardship for the citizens. He violated human rights. Corruption and financial mismanagement became an official policy while he embarked on a very expensive political transition programme which was later discovered to be a ruse.

THE ECONOMIC PROBLEMS HE CREATED

In 1986, Babangida's Government rejected a loan offer by the International Monetary Fund (IMF). He however accepted economic reforms that were far harsher than the ones proposed by the IMF. His programme was called Structural Adjustment Programme (SAP). It entailed deregulation of the banking and foreign exchange system which greatly devalued the country's currency Naira. He started a process of privatisation of government companies. His Structural Adjustment Programme caused economic ruin for Nigeria.

* There was a drastic fall in the economic growth rate.
* Inflation rose by more than 100 percent.
* Millions of Nigerians lost their jobs.
* Industries recorded very low capacity untilisation.
* Being an import dependent country, the greatly devalued currency resulted in high prices for imported goods.
* The standard of living of the middle class, especially the academics, professionals, civil servants, and small scale entrepreneurs fell sharply. The middle class was almost wiped out by SAP.
* Budgetary allocations to education fell by 40 percent and most tertiary institutions were in crisis.
* The promise to diversify the productive base of the economy with the aim of reducing Nigerian's dependence on the oil sector and imports became unrealisable. In fact, by June

1992, out of Nigeria's export earnings of $5.7 billion, oil accounted for as much as 97.1 percent, while non oil exports accounted for just 2.9 percent.
* With the devaluation of the currency, Nigeria's external debt burden rose by over 1,400 percent. The outstanding external debt which was N41.2 billion in 1986 rose to N600 billion in 1992.
* By 1991, the World Bank report put Nigeria as the 13th poorest country in the world.
* There were anti – SAP riots throughout the country.

**WIDESPREAD CORRUPTION AND FINANCIAL MISMANAGEMENT**

Treasury looting among senior officials of government became open and widespread. It is widely believed that by the time Babangida stepped aside from government in 1993, 3,000 officials had about $90 billion in secret Swiss accounts and about £75 billion in the United Kingdom. This explains why European nations are not willing to give Nigeria debt forgiveness. They are aware that Nigeria's criminally minded leaders have stolen huge funds from their country which are kept in richer countries of Europe and America.

A panel instituted by General Abacha's government with the late Professor Pius Okigbo as the Chairman, revealed that $12.4 billion earned by Nigeria from oil during the Gulf War was put in a special account and no satisfactory explanation was provided for its disbursement by General Ibrahim Babangida's government. A company was fraudulently paid by the Nigerian National Petroleum Company, NNPC, a staggering sum of $41.1 million for services not rendered. Efforts to try those involved in the big fraud were frustrated.

Two American journalists, Larry Gurwin and Peter Truell revealed that from a big deal of $1.5 billion made between Bank of Credit and Commerce International and Attack Oil, Government agents received $50 million gratification.

About £75 million undeserved gain was made annually by government agents from petroleum supply to ECOMOG peace keeping force.

The government did not properly account for its petroleum revenue through the NNPC and about $2.7 billion revenue from oil went to private accounts of officials of government annually.
s
A contract of $1.6 billion for Aluminium Smelting project in Ikot Abasi was embarked upon despite the advice of the World Bank and IMF against it because of the attractive kick-backs obtained by government officials.

## HUMAN RIGHTS ABUSES OF BABANGIDA REGIME

The freedom of the press was savagely assaulted in 1986, when a Nigerian journalist and a co-founder of the Newswatch magazine, Dele Giwa was brutally assassinated through a parcel bomb delivered to him by people believed to agents of the government. Shortly before his assassination, he was interrogated by men of the State Security Service. The police did not pursue the case and legal action taken against suspected agents of government by human rights group did not yield any appreciable result.

Many newspaper offices were closed for periods of time by the police, while thousands of copies of newspapers and magazines which published stories believed to be critical of government were seized and destroyed by the police.

Some journalists were bribed to write in favour of government and ignore its reckless financial mismanagement, its pursuit of ruinous economic policies, its assault on press freedom and its very expensive but dubious transition to democratic governance.

BABANGIDA'S DUBIOUS TRANSITION PROGRAMME WITH A HIDDEN AGENDA TO EVENTUALLY BECOME A LIFE PRESIDENT

On assumption of power in 1985, General Ibrahim Babangida promised to introduce a programme that would bring democratic government to Nigeria. His programme turned out to be a dubious one with a hidden agenda to eventually perpetuate himself in power.

And the dubious transition programme started in 1986 with the establishment of a political bureau. The bureau did its work for 15 months and the military government rejected its majority report which recommended 1990 as the terminal exit date for the military. It instead accepted the minority report which recommended a longer exit date of October 1, 1992 for the military.

Government set up a Constituent Assembly in 1988 to draw up a democratic constitution for Nigeria. It also created 589 local government areas for the country. It rejected the six political associations formed by various interest groups and instead formed two political parties which were financed and treated like government administrative departments. The National Electoral Commission was set up and billions of Naira was spent to fund the transition programme.

In keeping with the deceitful nature of the programme, the October 1, 1992 exit date for the military was later changed to January 1993. The date was again changed to August 27, 1993.

Party primaries were held by the two parties but the government cancelled the primaries and disqualified all the presidential aspirants.

Eventually, on June 12, 1993, Nigeria had a free, fair and peaceful election in which 12 million Nigerians voted and which was won decisively by Bashorun M.K.O. Abiola. It was the freest and fairest presidential election in Nigeria. However, General Ibrahim Babangida annulled the election and his action led to serious confusion and riots in the country until he was forced in his own words to step aside while a short- lived Interim National Government was put in place.

## THE INTERIM GOVERNMENT OF CHIEF ERNEST SHONEKAN

An Interim National Government was formed with Chief Ernest Shonekan, an experienced businessman and Chief Executive Officer of the biggest foreign company in Nigeria as its head, while General Ibrahim Babangida, who annulled the presidential election of June 12, 1993 stepped aside.

However, violent demonstrations continued in all the major cities against the unjustifiable annulment of Nigeria's freest, fairest and most peaceful election. Business activities and social life were paralysed for many days. The government, masterminded by the late brutal dictator General Sani Abacha, then a member of Chief Shonekan's Interim Government, became brutal and in one day, soldiers and policemen killed more than hundred demonstrators in Lagos. It was an unprecedented fascist repression. But the people were adamant and the demonstrations continued nationwide. In fact, the struggle was intensified when Nigerian workers obeyed the sit – at – home directive of a patriotic section of the Nigeria Labour Congress.

Petroleum workers fought gallantly for the de-annulment of the election, while Chief M.K.O. Abiola struggled for the re-validation of his mandate. Also, a Lagos High Court declared Chief Ernest Shonekan's Interim National Government unconstitutional. It was obvious to the public that Shonekan's government was not effective with General Sani Abacha who was General Babangida's right – hand – man dominating the Government. Abacha was Secretary of Defence in Shonekan's government and he did not accept the authority of the civilian head of government. For instance, shortly after the inauguration of the government, Abacha unilaterally removed a newly appointed Chief of Defence Staff, Lieutnant General Joshua Dongoyaro from his post.

Eventually, on November 16, 1993, General Sani Abacha forced Chief Shonekan to resign as Head of State, after spending less than nine months in government. Abacha formed a military government, dissolved the Interim National Government and all democratic institutions and formed a Provisional Ruling Council.

## THE MILITARY GOVERNMENT OF GENERAL SANI ABACHA (NOVEMBER 1993 TO JUNE 1998)

General Sani Abacha was one of the worst military dictators and tyrants who had ruled black African countries. In my judgment, he even surpassed the notorious Idi Amin of Uganda, Mobutu Sese Seko of Zaire in terms of wickedness, sadism and excessive greed. In terms of stolen wealth and unbridled corruption, he was entitled to a gold medal among African leaders who looted their countries' treasuries. He completely turned the affairs of Nigeria into that of his wife, children, brothers, relations and a few of his military collaborators and civilian politicians.

Abacha was a very deceitful man. He successfully marked his desperate desire to seize power and rule Nigeria for life. For example, in March 1992, at a reception in honour of the visiting Joint Chief of Staff of the US Army, Collin Powell, he said: "The present administration has taken bold steps to inculcate in members of the Armed Forces the notion that the ultimate power is in the ballot box and not in the barrel of the gun".

Also in February 1993, at the Murtala Muhammed Anniversary lecture, he deceived Nigerians when he said; "Ours will be the first military administration to openly declare that it will be the terminus of military rule in our history. We mean it".

He also successfully deceived Chief M.K.O. Abiola, the winner of June 12, 1993, federal election into believing that he, Abacha, was his friend and supporter as well as a democrat. This prompted Abiola to openly say that he and his party had trusted people in the Army. He was referring to Abacha who later seized power, put him, M.K.O. Abiola, in detention and refused all entreaties from Nelson Mandela, the Pope and other world leaders to release him. He successfully deceived Nelson Mandela that he would grant clemency to Ken Saro-Wiwa, an environmental and human rights crusader and eight other Ogoni leaders who were convicted by a kangaroo Court. Despite the promise to Mandela, he hurriedly executed the nine leaders on the eve of the Commonwealth Conference.

## ABACHA'S UNPRECEDENTED LOOTING OF NIGERIA'S TREASURY

Due to the overwhelming and all-pervading nature of Abacha's theft and fraud, it has been very difficult to know how much he, his family and collaborators really stole from Nigeria. But modest estimates put his worth and that of his family at about 10 billion US dollars and 5 billion British pounds.

The military government of Abdulsalami Abubakar, which took

over after Abacha's sudden death on June 8, 1998, announced on March 4, 1999, that the money so far returned by Abacha's family was N66 billion. This was a very small fraction of Abacha's criminal looting of Nigeria billions of dollars, British pounds and other foreign currencies as well as his choice property which have since been recovered by the new democratic government of Chief Olusegun Obasanjo. It does not also include the 1 billion US dollars the family has agreed to surrender this year, 2002.

One of the most straggering of Abacha's thefts which was arranged between him and his Ministers of Finance, Power and Steel, was the buying back of the debt of $3.1 billion owed Russia by Nigeria. One of Abacha's several companies, PANAR, bought and paid the Russians for this debt with $50 million. PANAR later collected the whole $3.1 billion from the Nigerian government after deducting the $500 million it paid the Russians, Abacha and his accomplices in this heinous crime against Nigeria, stole the balance of $2.6 billion.

On the maintenance of Kaduna refinery, the contract was inflated to $78 million and later to $214 million with $40 million kickback for Abacha.

Having deliberately incapacitated the country's petroleum refineries, Abacha embacked on massive importation of fuel through five companies, one of which was owned by him and three by his business partner, Chagouri and Chagouri, an international consortium owned by five Lebanese brothers. For every 300,000 tons of imported fuel Abacha made $600,000. He even imported a cheaper but adulterated fuel that was blended with pygas. The terrible fume and odour of the fuel led to the death of some Nigerians. Abacha made $300 million from fuel importation while his partner, Chagouri, was believed to have made $20 million. Abacha also owned a refinery in Ivory Coast.

## Post-Independence Helplessness and New Hopes

A contract earlier awarded at N72 million for Abuja stadium was re-awarded by Abacha on his seizure of power at the highly inflated cost of N25 billion.

He collected $144 million for an unexecuted contract to supply landing system at the airports and he also collected $9 billion for the unexecuted contract to dredge River Niger.

The Aluminium Smelter contract which Babangida government awarded for $1.7 billion (the price for a similar project in a Gulf country was less than $600 million), was raised to $3.8 billion by General Sani Abacha. His other thefts were very many and staggering, confirming his excessive greed.

Also, Abacha's family was deeply involved in the looting of Nigeria. A nationwide vaccination campaign for which the World Health Organisation suggested $5 million was awarded to Ibrahim Abacha, the dictator's son for $56 million initially and was later raised to $74 million. His son, Ibrahim Abacha, was linked with an illegal transfer of $2.2 billion out of the country in coded foreign bank accounts.

Ibrahim also got $200 million for an unexecuted Federal Housing contract to supply building materials, while he got another $32 million for an unexecuted contract to supply computers.

Abacha's young daughter won a N500 million contract for the printing of voters' cards which she printed very poorly. She was given another N500 million to print better cards.

Abacha's business partner, the Chagouri and Chagouri, made a fortune out of Abacha's looting and business deals. The company is reputed to be worth more than $20 billion.

## The Worst Specimen

I was further convinced that some Nigerians are the worst specimen of the black race by a recent incident. With billions of pounds and US dollars stolen by General Sani Abacha and his family yet unrecovered some Nigerians harassed the present elected President to release the dictator's son, Muhammed Abacha, who was facing trial for murder and huge thefts of public funds. On his release, he was welcomed to his home State of Kano as a hero with great pomp, noise and fanfare.

He also denied the undertaking made on his behalf to refund more than one billion US dollars to the Government. This very sad situation occurred in Nigeria at the time when China, the most populous country of the yellow race, publicly executed a senior government official for stealing about $400,000 of public funds.

### Abacha's Human Rights Abuses, Terrorism And Brutal Dictatorship

#### Nigerians Who Were Assassinated By Abacha And His Agents

* Chief Alfred Rewane, a septugenarian leader of the NADECO opposition group. He was assassinated in his bedroom by Abacha's agents.

* Alhaja Kudirat Abiola, wife of the detained president-elect, Chief M.K.O. Abiola. She was murdered in Lagos by Abacha's death squad.

* Alhaja Suliat Adedeji, believed to have been murdered for making some derogatory remarks about the sanity and troubled mental history of the bestial dictator, Sani Abacha.

* The son of Chief Olu Onagoruwa, the former Attorney-General in Abacha's cabinet, killed as a punishment for his father's resignation from the cabinet.

* Rear Admiral Emmanuel Omotehinwa (rtd), a close associate of one of the exiled opposition leaders, Lt. General Alani Akinrinade (rtd).

THOSE WHO SURVIVED HIS ASSASSINATION ATTEMPTS

* Senator Abraham Adesanya, a leading lawyer, politician and leader of the opposition group, NADECO
* Mr. Festus Ibru, publisher of the Guardian newspapers and one-time minister in his cabinet.

THOSE HE IMPRISONED

He imprisoned thousands of Nigerians, including Chief M.K.O. Abiola, the winner of June 1993 presidential election, Chief Frank Kokori, Chief Milton Dabibi, Dr. Frederick Fasheun, Chief Olu Falae, Otunba Olabiyi Durojaiye, Hilary Ojukwu, Turner Ogboru, Ayo Opadokun, Olisa Agbakoba, Polycarp Nwite, Professor Akinjide Oshuntokun and Malam Shehu Sani.

THOSE HE DROVE INTO EXILE

He drove several opposition political leaders and human rights crusaders into exile. They include Chief Anthony Enahoro, elder statesman, eminent politician, veteran journalist, who moved Nigeria's motion for political independence and leader of the opposition group, NADECO, Professor Wole Soyinka, Nobel Laureate and a leader of the Liberation Council; Bola Tinubu, Air Commodore Dan Suleiman, Lt – General Alani Akinrinade (rtd); Col. Sambo Dasuki, Chief John Odigie – Oyegun, Raph Obioha and Ledum Mittee.

THOSE JAILED AFTER KANGAROO COUP TRIALS

In 1995, he jailed 41 persons, including the present democratic President, Chief Olusegun Obasanjo, and Obasanjo's former deputy, when he was military Head of State, General Shehu Musa Ya'radua and some journalists after they were all convicted for a phantom coup.

He later, in 1997, sentenced another group of 16 to death and terms of imprisonment for the second fake coup. Those given death sentences included his second in command, who initially helped him to consolidate his hold on power, Lieutenant – General Oladipo Diya, two of his former ministers, Major General A.I. Olanrewaju and Major General A.K. Adisa. He also sentenced a journalist, Niran Malaolu, to life imprisonment.

He detained several other Nigerians, including Chief Bola Ige, late Federal Attorney General and Minister for Justice, Alhaji Lamidi Adesina, now the executive governor of Oyo State, following riots in Ibadan and other cities over his plan to become a life President.

He then used stage-managed bomb explosions as excuses to detain more of his perceived enemies.

Abacha closed many newspaper houses, detained several journalists, seized and destroyed thousands of copies of newspapers and magazines during his regime of terror.

ABACHA'S PLAN TO BECOME NIGERIA'S LIFE PRESIDENT

In furtherance of Abacha's resolve but inordinate ambition to become Nigeria's life President, he organised a fraudulent transition programme. He set up a National Constitutional Conference of 369 delegates, out of which 96 were hand – picked by him as government nominees who were to do his biddings. Only 123 members were needed to form a quorum. With his 96 nominess in attendance only 27 of those elected in an election, boycotted by a large majority of Nigerians, needed to be in attendance. The teleguided constitutional conference gave Abacha complete freedom to determine his own exit date from power. A leading northern member, General Shehu Ya'radua, who had earlier master – minded a resolution by the conference asking Abacha to handover to a democratically elected government in 1996, was later arrested, falsely charged for a coup det'at, imprisoned and killed in prison when he was forcefully injected with a deadly substance.

The conference report was re-drafted and tampered with by the government and the resultant constitution was vague and confusing but clearly prepared to accommodate his ambition to become Nigeria's President for life. The various transition agencies he set up were headed by his lackeys and sychophants who believed in his self- succession programme. He set up five political parties which he manipulated at will, and organised some sham elections. He was picked by the five political parties as the sole candidate for the presidential election.

Tension was very high in Nigeria, as leading politicians, lawyers, human rights activists, trade unionists and others rose stoutly against his self-succession plan. A group of eminent Nigerians, initially eighteen, the number rose later to thirty-four, expressed their strong disapproval of Abacha's life president ambition.

Fortunately, for Nigeria and Africa, the country was saved from what would have turned out to be one of the bloodiest civil wars in history. Abacha died suddenly on June 8, 1998, while he was with two Indian prostitutes. The death of the terrible tyrant led to widespread jubilation by millions of Nigerians. World press report confirmed that Nigerians gave the most widespread jubilation ever recorded on the death of any leader in history.

## THE ROLE OF THE WESTERN WORLD IN THE REGIME OF THE TYRANNICAL NIGERIAN DICTATOR ABACHA

One other evidence of the hostile attitude of the West towards many troubled black African countries was demonstrated towards the end of Abacha's repression and criminal looting. Evidence was given at the Oputa panel set up by the present democratic government, that Western multi-national companies contributed money for the realisation of Abacha's self – succession plan. They contributed money at a time blood was flowing in the streets of Nigeria, with the country engulfed in serious uncertainty, tension and anxiety. It was at a time when if his self-succession bid had suceeded, Nigeria would have faced such a chaotic situation that would have put the whole of the West Africa sub-region in total confusion. The policies of the Western monopolies and their governments are always determined by criminal self- interest and perpetual economic exploitation of black Africa's resources. Their policies have nothing whatsoever, to do with the well-being of black Africans.

## GENERAL ABDULSALAMI ABUBAKAR'S GOVERNMENT

With the sudden death of Abacha, which saved Nigeria from an impending tragedy, General Abdulsalami Abubakar emerged as the military Head of State. Most Nigerians were completely disillusioned by the criminal looting of the country's treasuries, the terrible human rights abuses and the deceitful and fraudulent transition programme of Ibrahim Babangida and General Sani Abacha. Although Abubakar promised to hand over to a democratically elected government in ten months, his promise was accepted with caution. But it was in the area of treasury looting, free-for-all corruption and squandermania that Abubakar's regime justified the pessimism of Nigerians about military rule. In the area of corruption and theft of public funds and property, Abubakar with his military and civilian collaborators in government, constituted an unmitigated disaster to Nigeria. They were as bad as their military predecessors in their flagrant abuse of office and the perpetration of fraud and corruption. In fact, some discerning observers insist that though the regime spent less than a year in office, it looted Nigeria treasury of more funds than any of the former military governments.

### CRIMINAL TREASURY LOOTING, SQUANDERMANIA AND ABUSE OF OFFICE BY ABUBAKAR'S REGIME

Shortly after Abubakar came to power, the National Economic Intelligence Committee, NEIC, led by Professor Sam Aluko, disclosed to utter shock and dismay of Nigerians that $50 million had been found missing from Nigeria's foreign reserves.

Without giving any credible details, Abubakar defended the theft by claiming that the money was given to some unnamed African countries.

With a deluge of outrageously inflated government contracts, the regime looted billions of naira of public funds. In fact, reckless spending through dubious contracts was so alarming that the government spent 4 billion dollars from the country's $7 billion external reserves in a few months.

It embarked on a hurried and dubious privatisation of major public companies which received widespread condemnation from the public. But for the defeaning outcry of the public and media, the regime would have used the stolen billion to buy up public companies through government officials. One of such widely condemned secret privatisation deals was the plan to mortgage the Nigeria Airways to a private British company, Virgin Atlantic Airways.

Reuters News Agency disclosed in May 1999 that a huge sum of N60 billion would be spent by General Abubakar's government in 26 days. The following were some of the outrageously inflated contracts awarded by the regime.

* It spent ₦24 billion on the construction of the Defence Headquarters.
* It awarded a ₦15 billion contract for the construction of the Central Bank of Nigeria.
* Police headquarters contract was awarded for ₦12 billion.
* Before the International Youth Championship was held in Nigeria, the regime of Abubakar provided the National Electric Power Authority (NEPA) with a huge sum of $375 million to prevent the epileptic power supply during the Youth championship.
* The money was to be used for NEPA's rehabilitation of its power stations. The $375 million was misused by government functionaries and their collaborators because there was no appreciable improvement in power supply throughout the championship. In fact, all the eight stadia used for the championship obtained electricity through generating sets.
* Perhaps the most outrageous abuse of office by General Abubakar, his service Chiefs and others was the one reported by AFRICA CONFIDENTIAL. Leading members of the Government awarded themselves oil exploration blocks and oil lifting contracts shortly before their exit from government. Each allotee would obtain $3 million without any investment whatsoever and by merely selling the allotted block. However, the civilian government of President Olusegun Obasanjo on assumption of office on May 29, 1999, cancelled the oil licences awarded themselves

by the outgoing regime. It also suspended all contract awards, approvals and appointments made by the Federal Government from January 1, to May 28, 1999. They were all made subject to review.

* General Abubakar's government awarded a contract costing a staggering sum of N3.2 billion through the National Maritime Authority in very controversial circumstances. An official who stoutly opposed the contract award was relieved of his post while another was arrested.

GENERAL ABUBAKAR'S GIMMICK

Like the case of the kettle calling the pot black, the thoroughly corrupt government of Abubakar, three days before its exit from power, published a military decree which listed funds and properties to be forfeited to the State by the late General Sani Abacha. The funds ran into billions of naira and several thousands of foreign currencies.

Those who forfeited several billions of naira and choice properties include Abacha's National Security Adviser, Ismail Gwarzo, Anthony Ani, Abacha's Finance Minister, and Bashir Dalhatu, his Minister of Mines and Power. The important question many discerning people had asked Abubakar was: "What moral right had Abubakar to condemn others when he and his colleagues in government had not surrendered billions of naira stolen during his tenure?"

NIGERIA IS STILL IN DANGER

Many Nigerians, especially the leading political leaders and human rights activists who fought several battles against the military governments' squandermania, corruption, abuse of office, repression and manouver to stay in power indefinitely, are now making a fundamental mistake. They have, since the return of civilian government in May 1999, embarked on an orgy of self-congratulation on their hard-won victory over military tyranny and misgovernment. Many of the freedom fighters are now complacent.

But if the truth be known, Nigeria is still in danger for four reasons. One, our country cannot be an exception to the normal course of justice throughout the world as far the military and political leaders who betrayed their countries, brutalised and pauperised their citizens are concerned. In the Phillipines, Indonesia, Uganda, Ethiopia, Central African Republic and others, corrupt and tyrannical leaders have been firmly dealt with by their countries. Some fled into exile. Some died in exile. Some were imprisoned. And in many cases, their loots within and outside their countries, were recovered.

But in Nigeria, it appears many people are unaware of the grave danger which the present situation in which three former military rulers – General Babangida, General Buhari and General Abubakar who have refused to be made accountable for their economic mismanagement and grave human rights abuses poses. The only past military leader whose family, collaborators and friends have been made to refund part of their looted billions was General Sani Abacha. This has been so, possibly because he is dead. The three other generals defied summons by the Justice Oputa Panel to explain the serious allegations made against them by many witnesses. They have obtained safe haven in legal technicalities. They still loom large in the affairs of Nigeria and even still aspire to come back to power. They still decisively decide on the pace and course of events in our unfortunate country.

My candid view is that unless Nigeria deals firmly and openly with these leaders on their past misdeeds, come centuries, Nigeria cannot have genuine peace, unity and leadership accountability.

*Post-Independence Helplessness and New Hopes*

Secondly, Nigeria is still in danger because no national leadership since independence, including the present civilian government, has found any meaningful and far – reaching solution to the intractable problem of grinding poverty among the masses. And the poverty situation has been growing worse and intolerable every year. They also have no solution to the problems of unemployment among millions of youths. Already, the disillusioned and hungry youths are making the country virtually ungovernable through widespread riots, ethnic and religious disturbances, sabotage of petroleum pipes and day and night robbery operations. This situation may eventually lead to a bloody revolution or the emergence of a dictator that would be more ruthless and far worse than any of those we had in the past. But if Nigeria is lucky, he may be a benevolent dictator motivated by the urge for radical changes, meaningful improvement in the well-being of Nigerians and the cleaning of the Augean stable.

Such a dictator who must be incorruptible and be ready to die for his country, will be able to squarely face the threat of foreign debts through which Nigeria has been enslaved.

Thirdly, a fundamental problem that may lead to Nigeria's eventual disintegration, peaceful or non-peaceful, has been and is being treated with levity by the past and present governments. The problem is the failure so far to squarely face the issue of convening a national conference, where all Nigerian nationalities would be brought together to decide how they really want to be governed. Nigeria urgently needs a conference, sovereign or not, where a true federation with greater autonomy and clearly defined functions for the federating units, would be agreed upon.

The contraption christened Nigeria by the British was initially a loose federation with the regions and the centre having clearly defined autonomy, based on exclusive, concurrent and residual legislative functions. With the long period the military ruled the country, the soldiers bastardised the constitution and turned the government into a unitary one with an all-powerful centre. This was done without the people's consent but for the convenience of military's system of central control and command. This normally will have to be critically examined and redressed at a national conference.

Any further delay in summoning the conference is dangerous. It has been one of the main reasons for Nigeria's recurrent predicament since its attainment of independence in 1960. It is believed that it is part of the Northern section of the country that is resisting all attempts at the convocation of a national conference. Unfortunately, the more this is done, the clearer it will become to the Southern and some other parts of Nigeria that the section which is resisting devolution of power must have been taking undue advantage over other sections by perpetuating hegemony through a forced and unstable unitary government.

It will be extremely short-sighted if Nigerians don't realise that sooner or later and possibly sooner than later, we may go the way of the USSR, Yugoslavia and Checkoslovakia. If these countries, with their several years of strong central governments, ideological cohesion, monolithic systems and strong leaders broke up under the pressure of their nationalities, Nigeria must realise that time is already running out for it on this issue.

The forth reason why Nigeria is in danger is the anti-people activities of the political and government leaders in the present democratic dispensation. The pomp and peagentry displayed regularly by political leaders, the outrageous salaries and allowances paid public office holders, the expensive housing and transport facilities provided for them, especially by the Federal Government and the National Assembly, run counter to the

*Post-Independence Helplessness and New Hopes*

overwhelming poverty among the masses of a country confirmed to be one of the poorest in the world. With the affluence displayed by public men in Nigeria, it is difficult to believe that theirs is a country where about 80 percent of the citizens live below poverty level, and who spend less than one dollar a day. Worse still, the House of Representatives leadership has fought the Executive arm of Government to a stand still on its total refusal to allow the country's Accountant General to check how much the House had spent since 1999 to date. It has refused to be accountable to the public.

It was unrealistic, short-sighted and inhuman that the Salaries and Wages Commission appointed by the present civilian government recommended earnings that are completely out of tune with the poverty and deprivation in the country. Ironically, too, the National Assembly members, especially members of the House of Representatives who should fight for the interest of the poor masses, have paid themselves fantastic salaries and allowances not recommended by the Salaries and Wages Commission. This is an intolerable situation which, if not remedied, will put Nigeria in another serious blind alley.

Recently, it became obvious to majority of patriotic Nigerians that our ever tottering country is now clearly travelling down an inclined plane. The Upper House of Nigeria's National Assembly, the Senate, which is expected to comprise matured and successful elders, threw all caution to the winds when to the consternation of most Nigerians, it pardoned all its members, who had earlier been indicted of crimes like stealing and misappropriation of billions of Naira of public funds by the Senate's own two panels of enquiry.

It is tragic that the Upper House of Nigeria, a country which the world has adjudged as one of the two most corrupt countries in the world, has now legalised unbriddled corruption and theft by public men.

It means that sooner than later, a man like the former president of Ghana, Jerry Rawlings, may emerge in Nigeria and summarily execute corrupt public men, who had brought international odium as well as economic ruin to our country and the present National Assembly leadership may be in the forefront of those who would face the firing squads, if it did not rescind the legitimacy it had given to public theft in our country..

CHAPTER TEN

# 1976 EDITION
# THE BLACK MAN CAN MAKE IT

ONE major problem of the black man is that he is today not aware of his basic human weaknesses and problems. And his lack of any serious awareness of his weaknesses dates back to centuries. A few blacks who are and have for long been aware that we are our own worst enemies have not been able to do anything concrete about our limitations. Some of my fellow blacks are too frightened to talk about our basic problems. A few that have written on our weaknesses and problems of backwardness have only looked for an easy way out of our complex situation.

Others blame the slave trade, the kindness of nature, colonialism and neo-colonialism for our underdog position in the world. They look for scape-goats. But unfortunately, we have never realised that there was hardly any problem the black man faces or has faced - slavery, colonialism and neo-colonialism - which other racial groups like the Chinese, Japanese and even Europeans, did not face in the past. The problem of our backwardness is more with us than our so-called oppressors. For many years, I have closely observed my fellow blacks in Nigeria and other African and Caribbean countries. I have also closely observed the white and yellow races in Europe, Asia and Africa during my journeys round the world as a journalist and later as an editor. I have now come to the conclusion that we have some weaknesses that are peculiar to us. Although we are as intelligent as other races, yet, our life outlook has been conditioned by factors which are very difficult to fully understand or explain no matter how hard one tries.

One of our greatest weaknesses is our lack of self-discipline both as individuals and as a society. I believe that if we must make it as a race it is discipline that we must foster and cling to. It is with discipline that the black man can achieve the much-needed colossal re-orientation of social attitudes and a new way of life. Today, the black man sees his new African or Caribbean nation as a Galilee, a place of peace and rest. He sees his poor country as a land of new horizons, where everything is new and nothing is impossible. But unfortunately he bears a very heavy cross. That cross is indolence. It is laziness. It is indiscipline. Hard-work, diligence and discipline are completely lacking among us. We blacks generally regard our work as drudgery.

We do not believe in doing our little bit well. We have not appreciated the fact that whether we are night soil men, labourers, farmers, teachers, journalists, soldiers, policemen, clerks or factory workers, we should all regard our work as a meaningful form of self-expression. We do not take pride in our jobs.

Our poor attitude to work and indiscipline also affect our attitude to our countries. We have never learnt how to sub-ordinate self to the good of our country. We can't put our nation before self. When a white man works very hard, even in a capitalist country like the United States or the United Kingdom, behind his desire for personal gain and wealth through his resourcefulness is a strong desire to leave his country better than he found it. He may want to become a millionaire but deep down within him is a determination to donate generously to charity or institute a philanthropic organisation when he makes it. Hence, the world is blessed with Ford, Rockefeller, Thompson and other Foundations which have helped and enriched the lives of millions of people throughout the world. But to the black man, self is the Alpha and Omega of all his lofty endeavours and ambitions. He is very selfish. The result is that hard work among the blacks often has negative effects on the overall national progress because in every black society, a man who has worked very hard and made it usually judges his importance and achievements by the number of mistresses he comfortably keeps in well furnished flats and how frequently the cars of such mistresses are changed. The black man reckons his importance by the number of houses he owns and not in the number of things he creates or in the number of difficult tasks he performs in an effort to guarantee a better life for posterity. His lack of discipline also affects his attitude to the laws of his society. He uses his ingenuity to break any law. And he does so with impunity because both in our face-to-face traditional societies as well as in our modern independent nations, the law is a respecter of persons. The law maker in fact makes it so. The sons and daughters of the chiefs and the wealthy were in the past allowed to commit any crime known to man and get away with it.

It was normal for them to exploit the slaves and the poor. They could raid markets, collect rents on the land and live entirely on the productivity of other citizens. Today among citizens in the new black states, the disregard for the law of the land which stems from our basic problem of indiscipline even affects our observance of the simple rules of hygiene. People urinate on the side-walks in the city centres even when public toilets are available. Public conveniences are carelessly used when available and our refusal to obey simple rules is revealed in the black man's reckless driving habits, the refusal or inability of law enforcement agents to enforce the rules and the resultant unnecessary deaths on our roads. Law enforcement is difficult and justice is openly miscarried because in many black states a highly placed citizen who commits a serious offence like manslaughter or theft is easily set free. As soon as his old school mates, secret society colleagues, ethnic relations or social club members learn of his offence, they will intervene promptly on his behalf. The result is that either the police or the director of public prosecutions is influenced not to bring the case to court. And if the case is heard in court, the judges, no matter how highly placed, are influenced to pervert the course of justice and protect the individual.

One other glaring weakness of the black man is that he is very selfish and individualistic. We hardly form partnerships which can last for 20 years. We are always anxious to cheat our partners or neighbours or fraudulently convert to our own use that which belongs to others. Besides, we don't wish ourselves well and we destroy our best citizens. Among the whites and yellows their best people, the Mao Tse Tung, Andrei Gromyko, Henry Kiesinger or George Best, are consciously protected and encouraged by the society. All their faults and weaknesses are played down relative to their achievements which are emphasized. Their outstanding attainments and personal qualities are emphasized. But among us, the man who is doing very well or has made it must pretend to his fellow blacks so that he may not be destroyed. He exerts much energy in an attempt to pretend that he is not so successful so that he may not be destroyed. Whatever mystical powers we have, like the powers of witch-craft, are not used to foster creative activities and promote inventions. They are used to harm, incapacitate or destroy our fellow blacks. Worse still, mediocre or intelligent but extremely fraudulent citizens have in general, always had the crucial and final say in the affairs of black societies. This was the situation centuries back. It is the same in our modern societies. The best people are either destroyed, subjugated or at best just merely tolerated.

## The Black Man Can Make It

But very poor leadership appears to me as the black man's greatest problem. It is sad to admit that with only a few exceptions the black race is ill-served by all sorts of poor leaders who have emerged since the attainment of independence by many black states. The white and yellow races have produced so many giants like Ho Chi Min, Mao Tse Tung and Winston Churchill, who were a tower of strength to their country men and humanity. But the black man's home continent has produced only a few Kwame Nkrumah, Julius Nyerere, Patrice Lumumba, Murtala Muhammed and Sekou Toure who had either been destroyed or are seriously handicapped. As shown in chapter nine, very few black leaders could stand up for the genuine rights of their peoples, especially when imperialist interests are involved. Many black political leaders have a narrow concept of what constitutes a life of fulfillment. They have no lofty dream of leaving their country better than they found it. Above all, our leaders are corrupt. They abuse their official positions and corruptly enrich themselves. A situation has therefore emerged in many of the poor black nations in which any talk of probity and uprightness in public life is just a mere academic exercise.

Lack of originality is our other major problem. The black race immitates the other races. We are copycats. Slavery, colonialism and neo-colonialism do not constitute any valid explanation for the failure of the black man to find original solutions to his several problems. They are not sufficient explanation for our failure to change our environment and make it a better place to live in. Afterall, slavery and colonialism had always been the rule since the dawn of history. If the black man had been original, if he had the right type of leadership, his oppression and exploitation in the past could not have constituted a permanent hindrance to his progress. The USSR, China, Japan are a few of several examples of nations with overwhelming problems in the past, but which, with originality and leaders who exercised genuine gifts of leadership, became great nations. For instance, as late as 1917, the USSR was correctly described as a "semi-colonial appendage of Western Europe." A large proportion of her economy was stimulated by foreign enterprise and financed by foreign capital. Like the present day Nigeria, modernisation was partial. The mass of the Russians lived in a stagnant and depressed countryside. But when the Bolsheviks obtained power in 1917 they knew what to do with it. Russian leaders refused to go by any precedent, it only learnt from the pitfalls in the pragmatic and experimental approach of the West to modernisation. At great sufferings and sacrifices to the Russians, especially the Kularks and others in the rural areas, that country embarked on total savings, total planning and total regimentation. The Bolsheviks compelled the USSR to save about 30 per cent of her national income every year. England saved between 15 to 19 per cent of her gross national income during her own period of capital accumulation and industrialisation. Russian leaders ignored the views of Western theorists that the saving of 10 per cent of national income is sufficient for the take off period. The Soviet leaders decided on 30 per cent. They were original in all the plans they made and this explains why the agrarian and industrial transformation which took England, as a pioneer, more than 300 years to achieve took the Soviet Union less than 30 years.

And China, with her dedicated and imaginative leadership achieved even more spectacular results in rapid modernisation. The main reason for China's "miracle of progress" is that although Chairman Mao Tse Tung was one of the world's most influential Marxist philosophers, yet, he insisted that theories are relevant when they are made to serve the peculiar needs of a people and only if a country has a clear idea of where it is going. This explains why in 1949, when victory came to the communists with the Chinese energy already terribly sapped by the most stupendous guerrilla operation in history, Chairman Mao Tse Tung made a public declaration that his giant country, which contains one-fourth of the human race, would become a great world power within a few years. This declaration was made when China had immediately behind it about 160 years of weakness and foreign domination and at a time when the country had experienced 40 years of internal and international wars which decimated her vast population and virtually destroyed her economy.

For despite China's pre-5th Century civilisation, she had become an under-developed country by 1949. And some years before the end of the civil war, pieces of Chinese territories were subject to concessions to other countries. The British also controlled taxes and duties as late as 1930, while more than 60 per cent of China's trade was controlled by the Japanese and British foreign firms owned 45 per cent of the country's textile industry and about 50 per cent of her coal production. By 1930, postal services were still largely in the hands of the French.

But on June, 2, 1950, the Chinese Communists embarked on a gigantic agrarian reform which changed the land-owing class into a landless class and gave the landless peasants the confiscated land .300 million peasants benefitted. The government was in control of the 99.6 per cent of the vast growing economy by 1956. The agricultural reform was supported by an elaborate programme for rapid scientific and technological development. So that by December 1968, when Chinese atomic scientists launched the country's eighth nuclear explosion, China had emerged as a military and world power within two decades of the end of the civil war. She thereby compelled her acceptance by the Western powers on the basis of genuine equality.

Japan is another country where originality and right leadership had helped to ensure her rapid transformation into an industrial power. Japan suffered great destruction during the Second World

War. But she quickly regained strength, learnt from everywhere in the world and improved on all things produced by others. Within a few years, Japan became a leading nation in steel production, ship-building, automobiles and the most sophisticated electronics. The fantastic progress is a continuing one and it was in fact, predicted that Japanese economy might outgrow that of the United States by 2,000 AD. Japan is already ahead of Britain and the United States in education with 10 per cent of her young men in universities.

And although that country occupies only 14 per cent of the land area in Asia and had only 5 per cent of the total population of the sub-region, yet, she produces 95 per cent of Asia's motor vehicles and 75 per cent of the region's steel requirements. Japan possesses about 90 per cent of all the TV sets in Asia, 35 per cent of the area's radio sets and about 68 per cent of all the telephones in the region. Besides, she is the third most powerful industrial nation in the world. And strangely enough, Japan's land area is only 142,800 square miles while Nigeria is two and half times her size with a land area of 356,000 square miles. It is neither area nor large population that counts, otherwise, India would have become the true industrial and technological giant of Asia and not Japan. Japan achieved rapid progress based on an original ideology and a peculiar way of life. One is the Japanese fanatical love of labour and the other is their absolute devotion to their places of work.

### The way Out of the Black Man's Dilemma

Then the all-important question: which then is the way out of the black man's dilemma? The starting point is for us to admit that we have some basic human weaknesses that are peculiar to us and we should do something positive about them. The black man should stop looking for scape-goats. Rather, he should admit the fact that he is his own worst enemy. This is the only way he can make meaningful impact on the rest of the world. There is nothing basically wrong in the present cultural awakening among the blacks in different parts of the world. But this should not be an end in itself, because that would be most dangerous. For the blacks would be regarded as vain and unrealistic peoples if the wish to protect and cherish their much-vaunted black civilisation is so great that it takes precedence over the basic problems of the masses throughout the world. These are poverty, ignorance, superstition and mental slavery. It's also an indication that it doesn't matter to us if we remain the world's underdog forever. As I see it, the most crucial point is that whatever we black men and women, have discovered to be our achievements in the past, even if these are very modest, must be used as a source of strength for our present and future. We must lay down new paths for our future, politically, economically and culturally. But we cannot use whatever is good in our past to reshape towards new goals and purposes if we live in a world of illusion about our past.

One other thing we must do is to consciously encourage our best citizens instead of seeking ways and means to destroy them. The blacks should discover and reward talents. The present situation where mediocres usually have the final or most decisive say in black man's affairs should be discouraged if we will ever make any meaningful progress. We should also learn to wish our fellow blacks well. We must seek original solutions to our complex problems. It means we should realistically compare ourselves with the other races of the world in terms of our obvious backwardness. We should find out why Africa has realised just very little of its natural potentials and why a great deal of Africa's present wealth goes to non-Africans, who dwell mainly in Europe and America. If we want civilisation which is an inheritance of the entire humanity to move a step further, if we want civilisation to advance higher than Europe and Asia have brought it, we must be original; we must invent and make discoveries. We must work out new concepts and discourage the idea of our being the poor immitators of Europe. We must have a mental revolution that will reject the thought-pattern of Europe. This is what every average black man or coloured person is demanding in an un-equivocal manner. The black masses throughout the world want to determine for themselves the kind of political, social and economic systems they will live under. This requires originality. It entails the need to challenge and change the existing imperialist and neo-colonialist systems and all our values, beliefs, traditions and institutions which are inimical to our progress. It all means black nations like Ghana, Guinea, Tanzania, Guyana and Nigeria since July, 1975, with leaderships that possess great heart and foresight must strive harder to give their nations self-reliant and modern economies that are based on black man's original ideas and solutions.

## Nigeria's Great Responsibility

By virtue of her population and wealth, Nigeria is the greatest source of hope for the black race. If Nigeria, which is the richest and most thickly populated black nation on earth, does not make it, I believe that the black man can never make it anywhere in the world. But to make it, my country needs the right type of leadership for many years to come. She needs leaders who will see things steadily and see them whole; men and women who will know that the world is neither their master nor their servant, men and women who will accept their limitations and be creative within those limits.

Men and women of intelligence and uncompromising integrity must have the final say in the affairs of my country and rule her for several years to come. These leaders must have a great deal of self-discipline, selfless spirit, vision and a deep appreciation of the black race's basic problems. Leaders who possess these qualities could infuse into the Nigerian elite and masses the discipline and massive re-orientation of our life outlook that is so badly needed. They must mobilise our people and resources, fight and completely destroy neo-colonialist interests, put the greatest emphasis on education, science and technology and build a modern self - reliant economy that will be based on the imaginative adaptation of socialist ideas to our peculiar circumstances, until Nigeria becomes a great modern nation like China, USSR, or Japan. And if the leaders of small nations like Sweden, Switzerland and Denmark could transform their countries into prosperous, industrialised modern states where abject poverty, squalor and ignorance no longer exist in any form, there is no reason why political leaders in Nigeria in particular and in countries like Ghana, Tanzania, Guinea, Zaire and Zambia cannot transform their countries into modern nations within two or three decades. The most important requirement Nigeria and other black countries must have in order to make it is a modernising elite who could demonstrate genuine gifts of leadership.

Nigeria will also need a decisive revolution in education in order to effectively meet her leadership responsibilities. Examples in different parts of the world have shown that we can wipe out illiteracy within two decades and by doing this we would have taken the most vital step on the road to modernisation. In this respect my country has a lot to learn from the rest of the world. For instance, in 1788, Denmark operated under a feudal law which prevented "all males over the age of four to move from the place of their birth." Denmark had few national resources and her main asset was her fertile land. And by 1850, she had just a subsistence economy with her agricultural products being mainly for domestic consumption. She sold very little exportable produce. But within a few years, Denmark became a model to the world in co-operative development and methods. Her farming became completely modernised. She became an important industrial nation and her engineering products were soon in great demand all over the world.

The result was that by 1954, Denmark was ranked sixth among the countries with highest income per head in the world. The secret is simple. It was education that played such a decisive role in the transformation of Denmark. For in 1814, Denmark took a far-reaching step when she embarked on one of the most gigantic educational programmes in Europe. A royal decree was promulgated. It made schooling compulsory for all children, sanctioned the establishment of state schools in all localities and stipulated a heavy fine for parents who did not keep their children at school.

Education also played an important role in the "Russia's miracle of development." For by 1917, the Union of Soviet Socialist Republics was, like the present day Nigeria, a country where the modern sector was foreign-dominated with the mass of the people living in a stagnant and depressed country-side. But when the Bolsheviks obtained power in 1917, they decided to raise educational standards and they gave formal and political education the highest priority. The result was that in the 1966/67 school year, the total school population was over 50 million. With more than four million, the USSR in 1967, had three and half times as many university students as Britain, France, Western, Germany and Italy put together. And this was a country which had only 127,000 university students by 1917. Since 1917, 100 million people, children and adults have been taught how to read and write. Illiteracy has been wiped out. Education is free and compulsory. Hence, education and the mobilisation of internal resources turned the Soviet Union into a giant in industry, science and technology within a few decades.

And a major explanation for the success story of China was that huge country's original approach to education. During my stay in China in 1973, I noticed that every Chinese youth who passes out of the middle school- an equivalent of Nigeria's Higher School

*The Black Man Can Make It*

Certificate course-must spend compulsory two years in either a public farm known as the commune or in a factory. He will work with other farmers and factory workers. During this period, he is expected to work diligently and use his knowledge of biology, physics or chemistry to produce fertilisers, generate electricity or carry out other inventions. He must prove that he is extremely hard-working and creative and that he has a lot of political consciousness before he could be allowed to proceed to the University. At the end of two years, every farmer or worker in the commune or factory to which the youth is attached would write a report on him showing whether university education can make him be of greater use to China. No university in China will admit him if the report shows that he is neither creative nor willing to labour diligently for the greatness of China. And if the report shows that a particular youth is outstanding or has invented or improved many things that enriched the lives of the local people, he would, in addition to automatic scholarship, be paid full salary while undergoing his course at the University. To my mind, if Nigeria is to successfully meet her heavy obligation to the black race, she must move further than her present free universal primary education scheme. Education at the primary level should be free and compulsory while post-primary education including education at the University and Polytechnic levels should be free at once. The rewards will come in great abundance. Also, the philosophy which underpins our present educational system should be completely overhauled. The curricula and methodology of instruction should be changed from its present foreign concepts to reflect our culture and our country's aspirations. The government should draw up new syllabi and commission the writing of textbooks which should totally reflect our country's background, history, and a new aspiration to become a giant, modern black nation. On no account should non-Africans be allowed to have a say in the design and execution of our free education programmes. Foreigners should also no longer be allowed to hold key administrative positions in our post-primary institutions.

Another important step Nigeria must take if she is not to betray the black race is to become an atomic power as soon as possible. If France and India had been so desperate in becoming atomic power, Nigeria should be more desperate in becoming one. For one thing, our need is greater than that of France and India. For another, with our explosion of nuclear bombs, especially if we explode ours before South Africa does it, Nigeria would put the black race everywhere on the threshold of a new era. We would also frighten South Africa more than our military strength today frightens her and her allies. And Nigeria is in a strong position to become a nuclear power. We have the money and we have many Nigerians with a touch of genius. With the acquisition of atomic power Nigeria will also record other spectacular achievements in science and technology and destroy the sad fact that it is only the black race that has not joined the atomic power club. The Mongolian race joined through the Chinese and lately the Indian atomic explosions. It may be argued that Nigerians are so poorly fed, poorly clothed and poorly housed that it would be unwise to divert our resources to nuclear experiments. I believe it is a serious mistake to under-estimate the importance of nuclear capabilities to Nigeria. It would give Africa and the black race a new identity. It would also give us a leap forward.

A good example of a nation that obtained such a leap forward in nuclear science and technology is China. During the Korean War, China was under the direct threat of America's atomic weapons. Nuclear threat partly forced China to negotiate the 1953 Armistice. But in 1954, Chairman Mao Tse Tung asked all his country's citizens studying and doing research in the Western countries to return home. The crusade began. The Institute of Atomic Energy, the Academy of Science and the Institute of Dynamics were strengthened. There was total mobilisation. The interesting story which the great Chinese atomic scientist; Tang Pa Check, told his colleagues of the International Atomic Energy Agency in Vienna reveals how a nation with the right leadership, will and a sense of direction can attain so much within a short time. It was the story of how Chairman Mao Tse Tung one day summoned Chien Sanchiang and told him that China's highest interest demanded that she must have her own atomic bomb by January 1, 1965. Chairman Mao's target was immediately accepted as a challenge by Chinese scholars. The result was that Chien and his team exploded the first Chinese bomb on October 14, 1964, two months ahead of the target set for the nation by Chairman Mao. And with great pride in their achievements, Marshall Nie Jung-chem, the overall head of Chinese atomic weapon development told 353 scientists from 43 countries of the world in Peking in 1964: "Modern science is no longer the monopoly of Western countries." It is my belief that Nigeria should be able to tell the rest of the world before a decade that atomic power and modern science are no longer the monopoly of the white and yellow races. The Chinese atomic scientists' determination was quite spectacular. For as a present for Chairman Mao's 75th birthday the country's eighth nuclear device was exploded on December 27, 1968. So within 20 years, the Republic of China became the third greatest scientific power in the world with only USA and USSR ahead of her. A world super-power was born. China, a country vilified, ostracised and ridiculed for years had won world recognition and acceptance through self-reliance, purposeful leadership and a total national commitment. A black nation must become a nuclear power within a decade. And my country, Nigeria, is that nation.

Nigeria should also work hard to become a giant in science and technology. For there are in this country, brilliant men and women physicists, engineers, chemists, mathematicians, technicians and pilots - who are all Nigerians with creative energy. We missed a unique chance in our history to tap the resources of our local genuiuses of our civil war. We did not use the experience and creative talents of men and women of the Research and Production (R.A.P), who, during our civil war, in desperation, produced our country's first rocket from rusty mild steel pipes. Reports confirmed that the anti-aircraft rocket invented by the men of RAP in "Biafra" had almost 5,000 feet (nearly a mile) range. These Nigerian scientists were improving their designs in a bid to produce a 10 mile rocket when the Nigerian civil war ended. They invented many other products; batteries, petrol, beer, explosives etc. In a war situation, these scientists received every encouragement from the Biafran leadership.

They were not hindered by bureaucratic red tapes. They had direct access to the rebel leader, Odumegwu Ojukwu. I believe that Nigeria has men and women whose talents and resourcefulness could be fully tapped for our nuclear experiments and other great scientific achievements. These Nigerians were either trained at home or in different parts of the world. And apart from the men of RAP who invented Nigeria's first rocket but are today unknown and unpraised, I discovered some other brilliant young Nigerians at the Kainji Dam site in the Kwara State of Nigeria in 1973. During my visit to Kainji, I discovered that the maintenance and operation of the electricity supply at the multi-million hydroelectric dam was entirely handled by Nigerians. Young and confident Nigerian engineers and technicians were in firm control of the giant complex. The Nigerian government brought in a group of Canadian experts who were given definite instructions to train, in a record time, Nigerians who today successfully maintain the Kainji complex. It means one surest way for Nigeria to become a great industrial and technological nation is for her to compel the foreign firms who are now building our roads, flyovers, bridges, factories, iron and steel complex and other national projects to train Nigerian engineers, scientists and technicians who would handle similar projects in future without foreign assistance. Nigeria could still buy foreign machinery and equipment before our iron and steel complex goes into production.

And as Sudan's Major General Joseph Lagu, leader of the Anyanya Southern guerrilla, who led the seventeen-year secessionist war in the Southern part of his country told me in the Sudan in 1973:

> *"Nigeria is the basis of black African solidarity. In this, she has great responsibility. She is the most thickly populated state in Africa and with her population and wealth, Nigeria must assume a leading role in African politics."*

Indeed, our country has a great responsibility to Africa and the black world. And to discharge this responsibility successfully, she must acquire nuclear power, become a giant in science and technology, encourage and sustain the right type of political leadership. This is how she could give the world's black peoples the much-needed inspiration, pride and confidence in their past, present and future.

### The Black Man's Dilemma

The foregoing story of the hope and problems of the black man has led me to one major conclusion. It is the fact that in all the crisis of the black man's story, there has never been a time when the need for truth in the examination of our dilemma was so critical. In the first place, the black man must admit the inconvenient fact that there is no single profound technological breakthrough by any black nation or individual that mankind has inherited throughout history. Since the attainment of independence by the new black states we have become a victim of illusion as regards our importance in the world. We naively believe that because independent Nigeria, Zaire, Guyana and others are members of

*Black Man's Dilemma*

the United Nations Organisation where they can freely condemn everybody and everything the black man is therefore equal to the Caucasian and Mongolian races. It is true that to suggest in 1930 that the former Nigerian Head of State, Yakubu Gowon, would be an honoured guest of the Queen of England or that President Mobutu Sese Sekou would be an honoured guest of the King of Belgium, would shock even the greatest optimist. But today this is not important. The crucial question is the black man's glaring backwardness and the fact that this backwardness is so persistent and recurrent. Some scholars have said that no black country has made a breakthrough to modernity because of our five centuries of harrowing experience in slavery, torture, colonial exploitation and neo-colonialism. There is a point in this. We were subjugated, exploited and dehumanised. Unlike the Chinese who, centuries ago, invented the gun-powder and printing, or the Japanese and the Russians who have made it in technology because they had politically settled states, the blacks have always peoples without politically settled minds. The slave trade and the colonial past have dehumanised us in culture, in our way of thought, in attitude to work, in our appreciation of what constitutes a life of real fulfillment and in our naive failure to appreciate the extent of our grinding poverty. We have become the world's underdog. Ours remains the only race that has not made it in history. We could not match the outstanding contributions of the other races to human civilisation which is mankind's common inheritance. And we suffer from the world-wide notion of black inferiority.

The result is that the black man today faces a serious dilemma. He is behind the rest of the world. He is very backward. But the few black states like Nkrumah's Ghana, Guinea, Guyana, Tanzania and Nigeria since July 29, 1975 coup de tat, which have right leadership, and are making efforts to be self-reliant, original and progressive, are being hindered by white conspiracy. Imperialists interests regularly organise economic sabotage, internal disaffection, campaign of calumny by the Western Press and in the case of Guinea occasional frontal military attacks by foreign based Guinean dissidents. Also, countries which don't face white sabotage have poor, selfish and corrupt leadership. This then is the black man's dilemma. Two difficult paths lie before the black nations of the world. They can tread the well beaten path, continue to adapt the established systems and follow the trial and error approach of the West to development. In which case, they will prod on and remain neo-colonial. This is what can satisfy the white man and save our countries from his sustained sabotage. It is also the easier option but one that is against the best interest of the black race. By using other people's ideas and old formulas, it means the black man can never make it. He will remain the world's underdog and his race will continue to be looked down upon by the other races. The other option for the black nations is to find original solutions to their complex problems of indiscipline, abject poverty and poor leadership. They should refuse to remain poor immitators of the white race. Education, discipline, self-reliance and the right leadership should form the basis of such a new position of strength. Admittedly, it is a more hazardous option which will encourage Western imperialists to strengthen their sabotage against our young nations. But from my observations during journeys to China and other Asian countries, to the United States and South America and to several European and African countries, I have come to the conclusion that as black peoples we must do a lot of original thinking, accept our limitations and peculiar weaknesses and look for a drastic, preferably our own peculiar way, out of our basic problems. The black man can make it. But we need the hurricane of change known as revolution. And ours is a race against time. Time is running out.

*Black Man's Dilemma*

CHAPTER TEN

# REVISED EDITION

# THE BLACK MAN CAN MAKE IT
## AN UPDATE

Since **Black Man's Dilemma** was published in 1976, I have become fully convinced that the youths and elders, especially the educated youths, in black African countries, should be more vigilant and desperate in exposing and checking the excesses of their rulers. They should, by all means, prevent the type of reckless misrule, treasury looting, squandermania, corruption and tyranny of the past rulers, who brought economic and political ruins to their countries. Black youths and elders should embark on fierce and sustained battles with corrupt, greedy, selfish and incapable leaders. The resistance may be in form of massive city demonstrations, with constant and widespread education and mobilisation of the citizens. Concerned democrats and human rights crusaders should confront law enforcement agencies who may disrupt democratic assemblies, rallies and demonstrations.

Also, highly educated, successful and rich black American leaders have a crucial role in bringing rapid and orderly development to black Africa. They could give scholarships to carefully selected youth leaders from black Africa. These youths, would, while in the U.S.A; be deliberately exposed to the ways in which American society enforces the fundamental rights of its citizens. They will observe how all forms of injustice to citizens are checked and how public men in the executive and legislative arms of government are made fully accountable to the electorate. On their return to Africa, the fully exposed youth leaders will ensure that misgovernment and tyranny are no longer tolerated in their countries. They will become crucial catalysts for decisive change in their countries.

Successful black Americans also owe it to their Africa motherland to assist black Africans in resisting any further usurpation of power by the military in all African countries. They should also exert pressure on the United States Government to help African countries in dislodging self-seeking military adventurers. Black leaders in the United States should strive to effect a radical change in the policy thrust of the US Government towards black Africa. America should no longer support corrupt, oppressive and inept African leaders. Afterall, considering the stiff sanctions which the United States always imposed on American Presidents who made mistakes that offended American sensitivities and norms, it would be unjust, unfair and contradictory if the same USA supports corrupt, rapacious and tyrannical rulers in the under developed and poor countries of black Africa. Supporting oppressive and corrupt leaders in these countries can lead to a revolution by the masses of these poor countries, in which all the investments of America and the Western World would be in jeopardy, while American minions and puppets would be swept away. The type of revolutions that swept away many leaders in Eastern Europe can surely occur in black Africa, when the masses, in their rage and desperation, decide to slash back at their oppressors. Furthermore, it belittles the status of the United States as the only super - power in the world, the richest and biggest advocate of democracy if through its backing of callous, corrupt and visionless African leaders, the masses in these poor countries are kept in abject poverty, ill-health and ignorance.

Moreover, it is in the best interest of black Africa and the black race, if courageous, educated and public-spirited leaders who have original ideas on how their countries can be rapidly transformed without being teleguided by the IMF/World Bank and the Western World, participate actively in politics. They should grap political power in their countries.

These new black African leaders should be original and ignore all precedents in their resolute and patriotic pursuit of their endowed but poor countries' search for spectacular economic, social, educational and political transformation.

For instance, China became a world power despite the isolation, the jeers and pessimism of the Western countries. With originality, Japan became an industrial giant in the world and the former USSR became a super-power and the greatest rival of the United States without the ill-motivated Western world monitored and progress retarding prescriptions of the IMF and World Bank.

I believe that with its vast natural and human resources, especially its highly educated population, Nigeria can become a medium world power with its own atomic energy within fifteen years. And unless and until Nigeria which is the most thickly populated black country and the most naturally endowed in the world becomes an atomic power, the black man will continue to be merely tolerated by the other races.

And with far-sighted, acutely intelligent, highly educated, gifted, bold and intensely patriotic leaders, Nigeria can earn double from palm kernels, palm kernel oil, palm oil and tropical fruits in twelve years what it now earns from petroleum. With an imaginative agricultural reform, Nigeria can become self-sufficient in food and raw materials requirements in eight years, with the country becoming one of the biggest exporters of food items in the world.

With a gifted Nigerian leadership which is fully aware of recent history of economic miracles in different parts of the world, a better variety of groundnut and cotton for the North, cocoa for the West and cashew nuts for the South East and the West, could be obtained with millions of Nigerian farmers encouraged through subsidies to plant millions of these cash crops. With this done, our country's suicidal reliance on one product will end because Nigeria can earn three times what it now earns from petroleum from exported groundnut, cocoa, cotton and cashew nuts. These products fetched our country millions of British pounds during the colonial era and for some years after independence.

Besides, every town and village in Nigeria can enjoy uninterrupted electricity supply in three years through the use of solar energy, with Nigerian villages becoming transformed through industrialisation and scientific farming. But the question that is as many-layered as an onion is: Will the Nigerian system and factor allow leaders who have genuine gifts of leadership, leaders who are original, visionary and intensely patriotic to get to the country's apex of political leadership? It can be done if a crop of highly determined leaders can massively mobilise the citizens thereby neutralising the effect of billions of stolen funds which those who ruined Nigeria in the past will spend during elections. The electorate could be advised to collect the stolen money from Nigeria's former military rulers and their civilian collaborators but still decisively reject them at the polls.

The Democratic Republic of Congo is another greatly endowed African country that can become a medium world power and achieve a spectacular breakthrough to modernity, with the right leadership. The black majority rulers of South Africa could also help in the rapid economic transformation of black Africa by exposing them to the high level of technology and industrialisation she now enjoys.

One other area through which blacks can make it is through political education for the masses with the aim of exposing them to the acute nature of their needless penury and suffering in the midst of plenty. They should be made aware that their countries should have nothing to do with poverty if they have the right type of political leadership.

The campaign against corruption should be vigorous and emphasised among all the strata of the society. The campaign should be given greater attention among students of tertiary institutions, secondary and primary schools and even at the nursery schools level. Adults, youths and children should on daily basis, be made to appreciate the grave danger which the society at large and individuals face through corruption. Courageous citizens who expose corrupt practices among government officials, law enforcement agents and private companies should be protected, rewarded and honoured by the State for their courage and patriotism. The campaign should also extend to churches, mosques, clubs, and societies.

Above all, black leaders who occupy important positions in black African countries and in diaspora could give our race a new sense of pride and genuine acceptance if they fully understand and embrace the idea of what constitutes a life of true fulfilments.

It must be stressed that a truly fulfilled life is not recognised by the amount of wealth and property illegally amassed at the expense of fellow citizens or the undisciplined life of opulence and extravagance led without serious concern for the well being of the under priviledged members of society. A life truly fulfilled is one in which we leave our society better than we found it, it is a life dominated by self-discipline, and selfless service. It is a life dedicated to the advancement of the frontiers of science, education, technology and health through endowments created with our wealth and resources for which we would forever be remembered when we are no more.

Finally, blacks in Africa and diaspora should give their race a new image through the cultivation of traits of discipline, great industry, honesty, self-respect and public spiritedness. Through this, we shall become proud representatives of our race. We shall be able to raise our heads high everywhere in the world.

# BLACK MAN'S DILEMMA

## REVISED EDITION

## UPDATE OF EVENTS 1976 - 2002

*APPENDIX I - VI*

# APPENDIX I

Black Man's Dilemma
Revised Edition
Update Of Events, 1976 to 2002
The State Of The Nation - *A Weekly Column*
By
Dr. Tai Solarin
First Instalment
Published in the Nigerian Tribune, Monday,
January 11, 1982

> Black Man's Dilemma
> *Areoye Oyebola*

WHEN Areoye Oyebola dropped his bomb, *Black Man's Dilemma* in 1976 and as it exploded under the sophisticated nostrils of Nigeria's ivory tower historians, I laughed as they took their bows and arrows, squatting in all available dark corners to direct their missiles into poor Areoye Oyebola's jugular veins. I was otherwise engaged and so did not join him at the battle front as I should have done, thus postponing my contribution by as long as five years.

However, five years delay is nothing as Black Man's Dilemma is going to be hotly debated for the next 25 years at least, by those black Africans and their European sympathisers who earned their professional chairs by "What we have we hold" truism of the tremendous contributions of the Black African to the world culture.

Have you, revered reader, ever heard of the Quakers or Quakerism? The original Quakers got their name because much earlier on in their "Church" somebody would suddenly start to shiver, to "quake", having been possessed by the spirit! And he or she would tell so many outrageous things that the "spirit" has spat out through him.

Today, however, the Quakers do not "quake" anymore. They think it is silly and so have outgrown "quaking". In other words, they now believe, even if they do not openly tell the world, that "quaking" was staged over the years.

When several years ago, I went to the wedding in Lagos, of one of the sons of my esteemed teacher, now Chief Odebo of Ogere in Ogun State. I was startled to find a pretty girl looking 21, a few benches to the front of me, falling down shivering, I thought she had fainted and I was about to dash out to help her up when one of the officials went near and cleared the kiddies who were standing too close. She was quaking. I nearly burst into laughter, but that would have hurt the feelings, the religious feelings in Celestial Church of Christ. I, therefore, discreetly looked away.

I supposed, sometimes in the future, the Celestial Church members would, as the matured quakers of today, stop quaking, too!.

That is how I have found all the platitudes of the defenders of the great black man's cultural contributions into the pool of mankind's output.

*Appendixes*

"Charity," we are told, "begins at home". I come from Ikenne, in Ogun State, I dont think there was a single house here in Ikenne 200 years ago. My father, I was told, built the family house that I met there. My father travelled in from Ijebu Ode and stopped to pass a night in Ikenne which he instinctively liked and took to from that night. He met a few other people there who came in just as casually as did my father.

There is a big ditch near the town, running several miles towards Ijebu-Ode. As there is no written record of any type, nobody knows how the pit got there or for what purpose it was dug there. For that age of universal bellicosity, it probably was dug as a defence line to bait enemies into. Nowhere in the whole of Remo is there anything to suggest antiquity that dates beyond two hundred years back.

That statement holds true of the whole of Yorubaland that includes Ile-Ife. (Ile-Ife is the cradle of the Yoruba race). Outside Opa Oranyan at Ile Ife what else is there. With no written record of any kind, any stories of Opa Oranyan would be old wives tales. There, of course are the bronze heads.

They might have been brought there by the immigrants. If made there why did such an art come to abrupt truncation? If bronze ore was available there deep in the in the soil why has none been extracted since?

Spread the net to cover the whole of Nigeria - the whole of West Africa - continue the belt to cover across the world from latitude 20 degrees North of the Equator to latitude 20 degrees South of the Equator. Anybody who takes a casual look at the world map and places netted in by the lines of latitudes named, would find the possible exception in India and Indo China. But one would be quickly reminded here that it was the downward sweep of the people from China and Northern India that changed the situation in those areas. The conclusion I want to draw here is that the world's torrid, humid and mosquito fettered tropical lands have contributed least, if any thing into, the culture of humanity. It is here I want to come to the aid of Areoye Oyebola. Had Oyebola in his wide research come across the American geographer, Huntington, he would have tempered his righteous indignation against the black man that inhabits the tropical lands.

In one of the several volumes of Huntington analysing the where withal of human progress, he followed up the progress of a generation of people that left Europe for the Western World. Some of these people settled in Canada. Another group of the same people settled in the United States of America. The third group of these same people settled in Haiti (East of Cuba and just north of latitude 20 degress of the Equator).

After a set of time, these immigrants into Canada, U.S.A. and Haiti were checked on. Huntington reported that those who settled in Canada had made progress but that such progress was tempered with the fact that these new Canadians had Britons to rely on and quite a few of their problems were solved for them from the old country. Those however, who settled in the United States had soared triumphantly high. They had battled against all odds, bad Winter, cruel Summer, flood, high winds, everything. Those, however, who settled in Haiti had slumped. They had achieved nothing. Huntington quoted a teenage girl as saying "here, you feel like doing anything, like doing nothing, nothing." And so these Europeans settlers, same stock of people as settled in Canada and in the United States slumped, in human barometer, after having being battered by the uncompromising, acidic sledge hammer of the tropical climate.

*Appendixes*

Let me, at this point go up at a tangent and correct a special theory, where I think, Oyebola erred. Oyebola finding the great difference there is between the tropical man transplanted by slavery into the stimulating geographical environment of the colder latitudes of North America and his kith and kin back home in West Africa, concluded that it was the most intelligent men and women that were taken away.

The reverse, however, is the truth. Oyebola would accept that anytime there was a raid, it was the most intelligent who would be most alert and would know how to melt miraculously away. A subdued whistle, a gesture from a neighbour, a quick clap of the hands and the most intelligent has evaporated. By and large it was the stupid and slow of foot that got quickly roped off and carried away as slaves.

Of course, a few intelligent ones would be unlucky to fall as prey to the slave traders. It was some of these very intelligent ones who felt too proud to be caught as slaves that leapt over board mid Atlantic. The unintelligent ones capitulated unconditionally. And anybody who sees the pictures of the slaves would easily agree they always look stupid, because they were unintelligent.

Now we come to the crux of the matter. If most of the slaves taken away across the Atlantic, were as explained above, the most unintelligent, why did they prove so much better than their most intelligent kinsmen left behind in West Africa?

The reason is easy to proffer. They had to live, there in America, cheek by jowl with the more virile neighbours - the white. The slaves either screwed up their courage and worked, or threw up their arms in surrender and foundered. Generally, they had no choice. They would either work or get shot. These new conditions they found themeselves working under were unkown to those men and women they left behind back home in West Africa. If all the Black Americans in the US today, and these are the descendants of the people I said were generally unintelligent, were flown back to West Africa today to compete for whatever jobs were available for anybody who qualifies, only very, very able ones amongst us, home based black Africans, would get any job. Ayodele Awojobis, (Awojobi is the late brilliant professor of Engineering at the University of Lagos, Nigeria) and these are very, very few - would get the jobs. I don't think I would. In the Washington D.C. post office which I saw in 1962 fully manned by Black Americans, I would be so much slower and pretty stupid as compared with anybody else in the service of that post office. Not a single man or a woman in the General Post Office on the Marina in Lagos, Nigeria would qualify to work beside the Black Americans. He is simply so fast, so deft.

# Black Man's Dilemma
## Revised Edition
## Update Of Events, 1976 to 2002

*The State Of The Nation - A Weekly Column*
*By*
*Dr. Tai Solarin*
*Second Instalment*
*Published in the Nigerian Tribune,*
*Monday, January 18, 1982*

> Black Man's Dilemma
> *Areoye Oyebola*

IN China, I visited the Great Wall and had my photograph taken, standing around where Bertrand Russell stood some 60 years before when he visited same wall.

Emperor Chin Shih Hunag Ti, after uniting the different parts of the country into an empire in 228 B.C., took over what his predecessor had built of the Great Wall and he lengthened and fattened it into the impregnable fortress it is today. It ran for 1,500 miles, some 600 miles of which were built during his reign. We are told that the last thing that any astronaut recognises from the terrific distance that separates him from our earth is the Great

Wall. The Chinese writing was there long before the invention of writing as it is known in the West saw the light of day. In many parts of China you are shown bold indelible Chinese writings carved out on huge granitic bolders. Most of them date back to 4,000 B.C. The Pa Li Chuan Pagoda near Peking was built in the 13th Century. Whilst the Pei T'a (north tower) at Fang Shan was built in the 8th Century.

It does not matter where you turn in China, antiquity hits you flat on the face. You would need more than an atomic bomb to obliterate the Chinese past, or, to put it in the language of our subject, Chinese Culture.

Last August, I sat on a chunck of a pillar in the old city of Corinth in Greece, listening to our guide describe what the place, now in ruins, looked like in the ancient country that Greece is. So many new development projects have to be re-located for, invariably, the sites chosen for them are suddenly found, as the foundations are dug, to be underlain by some hitherto unknown ancient edifice.

Everywhere you go in Asia (north of 20 degrees Latitude) or Europe you find antiquity staring hard at you and you cannot keep asking yourself, where, in your own part of the world, are any parallels to what you see.

We have read of a few temerarious Africans years ago, crossing over the Mediterranean Sea and inflicting defeats on some Southern European countries. One would like to know what the climatic conditions were for those highly spirited men unleashing death and destruction on some parts of Europe.

There have been fluctuations of climatic conditions over several areas of the world but there has been nothing to suggest that the tropical lands as we know them today were ever subjected to the

*Appendixes*

ice age ordeals that are evident in most of the countries of northern Europe and Asia. There is evidence that the Sahara Desert of today, with a size three times that of Europe, was once covered with tropical forests. And tropical forests have chronically carried nothing but death at their trails. In other words, even in its palmy days, the Sahara never had a people with a civilisation that left anything to posterity.

We are now in the position to say it is the climate, more than anything else, that makes a progressive people. At birth, all men start at zero. Nature has been ever so generous that intelligence whereever it abounds in good measure, continues to remain with families that have them even if they are not going to make use of them, depending on where in the world such people are born.

Had Winston Churchill been born into a family in Iran, he would not have had lesser intelligence than he had been born with in England, but as an Iranian, the best he could have become was a hot moslem gospeller, and, in his quintessence, an Ayatollah Komeini. Had Ayodele Awojobi, a brilliant Nigerian professor, been born in Germany, he would have put man on the moon earlier than Von Braun did. Instead of his time being wasted in Nigeria in trying to resolve the unholy tangle in the Anatomy Department of the University of Ibadan, or breaking his heart in trying to figure out the dimension of corruption in the Federal Government of Nigeria.

Areoye Oyebola soliloquizes "No where in Africa can one find the type of heritage I have seen in Europe and Asia. And the intriguing questions that have persistently crossed my mind are; what efforts were my black ancestors making when such great architectural, aesthetic, technological and scientific achievements were taking place in Europe and Asia? Did my black ancestors achieve any original and durable form of political and social organisation comparable to those written records I have seen in Europe, Asia and North Africa?" (P. 22 of the first edition, and page of the 2002 edition.

My answer to each of the questions above is in the negative, and I go further to say that had there not been the 20th Century means of communication by sea, by air, by the telephone, the radio, the television, the video, the newspapers, the shrinkage of our world as it is, things in the tropical lands would have continued to be as they were during the previous one thousand years. The Concorde alone shakes man more to the reality of life than is possible by any other thing. A letter written in Paris and put into the Concorde would arrive at its Los Angeles destination on a date before it was written.

Even if the tropical man doggedly refuses to rise up to the demands of the 21st Century he would be forced to accept them. I have, somewhere in my house a cutting from the NEW NIGERIAN where a Nigerian motor cyclist delicately planted a crash helmet on what that paper called his "cultural cap." The motor cyclist was only feebly clinging to the shadows of an assumed culture. Take that same motor cyclist out of Kaduna and put him alongside other motor cyclists on Eko Bridge in Lagos, Nigeria. He would quickly find he would have to shed not only his "Cultural Cap" but also his voluminous gown.

A few years back, a newspaper reported that Fela Anikulapo Kuti, a famous Nigerian musician, had imported some musical instruments to the tune of N20,000. Without those instruments, manufactured in Europe, Fela would have made no name for himself as an exponent of some intrinsic aspects of African music. Would we condemn Fela for importing these musical instruments and ask him to make do with what there are locally, of indigenous musical instruments?

*Appendixes*

The Senior Medical Officer in Shagamu State Hospital, Dr. Oke keeps me alive by treating my asthma with drugs, all of which are manufactured in Europe and America. Would I stop taking advantage of his treatment and wait until somebody in this tropical climate comes up with a local cure?

The same NEW NIGERIAN I referred to earlier on reported sometime ago that our culture was being exterminated by foreign influences. It has not dawned on that paper that culture, if indeed, it is culture, is impossible of extermination. You go through Rome or Athens or Peking in the middle of the night and you are awed by a culture that is perennial and incapable of being eroded, let alone exterminated. Our gowns, our tall caps, our dances, no matter how titillating, are all tinsels of culture. The FESTAC, (Festival of African Arts and Culture) initially imposed on us by Gowon's military government but executed by Obasanjo's military regime was the greatest single item of calamitous waste that this country has ever experienced.

Areoye Oyebola laments that we are incapable of dealing a death blow on the mosquitoes that takes such a big toll on our lives, but he is more hurt still by the fact that we cannot invent a machine to pound the yam which only we eat.

Nothing is more soporific than the tropical climate. You don't have to bestir yourself too much in the tropics. Your land lady gives you a notice to quit your lodging, you can pass the next few nights outside, under the Eko Bridge. You would even get more fresh air there than your rented room provided. Whereas to be driven out of your lodging whatever time of the year anywhere in the high latitudes, you have to think and think fast, on how to get an alternative accommodation, or you get exposed to bitting winter or cold and stinging rain or high winds. There is one more area however, we have not looked into on how the high latitude human beings get their resourcefulness and invetiveness. It is from the wars. The greatest inventions that the high latitudes men have made have followed on the heels of devastating wars. The atomic bomb might have remained even untested for its potentialities for several decades were the Second World War not on.

Oyebola himself listed so many things that the Biafrans (Biafran was part of Nigeria that made a failed attempt to seceed) invented as war weapons, and tested very effectively in the Nigerian Civil War. But are we to artificially create wars to bestir the inhabitants of the torrid latitudes?.

There are, I think, only two alternatives open to us, residents of the world's tropical lands. The first is to accept all the benefits of science and technology which the occupants of the world's kinder climate have bestowed on humanity, and make use of them to make life more tolerable to ourselves and, at the same time, produce the agricultural products which only our climate could produce for the benefits of all mankind.

There is the second alternative. Huntington has said that the best climate in the world for the best of human performance, intellectually or physically, is somewhere in South of England. But all human beings cannot be settled there. The fact remains, however, that between latitude 20 degrees North of the Equator and 66 degrees north, and the same latitudes South of the Equator, human beings have come out in their best for mental and physical output. Get the present occupiers into the world's most depressing lands evacuated and allocated into the lands with stimulating climatic conditions. The tropical lands could then be communally owned by the whole of mankind, to be farmed for common benefit, and all their other natural resources put at the disposal of all mankind.

*Appendixes*

But neither of these is the answer. I submit the third alternative. A friend of mine, Dr. Sobomeyin who had been away for 20 years from our country is now back with enviable accademic qualifications to put his services a the disposal of Mother Nigeria.

He is afire with righteous indignation, and he wonders what we had been doing to have remained so pedestrian as a nation. I have lived for the past 30 years with the anger Dr. Sobomeyin is freshly exhibiting. It is attitude like his, like mine, like Eyo Ita's, like Ivan Ikoku's, like Sam Aluko's, like Chike Obi's, like Jegede's (Ikere Ekiti), like Ayodele Awojobi's, like Oluwole Awokoya's, like Mbonu Ojike's, like Areoye Oyebola's, that can fillip our country, Nigeria, from its position of time-hönoured stagnation and sterility to one of self-recovery and purposeful march towards acceptable, universal human progress.

*Black Man's Dilemma*

## APPENDIX II

Black Man's Dilemma
Revised Edition
Update Of Events, 1976 to 2002

Extracts From Engineer Reginald Dickenson's Views On Black Man's Dilemma, 1976 Edition, In His Book - African Ambit (Page 303-307) Published In 1995 By The Pentland Press Limited, U.K

THERE is an increasing sense of objectivity and realism amongst African writers and leaders. A remarkable African writer, who is both factual and constructive, is the Nigerian Chief Areoye Oyebola. In his book, *Black Man's Dilemma,* published in 1976 in Nigeria but as far as I can trace not generally available in the West, Chief Oyebola has made some of the most realistic and objective analyses of the problems of black Africa and the Negro race to be found anywhere.

I disagree with much of what Chief Oyebola has written, including his comments on colonialism, Russia and China and his suggested solutions to the problems existing in South Africa. Later events, such as the failure of communism in Russia and the human rights problems in China, have shown the shortcomings of the Russian and Chinese systems. The end of apartheid, and introduction of black majority rule in South Africa, has been achieved, but are the remaining problems, including tribalism, any closer to solution?

Chief Oyebola would undoubtedly also disagree with much that I have written from European and right wing standpoint. However, there is a surprising commonality about many of our opinions on the problems of independent Africa and the Negro race.

The coincidence of many of our views led me to get in touch with Chief Oyebola. We have corresponded by letters and telephone but have yet to meet. He and his publishers have agreed that I may quote freely from his book. Although I have hesitated about quoting him out of context, I feel that the following excerpts stand largely on their own and need no qualification.

> *There are three intriguing facts about the black race. They are facts which most black and "coloured" peoples and some liberal whites would prefer not to face honestly and squarely. One such fact is that no black country has ever made a breakthrough to modernity... The second intriguing fact about the black race is that it was the only race in history which had between 14.6 million and 20 million of its members physically transported as slaves from Africa to a completely new area... Equally strange was the active support which the African chiefs and middle class gave to the capturing and transportation of their fellow blacks to America... The third perplexing fact will undoubtedly arouse the resentment of my black and coloured brothers and sisters. Relying on the fact that the different races of the world came into existence at the same time I have come to the sad, but valid conclusion that the black man has made little or no contribution to world civilisation... I have*

*become fully convinced that the much vaunted black civilisation of ancient Ghana, Shonghai, Mali, Zimbabwe, Hausa/Fulani, Yoruba, Benin and other areas were quite inferior to the civilisation of other races... I regard the writings of Western liberal scholars and black historians on the greatness, glory and achievements of ancient African kingdoms, empires and emirates as a deliberate morale booster for the dehumanised black race...*

*Many Western liberals are aware of the fact that the white countries have a lot to lose if the black man faces the reality of his situation and if he accepts the fact that he hadn't a past that he can be proud of. The whites have a lot to lose if the blacks henceforth work hard to place their membership of the human family on the basis of genuine equality. White experts publish books about our past glory, grandeur and achievements. They've got willing disciples among black intelligentsia who have lost the candour of any critical self-searching... The absurd view has been expressed that colonialism and slavery led to the death of black Africa's cultural heritage. A culture can only die if a whole people can be exterminated as the Romans did in the annihilation of Carthage...Malcolm X was right to say that the Egyptian civilisation was African. But the ancient Egyptians were white and not "black" Africans.*

*One major problem of the black man is that he is today not aware of his basic human weaknesses and problems ..... Some of my fellow blacks are too frightened to talk about our basic problems.. Others blame the slave trade, the kindness of nature, colonialism and neo-colonialism for our underdog position in the world. They look for scapegoats. But unfortunately we have never realised that there was hardly any problem the black man faces or has faced, slavery, colonialism, neo-colonialism which other racial groups like the Chinese, Japanese and even the Europeans did not face in the past...*

*One of our greatest weaknesses is our lack of self discipline both as individuals and as a society. I believe that if we must make it as a race, it is discipline we must foster and cling to. It is with discipline that the black man can achieve the much needed colossal re-orientation of social attitudes and a new way of life... Our poor attitude to work and indiscipline also affect our attitude to our countries. We have never learnt how to subjugate self to the good of our country. We can't put our nation before self... One other glaring weakness of the black man is that he is very selfish and individualistic... The best people are either destroyed, subjugated or at best merely tolerated.*

*But very poor leadership appears to me as the black man's greatest problem. It is sad to admit that with only a few exceptions the black race is ill-served by all sorts of poor leaders who have emerged since the attainment of idependence by many black states... Many black political leaders have a narrow concept of what constitutes a life of fulfilment. They have no lofty dream of leaving their country better than they found it. Above all, our leaders are corrupt. They abuse their official positions and corruptly enrich themselves.*

I find an almost uncanny closeness between these extracts from *The Black Man's Dilemma* and what I had written earlier in my

*Appendixes*

original and these later chapters. In fairness, the extracts do not include much of the comment on dehumanisation and the negative attitudes adopted by the Western powers and societies toward the Negro race.

Chief Oyebola is concerned about continuing foreign domination, even after independence, and feels there is white conspiracy, imperialistic influence and sabotage at work designed to maintain white supremacy on a neo-colonial basis. Although I question this conclusion, I support the idea that, given the basic freedoms and rights of individual members of the population, independent African states should be free of outside influence and should learn from their own mistakes. However, where humanitarian or economic aid is required, there should be full accountability. One of my contentions in this book has been that the Commonwealth, which might be regarded as a neo-colonial system, should be disbanded.

I have been particularly impressed by the repeated plea for increased discipline and responsibility at all levels. I was reminded of my problems resulting from lack of social responsibility on the part of many of our Bantu staff in Nyasaland. I also thought of the vocation of my friend the bishop, who worked so hard to develop this sense. He was probably the most farseeing and wisest of us all in realising that this was the major problem developing countries faced in introducing a modern and responsible social structure and economy.

In considering this weakness in Africa, we should not overlook the failures and materialism of our present Western civilisations, where an "I'm all right Jack" attitude exists amongst many people. There is also a lack of pride in honest workmanship and a failure to accept responsibility. Selfishness predominates everywhere; people live to the maximum extent of their means with little thought of the future - "Social Security will always look after us." Lack of responsibility extends beyond the individual level to the national level, and our politicians, with a few exceptions, fail to face our national problems and, to remain popular, give us the leadership we unfortunately deserve.

# APPENDIX III

Black Man's Dilemma (Revised Edition)

Update of Events, 1976 to 2002

Black Man's Dilemma should become a Prescribed Reading For All Nigerian Secondary Schools

A Contribution To The Debate On Black Man's Dilemma, 1976, Edition

*By Professor J. I. Okogun* of The University of Ibadan.

I have read a number of reviews of Mr. Areoye Oyebola's book entitled: *Black Man's Dilemma*. Some of these encourage me or forced me a few months ago to read every page of the book. I am convinced that Mr. Oyebola exaggerated on a number of issues. He quoted from various authors alright, he underrated, ignored or heavily played down on negro contributions to civilisation as well as on past Negro achievements like as in the case of the Benin Kingdom. This attitude of pen was probably necessary to enable him write chapter four of his book - "Black Man's Negligible contribution to Human civilisation and then later to arrive at chapter ten of the book - "The Black man can make it" .......................... Perhaps the mistake of equating civilisation with technological advancement could have been avoided if the title of the book were "Black man's Dilemma In A Technological World".

## Review And Non - Review of Black Man's Dilemma

That having been said Mr. Areoye Oyebola must be congratulated for his courage to write *Black Man's Dilemma.* There is no doubt that he feels very strongly about the well-being of the black man on contemporary earth. In his book he has attempted to say loud and clear what he believes to be the root cause of contemporary Negro situation.

I am perturbed by the latest of the reviews of *Black Man's Dilemma* published in the Daily Times of 15th September, under the pen name of Adebayo Bello. The author of this review allowed his criticism of the book to degenerate into a subjective analysis; and in a way very close to the faults he saw in his review of the book. He failed, as expressed in the second sentence of his review, "............... to pin- point what philosophy Mr. Oyebola is trying to postulate" even after "Going through the book page by page." I must therefore refer similar readers and reviewers generally to chapter ten of Mr.Oyebola's book and more specifically to chapter seven, page 69 of the same book and I quote... "But such a leap forward requires a mental revolution on the part of all blacks in the world. This is the message of this book". One wonders then what edition is being referred to by that reviewer. Mr. Oyebola ably discussed his concept of this mental revolution in chapter ten of his book. The reviewer's quotations from pages 20 and 21 of the book which to the reviewer are inconsistent, are to me consistent than the reviewer's insistence that" The yardsticks for all these concepts are there for all to see in Western Europe and America." This statement is made by the reviewer inspite of his quotation from the book about travels in Europe and Asia. Perhaps Mr. Bello

*Appendixes*

should be reminded of Taj Mahal, Chinese palaces and Chinese books written several centuries before Christ, acupuncture, etc; Are these also Western? It is clear to the unbiased that *Black Man's Dilemma* considers that in a world ruled by technology, the civilisations of Asia and the East have been able to rise to the occasion without perpetrating a situation in which those nationals aid expatriates in eating up their national foreign currency through the development of insatiable appetites for values, materials and behaviour that are essentially Western. How else could Mr. Oyebola have assessed black man's technological achievement if not by comparison with other human species inhabiting Asia and Europe?

We are told ".... there is no basis for comparing a society striving to keep out heat with one trying to keep it in for instance; and secondly, what people have achieved at gun point can hardly be a test of their ability." Perhaps the reviewer has forgotten that the same people who have successfully struggled to keep in heat have achieved the feat of keeping out heat in the offices of top executives in Nigerian cities of Maiduguri, Kano, Ibadan, Lagos, Calabar etc. If a people's ability should not be measured when conditions best suited for the exploitation of that ability are created then we should all go back and learn lessons from the Renaissance, the scientific breakthroughs following on each of the world wars and explorations, the development of modern Chinese technology and the civil war episode here in Nigeria. It may be said that the black man of present day Nigeria does in fact need a kind of "gun point" for the envisaged take off. From chapter seven of *Blackman's Dilemma* it is clear that Mr. Oyebola does not hold views related to those on which Mr. Vorster (former Apartheid Prime Minister of South Africa) bases his apartheid system. Mr Vorster and his friends would be quite worried if the blackman took some of Mr. Oyebola's "mental revolution" recipe seriously. The next world war may be fought because the black man has in a self-conceited manner refused to take some of the steps outlined in *Black Man's Dilemma.*

## Wretched Of The Earth

It appears that the late Frantz Fanon and some Nigerians in their quoted; "Wretched of the Earth" wish the situation to persist whereby:

*Nigerians devise clever ways of eating up the national foreign exchange reserves by their refusal to develop their own products or accept the required discipline.*

*Nigerians sweat out their cocoa seeds, palm oil, unprocessed rubber, etc and receive back chocolate, margarine, tyres, etc. at over thrice the costs of the initial raw materials;*

*Nigerians sleep in air-conditioned rooms, drive air conditioned "Obokun" cars on Italian-built roads, while their country's petroleum is pumped away as cheap and as fast as possible, gas is flared; Nigerian iron and steel industry is built by the paternal Russia.*

*Nigerian technologists have to be trained by the massive exportation of Nigerians to friendly America, etc. and Nigerian "Tradomedicals" remain so secretive about their use of local herbs, that we have no opportunity of knowing and improving on their vanishing art.*

In conclusion, let Mr. Oyebola's *Black Man's Dilemma* be made prescribed reading for every Nigerian Secondary School child. The main suggestions in the book should aid the rapid achievement of those attitudes recently recommended to Nigerians by the Head of State (then General Olusegun Obasanjo) at Jaji and on several other previous occasions.

# APPENDIX IV

## Black Man's Dilemma (Revised Edition)

## Update of Events, 1976 to 2002

## Conflicting Comments and Reviews on the 1976 Edition of Black Man's Dilemma

THE ten lucidly written chapters of his new book reflect Mr. Oyebola's wide and varied knowledge of history, social science, economic and political problems of the Black Race.

Any reader would agree with me that the book is well written, the author's rather revolutionary ideas are challenging, his pithy witticism and penetrating inquiry should commend the book to those who read it for pleasure or to serious African students determined to unravel the truth about their race's contribution to world civilisation.

*MAJOR GENERAL I.B.M. HARUNA*
*FORMER NIGERIA'S FEDERAL COMMISSIONER FOR INFORMATION, AT THE LAUNCHING OF BLACK MAN'S DILEMMA*

The author of "Black Man's Dilemma", Mr. Areoye Oyebola, has not just written another book. He has raised controversy and provoked thought on an issue that exercises the minds of patriotic black men all over the world.

But the essence of the controversy lies not much in the dilemma that stares the black man full in the face as in taking the choice to overcome his disabilities and disadvantages and thereby come to his own among the races that inhabit our planet.

*BRIGADIER D. M. JEMIBEWON, PSC*
*FORMER MILITARY GOVERNOR, OYO STATE OF NIGERIA, AT THE LAUNCHING OF BLACK MAN'S DILEMMA*

May be Mr. Oyebola's extensive tour of other parts of the world in his journalistic career afforded him the opportunity to see many things; and we are better for it. For we are now sharing his experiences recorded in these few pages. I recommend the book to all those who have the courage to read self abdication.

*SUNDAY OGBOLE OF AHMADU BELLO UNIVERSITY, PUBLISHED IN THE NIGERIA STANDARD, JOS*

Mr. Oyebola's position is a subtle plea to "think tanks" in the young nations of Africa to wake up from our slumber and reorganise.

*EMEKA NNAMDI ASINUGO OF ENUGU, NIGERIA PUBLISHED IN THE DAILY STAR.*

*Appendixes*

My own idea, which Mr. Oyebola seems to portray in his book, is that the black race, especially the so called intellectual, is becoming megalomaniac.

We talk of African civilisation as if other races like the Chinese and the Incas of Peru had no peculiar civilisation of their own.

Hence, we resort to intercontinental primitive jamboree just to prove to the world that black men were once civilised.

The 20th Century has witnessed the Zenith of human inventive capabilities. The black man must come out of his autic shell before the turn of this century to avoid becoming a megalomaniac race.

*BENJAMIN O. BAYOWA*
*LAGOS, PUBLISHED IN THE DAILY TIMES*

Black Man's Dilemma, a book written by Mr. Areoye Oyebola, will for a long time, remain an object of controversy, debate and heated argument.

This is because the book strikes at the very basis of our existence as a race and tries to examine critically our past and present and the road to a glorious future.

*SEGUN ADELUGBA OF IBADAN*
*PUBLISHED IN THE DAILY SKETCH.*

This thought provoking book is a necessity in everybody's library, white or black..

I think it is an invitation to views and counter views, intelligent critiques and critical self-appraisal of the black man's position in the scheme of things.

*ATANDA ADEKUNLE OF IBADAN,*
*PUBLISHED IN THE NIGERIAN TRIBUNE*

Extremely rich in its bibliography and thoughfulness, "BLACK MAN'S DILEMMA" promises to be about the most controversial book ever produced by a black man on the race.

*TUNDE THOMPSON OF IBADAN*
*PUBLISHED BY THE DAILY SKETCH*

I admire Mr. Areoye Oyebola for his guts in speaking out his mind and telling us some home truths that we find convenient to sweep under the carpet. But his assumption that technological development with all it implies is the only yardstick of measuring a people's progress makes nonsense of much of what he has to say.

*MOHAMMED HARUNA OF KADUNA*
*PUBLISHED BY THE NEW NIGERIAN*

Many of Mr. Areoye Oyebola's judgements can be disputed, but he brings to the support of his thesis a mass of detailed information. And nobody could fail to be stimulated by so earnest and uncompromising a writer.

*DAVID WILLIAMS, A SEASONED BRITISH JOURNALIST, EDITOR AND WRITER. - PUBLISHED BY THE WEST AFRICA MAGAZINE, LONDON.*

I hope the book was not written to spark off unnecessary controversy just to gain attention, popularity and recognition, no matter the quality and quantity.

*DR. G. O. NZERIBE OF ENUGU*
*PUBLISHED IN THE NEW NIGERIA*

The book is nothing more than a tenuous web of half-truths and baseless logic which under the cloak of objective research, in fact produces a distorted, highly coloured and destructive picture of all that the black man has struggled to achieve.

### ADEBAYO BELLO OF LAGOS
### PUBLISHED IN THE DAILY TIMES AND NIGERIAN TRIBUNE

The review of Mr. Areoye Oyebola's book, Black Man's Dilemma by Mr. Adebayo Bello (that is the name of the reviewer quoted in the last paragraph) was very interesting. Mr. Bello should know it is very difficult to build but very easy to destroy. It does not cost us anything to criticise and condemn outright. Mr. Bello's review was packed full of abuses... He should realise that abuses are no arguments. Confused men only resort to abuses. In my opinion, the purpose of Mr. Oyebola's book is to ginger us up. He wants the black man to wake up from his slumber and be up and doing. The truth is always bitter.

### DEACON LAGUNJU BABALOLA OF LAGOS
### PUBLISHED IN THE DAILY TIMES AND THE DAILY SKETCH

The least one was tempted to do after reading through a purported review of Mr. Areoye Oyebola's book, *Black Man's Dilemma* by one Mr. Adebayo Bello was to dismiss it as a non-exercise. Or, heap abuses and libel on the person of Bello as he had done to Oyebola which of course, would mean displaying the same meanness which the said non-review had done.

Quite frankly, the black man has a long way to go to achieve self realisation.

### TOLA ADENIYI OF IBADAN, AUTHOR, JOURNALIST AND CRITIC, PUBLISHED IN THE DAILY TIMES

The excellent review by Adebayo Bello of Black Man's Dilemma has helped me to shorten my comment on the book written by Areoye Oyebola. At the suggestion of a friend, I had bought the book to read, unfortunately, I could not stomach the content beyond the first 40 pages.

## DR. L. N. ANIEBONA OF THE UNIVERSITY OF IBADAN PUBLISHED IN THE DAILY TIMES

It seems to me that Adebayo Bello's comments on Areoye Oyebola's book, Black Man's Dilemma, ran far off the mark as well as far out of proportion. The only significance is that Bello has promoted the sale of Black Man's Dilemma and thereby enhance Oyebola's prestige as a first rate writer.

Oyebola has endeavoured to arouse the black man from his slumber in order to rediscover himself and worth.

The black world should be grateful to Oyebola for providing an eye opener to black man's backwardness..

Mr. Oyebola should not relent but should continue to endeavour to educate the masses through his writing, taking solace in Manraivelli's wise saying that, "There is nothing more difficult to carry out, nor more doubtful of success, nor more dangerous to handle than to initiate a new order of things."

Areoye Oyebola has initiated some new order of things, let Adebayo Bello learn to be educated.

## KANMI ADISA OF THE UNIVERSITY OF IFE, PUBLSIHED IN THE DAILY SKETCH

*Appendixes*

Mr. Adebayo Bello's review of Areoye Oyebola's book could be dismissed as mere rubbish, the rantings of a mind that refuses to grow. People like the reviewer who prefer to take glory in ancient achievements will not be awake to the necessities and experiences of modern needs.

Mr. Oyebola is clearly one of our race's rare intellectuals with clear vision. He has done a meritorious service. I am one of those who are proud to own a copy of his book.

*OLU AKINTAN OF ABEOKUTA*
*PUBLISHED IN THE DAILY TIMES*

Adebayo Bello in his attempt to review Mr. Areoye Oyebola's Black Man's Dilemma fell victim of chauvinism, uncontrollable emotion and uncritical pride of the black man and therefore failed to convince most of his readers. His exercise was not a review but an outright condemnation of the controversial book. To him he sees nothing good or worthwhile in BLACK MAN'S DILEMMA. This makes his article uninteresting and unacademic.

Any unbiased mind or impartial reader will surely appreciate some of the points raised by Mr. Oyebola. Personally, it is a transparent truth to say that apart from his blackness, his religious superstition and taboos, the black man is yet to exert a lasting influence on world civilisation and prove that his race is no underdog.

*WILLY MASCOT ACHILIKE,*
*NATIONAL YOUTH SERVICE CORPS, KANO STATE,*
*PUBLISHED IN THE DAILY TIMES.*

Mr Areoye Oyebola's book is a commendable attempt at telling the black man that he is now in control of his destiny and must face the facts about his past and present realistically.

And any black man who intends to have a part in the future destiny of the black race would definitely gain from reading *Black Man's Dilemma.*

*ETTA IBOK, LAGOS*
*PUBLISHED IN THE DAILY TIMES*

*Black Man's Dilemma* is worth reading for the violent views and its politically provocative tirades against the black man.

*WILLY BOZIMO, LAGOS*
*PUBLISHED BY THE SUNDAY TIMES.*

Some years ago, I heard on a British Broadcasting Corporation Programme about a book written by a Japanese, telling his whole race about the physical ugliness of their beings. That book was not banned. It sold like hot cakes in Japan.

So, let it be with Areoye Oyebola's book. We will learn about our short comings from this book. Who knows, the black race may become the seat of the next unpolluted civilisation within a century.

*J.K. DURO OF JENTA, JOS*
*PUBLISHED IN THE DAILY TIMES.*

If you ask who is my man of the century in Nigeria, I will tip Chief Areoye Oyebola, journalist, educationist, author and lover of objective appraisal of issues.

I pick him because of his downright objectivity and frankness in his book -*BLACK MAN'S DILEMMA*. Chief Oyebola is the only one having the courage to express the truth about black's backwardness.

The blackman's no claim to any appreciable world invention and his deliberate rejection of modernity were lavishly x-rayed by The Chief. While the rest of the world are forward looking and making research for better future, we spend fortune reviving the crude aspects of those of our forefathers.

Revival of culture should not glorify in idolatory or be projected on radio and television to show barefooted artistes, dirty environments and dingy make-ups.

*KAYODE AWE,*
*PUBLISHED IN THE SKETCH NEWSPAPER OF MAY 30, 1983*

*Black Man's Dilemma*

# APPENDIX V

## Black Man's Dilemma Revised Edition

## Letter From A Ghananian Lady With Plan To Write A Book Like Black Man's Dilemma

Mrs A. B. Osafo Addo,
P. O. Box B. 186
Comm. 2
Tema - Ghana.

June 26th, 1984

**My Dear Mr. Oyebola**

I recently had the opportunity of reading your book, THE BLACK MAN'S DILEMMA. After reading it several times, I felt compelled to write to you to thank you for your wonderful work, and show my appreciation for your book.

I'm a Ghanaian, trained in West Germany from 1969 to 1980, and thus had the chance of travelling extensively to other parts of the world.

I returned to Ghana in 1980, and have since been desperately trying to write a book on the Black race, with special emphasis on the Africans. In fact your book has certainly inspired me to go ahead with my plans. Since I honestly want to discuss the Dilemma of the Black race, I felt it quite advisable to write to you for help and guidance for writing my book.

I am neither a journalist nor a writer and shall therefore need the assistance of an experienced writer. It seems we both have the same ideas and with your help I may one day be able to write something about our beloved race - BLACK RACE which may sooner or later inspire our people to try and compete on equal grounds with the other races.

In the hope of hearing from you soon.

I remain with best regards.

Yours sincerely,

Signed

**ADWOA BENEWAH OSAFO-ADOO (MRS)**

Appendixes

# MY REPLY TO MRS ADWOA B. OSAFO-ADDO OF TEMA, GHANA

Mrs A. B. Osafo Addo,
Dawhenya Clinic
P. O. Box B. 186
Comm. 2
Tema - Ghana.

July 27th, 1984

**My Dear Mrs. Osafo Addo,**

It was a joy to read your letter of June 26, 1984. Your kind words and gesture on my efforts in writing Black Man's Dilemma are also deeply appreciated.

I must confess that Black Man's Dilemma is just a little manifestation of very deep feelings and anxiety that I have nurtured for years on our dear race's predicament in a world that wants to go farther than the moon.

My dearest sister, I am most delighted that we had shared the same thought and anxiety for years. I know that our race would make it eventually but people like you and I must spend our time, energy and money in spreading our ideas until the forces of change become fiercely, genuinely and unpredictably at work among a race that has persistently remained the world's underdog since the beginning of history. A true revolution we must have.

I am happy to know of your proposed book. Please send me a summary of your ideas, a kind of resume of your book, so that I can give some ideas in areas of emphasis and make other suggestions. You can also send me a list of the books you have read or intend to read for any possible advice. You don't need to be an established writer or journalist to succeed. It is the sincerity of your ideas that is important and my publishing firm, Board Publications Limited, will assist you in editing.

I hope that you would have an opportunity to visit Nigeria in future so that we can exchange ideas on your proposed book.

Meanwhile I am sending, THE TYRANNY OF POVERTY, a booklet that contains some of the ideas I expressed in my column when I was Editor of the Nigerian Daily Times.

With kindest regards.

Yours Sincerely,

Signed.

**CHIEF AREOYE OYEBOLA**

# APPENDIX VI

## Black Man's Dilemma
### Revised Edition

## Update Of Events, 1976 To 2002

My First Letter To Dr. Kofi Annan, UNO Secretary General On Black Man's Dilemma To Which He Sent No Reply

### Scrictly Personal

Mr. Kofi Annan,
The Secretary General,
United Nations Organisation,
UNO Building,
New York,
U.S.A.

January 20th 1998

**My Dearly Beloved Brother,**

It is a great joy that you have made it to the headship of mankind's most important organisation, the UNO under the highly competitive and uncompromising scrutiny of all the races of the world. Hearty congratulations. The world is proud of you.

To say that you are very busy is a clear understatement. Even then, I earnestly plead that you should give this letter, my book, "Black Man's Dilemma" and the attached documents your personal attention.

And I wish that you also use your good and eminent offices to encourage the United Nations Educational, Scientific and Cultural Organisation (UNESCO) to take necessary actions on my request that UNESCO should be fair to the black race by giving me an opportunity to put my views on our race across to its experts, researchers and scientists.

My beloved Secretary General, I have a long standing and deep pain that our race is the world's underdog. And some eminent Africans shared my pains. They include the late Nigerian eminent statesman, Chief Obafemi Awolowo, who had two hours discussion with me when "Black Man's dilemma" manuscript was ready and the imprisoned former Nigerian Head of State General Olusegun Obasanjo, who gave me a seven page hand written appraisal of the manuscript before publication. The late President Ahmed Sekou Toure of Guinea wrote to commend my contribution. And so did Nwalimu Julius Nyerere of Tanzania.

As one of the very best from the black race, I know that you will agree with me that no individual, organisation, community or nation can make any meaningful progress without a sincere appraisal of his or its limitations and problems. Hence, I see the pressing need for the black race to critically and truthfully examine its backwardness vis-a-vis the other races of the world.

Finally, my dear brother, I will deem it a great priviledge if you give me an opportunity to meet you personally and share your thought on what you regard as a way out of our race's dilemma.

*Appendixes*

Meanwhile, I enclose with this letter and a copy of "Black Man's Dilemma" the following documents.

1. My letter of October 25th, 1997, to the Director - General, UNESCO, PARIS.
2. A UNESCO Director's reply dated December 15th, 1997.
3. My second letter to UNESCO dated January 13th, 1998.
4. My short general biography and short profile as a journalist.

5. Quotes from Black Man's Dilemma contained in a book published in 1995 - AFRICAN AMBIT - By Regained Dickenson.
6. Conflicting reviews and comments on Black Man's Dilemma when it was first published.
7. Short introduction to Black Man's Dilemma by New York subsidy publisher, Vantage Press Inc.
8. Newspaper cuttings showing remarks on Black Man's Dilemma by two famous Nigerian columnists - TAI SOLARIN AND KAWE.

I look forward to your kind reply.

My Fax No. is (02) 2413385, Ibadan, Nigeria.

With my warmest regards.

Very Sincerely,

Signed
DR. AREOYE OYEBOLA.

## MY SECOND LETTER TO DR. KOFI ANNAN, SENT TO HIM THROUGH UNO LAGOS OFFICE, DURING HIS JULY, 1998 VISIT TO NIGERIA. HE ALSO SENT NO REPLY TO THIS LETTER

Dr. Kofi Annan,
The Secretary General,
United Nations Organisation,
U.N.O Building,
New York,
U.S.A.

July 1st, 1998

**My Dearly Beloved Brother,**

Welcome home to Nigeria. I wish you a successful visit.

I sent you the attached letter, dated January 20th, with attachments by registered express airmail in January, 1998.

As the world's number one administrator, I have been expecting at least an acknowledgment of my letter from your high office. However, I concede that my letter probably didn't get to your reach.

But as this letter is very important to me personally and to the future of the black race in general, I very much plead with you to reply to my letter when you return to New York.

With my best regards.

Yours Very Sincerely,

Signed
DR. AREOYE OYEBOLA

*Black Man's Dilemma*

# BIBLIOGRAPHY

| | |
|---|---|
| ADAMS, Romanzo: | Interracial marriage in Hawaii. |
| AYAJI J. and ESPIE I: | (Editors). A thousand Years of West African History. |
| AKINJOGBIN, I. A: | Dahomey and its Neighbours. |
| AZIKIWE, Dr. N: | Liberia in World Politics. |
| AZIKIWE, Dr. N: | Renascent Africa. |
| BARNS, T.A: | An African Eldorado, the Colonisation of Africa. |
| BATTUTTA, IBN: | Travels in Asia and Africa. |
| BATRAWI, A.M.: | The Racial history of Egypt and Nubia. |
| BEECHAM, John: | Ashantee and the Gold Coast. |
| BENEDICT, Ruth: | Race, Science and Politics |
| BENNETT, Lerone Jr: | Before the Mayflower: A history of the Negro in America. |
| BOAS, Franz: | Racial Purity. |
| BOAS, Franz: | The mind of primitive man. |
| BOYD, W. C: | Genetics and the races of man. |
| BOVILL, E. W.: | Caravans of the old Sahara. |
| BROOMFIELD, A.W. | Colour Conflict. |
| BURNS, Alan: | Colour Prejudice. |
| BULLOCK, Henry Alan: | A history of Negro Education in the South from 1619 to the present. |
| CARMICHAEL, Stokely & Harmilton,: Charles V: | Black Power |

| | |
|---|---|
| CLARK, Kenneth B: | Dark Ghetto. |
| COMAS, Juan: | Racial Myths, UNESCO Publication. |
| COOLEY, W.D.: | The Negroland of the Arabs. |
| COULTHARD, G.R: | Race and Colour in Caribbean Literature. |
| CURTIN, P: | The Image of Africa |
| DAVENPORT, C.B & STEGGERDA, Morris: | Race Crossing in Jamaica. |
| DELAFOSSE, Maurice: | Civilisations negro-africaines. |
| DAVIDSON, Basil: | Which way Africa? |
| DAVIDSON, Basil: | Africa in history. |
| DU BOIS, W.E.B: | Black Reconstruction in America. |
| DU BOIS, W.E.B: | The Suppression of The Atlantic Slave Trade to the U.S.A. |
| DU BOIS, W.E.B.: | Souls of Black Folk |
| DIXON, R.B.: | The building of cultures. |
| DUNN, L.C.: | Race and Biology |
| DUNN, L.C.: | Heredity and evolution in human populations. |
| DUNN, L.C. & DOBZHANSKY, Theodosius: | Heredity, Race and Society |
| EGAREVBA, J.: | A short history of Benin. |
| FANON, FRANTZ: | Towards the African Revolution. |
| FANON, FRANTZ: | The wretched of the Earth. |
| FAGE, J.D.: | (Editor) Africa discovers her past. |
| FARNHAM-DIGGORY, S.: | Congnitive Synthesis in Negro and white children; Monography of the society for Research in child Development, vol. 35, No. 21970. |
| FLEURE, H.J.: | The race of mankind. |

Bibliography

GOX-BOURNE, H.R.: CIVILISATION IN CONGOLAND.
FREYRE, GILBERTO: The Masters and the Slaves.
FRAZIER, E.F.: The negro in America.
FRANKLIN, JOHN HOPE: From slavery to freedom: A history of Negro America.
GALBRAITH, J.K.: The Affluent Society.
GARDINER, ROBERT: A world of People.
GOLDEN, HARRY: Mr. Kennedy and the Negroes.
GROVES, C.P.: The planting of Christianity in Africa.
GRIER, WILLIAM H &
PRINCE, M. COBBS: Black Race.
HANKINS, F.H.: The racial basis of civilisation.
HAWKES, C.F.C.: Pre-historic foundations of Europe.
HAILEY, LORD: An African Survey.
HALL, R.N.: Great Zimbabwe.
HALL, R.N.: Ancient Ruins of Rhodesia.
HADDON, A.C.: The races of man and their distribution.
HERSKOVITS, M.J.: Man and his Works.
HOLLAND, WILLIAM L: Nationalism and the West.
HOLT, P.M.: Modern History of the Sudan.
HUXLEY, Julian African View.
JALEEP, P. The Pilage of the Third World.
JEFFREYS, M.D.W.: The Negro Enigma - In the West African Review of September, 1951.
JOHNSTON,
Sir Harry H: A history of the Colonisation of Africa.
KENYATTA, Jomo: Facing-Mount Kenya
KLINEBERG, Otto: Race and Psychology.
LABOURET, Henry: Africa and before the White Man.
LAWLER, S. D. &
LAWLER L. J.: Human genetics
LEGUM, Colin &

287

MARGARET:  
LEWIS, Artur W.:  

LEVI-STRAUSS,  
Claude:  

LEIRIS, Michael:  

LESTER, Paul &  
MILLOT, Jacques:  
LIND, Andrew W.B.:  

LINTON, Raph:  
LITTLE, K.L.:  

LITTLE, K.L.:  
LOMAX Louis E.  
LUTHULI, Chief Albert:  
MACMILLAN, W.M.:  
MASON, Phillip.:  
MALCOLM X.:  
MEAD, Margaret.:  

MONTAGU, Ashley:  

MOUMINI, Abdou:  
MYRDAL, Gunnar:  
NEEDHAM, Joseph:  
NEWMAN, Peter.:  
NKRUMAH, Kwame.:  
NURKSE, Ragnar.:  

PIAGET, J.:  
PIAGET, J. &

South Africa: Crisis for the West.  
Beyond African dictatorship, Encounter of August, 1965.  

Race and History, UNESCO publication.  
Race and History, UNESCO publication  

Les races humaines.  
An Island Community: Ecological succession in Hawai.  
The Study of Man.  
Race and Society: UNESCO Publication.  
Negroes in Britain  
The Negro Revolt  
Let my people go.  
African Emergent.  
Commonsense about race.  
An Autobiography.  
Cultural Patterns and technical change .  
Men's most dangerous myth: the fallacy of race.  
Education in Africa  
An American Dilemma.  
Science and Civilisation in China.  
British Guiana.  
Africa must Unite.  
Problems of capital formation in under developed countries.  
The origin of intelligence in children

| | |
|---|---|
| PIAGET J. and INHELDER, B.: | The Psychology of the Child. |
| PIFER, Alan,: | The higher Education of Blacks in the United States. |
| REUTER, E.B. | Race and culture contacts. |
| RICHARDSON, Ken & SPEARS, David.: | Race, culture and intelligence |
| RODNEY, W.: | West Africa and the Atlantic Slave Trade. |
| SELIGMAN, C.G.: | Races of Africa |
| SHAPIRO, Harry L.: | Race mixture. |
| SCHAPERA, I.: | The Khoisan peoples of South Africa: Bushmen and Hottentots. |
| SHINNIE, M.: | Ancient African Kingdoms. |
| SPENGLER, O.: | The decline of the West. |
| TOYNBEE, A.J.: | A study of history |
| UNITED NATIONS ORGANISATION: | Apartheid in Practice. |
| WAGLEY, Charles: | Race and class in Rural Brazil: UNESCO Publication. |
| WAGNER, G.: | The Bantu of North Kavirondo. |
| WATSON, Peter.: | How race affects I. Q. |
| WELLARD, J.: | The great Sahara |
| WHITE, Lelie, A.: | The Science of Culture |
| WOODSON, Carter: | The Education of the Negro prior to 1861 |
| WOODWARD, Mary: | The development of Behaviour |
| YOUNG, Whitney: | To be equal |
| YUTANG, Lin.: | Between tears and laughter. |

www.ingramcontent.com/pod-product-compliance
Lightning Source LLC
Chambersburg PA
CBHW061954180426

43198CB00036B/835